W9-CCR-949

AIR PHOTO INTERPRETATION for archaeologists

Frontispiece (overleaf):

Crop-marks near Little Bromley, Essex, 15 June 1976.

A complex pattern of geological and archaeological marks is made up of fossil ice-wedges, tree-pits from scrub clearance, square enclosures, ring ditches (some probably surrounding circular houses, others containing burials), old field boundaries, a possible windmill-mound, and filled-in gravel pits.

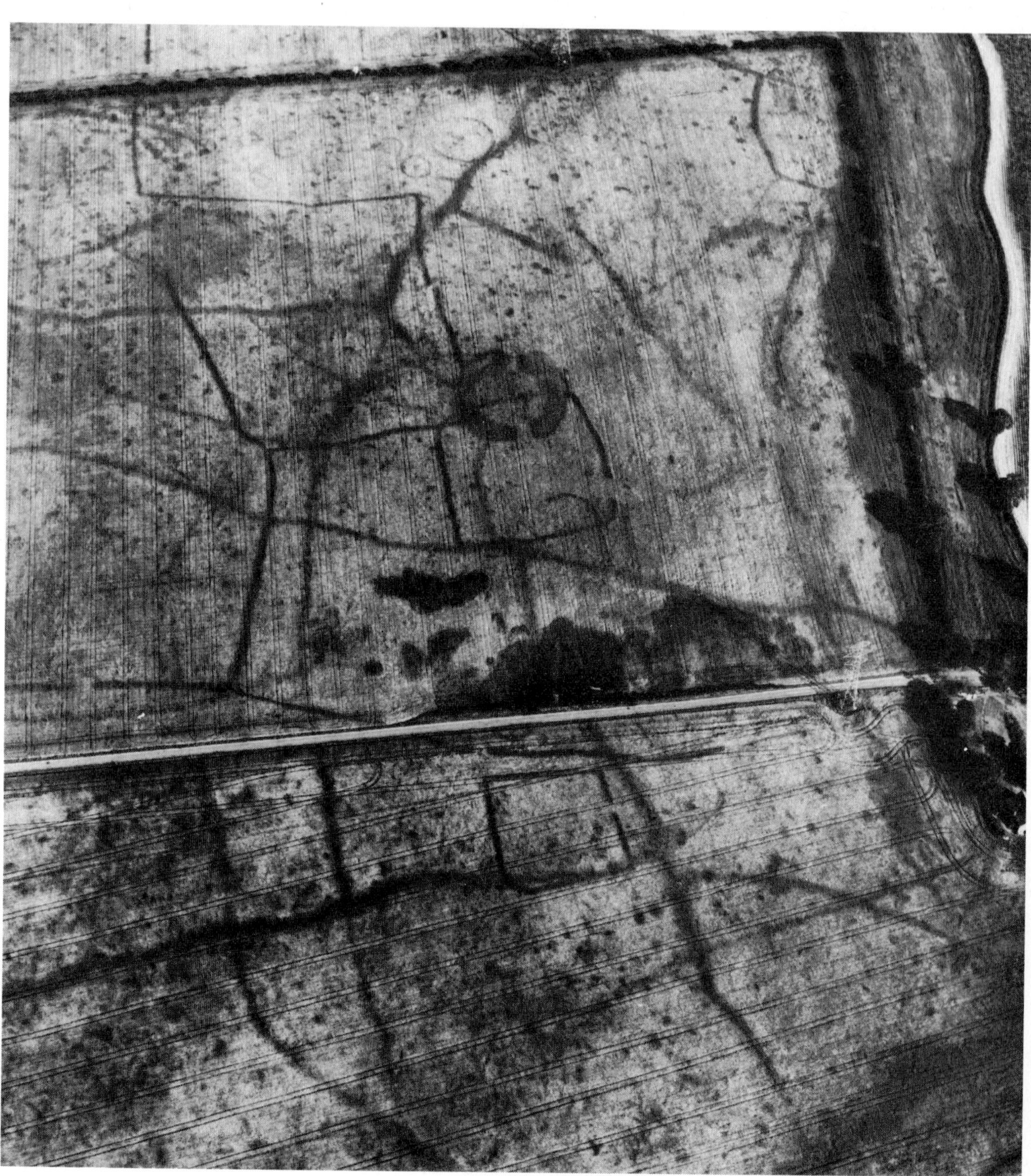

AIR PHOTO INTERPRETATION for archaeologists

D R Wilson

St. Martin's Press, New York

St. Martin's Press, Inc., 175 Fifth Avenue, New York, NY 10010
Printed in Great Britain
First published in the United States of America in 1982

ISBN 0-312-01527-5

Library of Congress Cataloging in Publication Data

Wilson, David Raoul.
Air photo interpretation for archaeologists.
Bibliography: p.
1. Photography in archaeology. I. Title.
CC79.P46W54 1982 930.1′028′5 82-10679
ISBN 0-312-01527-5

Contents

List of Illustrations

Acknowledgments

Figs 1–4 are by courtesy of the National Monuments Record (England) and are Crown Copyright. Figs 5–6 are from the Allen Collection in the Ashmolean Museum, Oxford; figs 17 and 28 are by Mr R. Agache; fig 27 is by Mr C. Léva, by courtesy of the Centre Interdisciplinaire de Recherches Aériennes, Brussels; and figs 78 and 118 are by Mr D. A. Edwards, by courtesy of the Norfolk Archaeological Unit. All the other photographs are from the Cambridge University Collection of Air Photographs.

The line drawings are by the author.

Preface

The value of air-photographs for archaeological research, conservation and planning has long been recognized, and such photographs are being ever more widely used by archaeological fieldworkers and administrators. Unfortunately, not all those who find themselves using air-photographs have had the training or experience to do so with real understanding. This is hardly surprising in that there are no established training courses in the archaeological interpretation of air-photographs, and until now there has been no handbook to guide those working on their own. *Air Photo Interpretation for Archaeologists* seeks to fill that gap. Its formal scope is limited to the landscape and archaeology of the British Isles, but the general principles involved are equally valid in western Europe and should be applicable, with only minor adjustments for local differences, throughout the temperate zones of the world.

It is truly remarkable that no one since 1938 has anywhere published a collection of air-photographs chosen to illustrate a representative series of archaeological sites in Britain. Such a publication would have had great general interest, as well as furnishing a valuable aid to identification. I am greatly indebted to my publishers for allowing me so many plates in which to show not only the appearance of a good range of archaeological sites, but also the non-archaeological features with which they are most liable to be confused. Recognition of the latter is essential to good photo-interpretation, yet it has received little systematic attention until now. Selected instances have been published by a variety of authors, but have been presented more often as amusing curiosities than as the basic material with which such interpretation is concerned.

The aim of the book is to be of practical use to the inexperienced interpreter, and nearly as much effort is devoted to warning him of possible misidentifications as to establishing the principles of sound interpretation. This reflects in a very real sense the practical experience of the author, who has had ample opportunity during seventeen years at Cambridge, working for the University's Committee for Aerial Photography, to make virtually every mistake that he describes. If the reader should sometimes feel that his propensity to foolish error has been overstated, he should take this as a sign that the author has been remembering some past blunder of his own.

In describing archaeological features an attempt has been made to avoid much use of relative terms such as 'large' and 'small' and to substitute absolute figures, even when these have to be very broadly defined. Thus, round barrows are described as having 'ditches with diameters ranging from 4m to more than 45m'. For many types of site such measurements are not available in the published literature and have been derived from a rapid survey of typical examples. It would be useful if corrections or extensions of these measurements could be sent to the author at Cambridge (address p 26).

It has not been possible to illustrate every type of site that is described, and reference has been freely made to air-photographs already published. All references to the existing literature follow the Harvard system, in which works are cited by the name of author and the date of publication; fuller details can be traced through the Bibliography (pp 206–8).

This book may be regarded as marking a definite stage in the development of archaeological photo-interpretation. For sixty years the data have been accumulating at an ever increasing pace. What we seem to have learnt in the process is assessed and set out here for the first time. But already the re-examination and systematic analysis of this great heap of data has begun. It will take a good many years to complete, but when it is done, we shall have a much sounder and more detailed knowledge of our material. Much that is now passed over or assigned to an undifferentiated miscellaneous category will then have been studied and classified. That day is not yet, however, and the present account must concentrate on the more obvious identifications that we can understand today.

I am happy to record my debt to those who have helped me in preparing this book by responding to my queries: Arnold Baker, Richard Bellhouse, John Hedges, Margaret Jones, Rodney Mackey, and Rendell Williams. I have also benefitted from the advice of a number of friends who have read portions of the text in typescript. These are Stewart Bell, Graham Douglass, Bob Evans, Graham Webster, Richard West, Rowan Whimster, Gay Wilson, and Liz Wilson; to them I extend my gratitude. I have not always followed their advice and the imperfections that remain should certainly not be laid at their door.

It has given me especial pleasure to be able to include in this book photographs taken by colleagues in France, in Belgium and in Britain: Roger Agache, Charles Léva, and Derek Edwards respectively. I should have liked to include more photographs, by other friends, but the need to select views to illustrate a great variety of specific topics led me inevitably back to the Cambridge University Collection, which, besides being my own place of work for seventeen years, has a more detailed subject-index than any other major collection of specialist air-photographs in the country. Without such an aid the illustrations for this volume could scarcely have been assembled.

Cambridge, 7 March 1982 D R WILSON

1

Air Photography and Archaeology

DEVELOPMENT OF AIR-PHOTOGRAPHY FOR ARCHAEOLOGY

Aerial archaeology as we know it today had its origins in Britain in the period between the two World Wars. The history of its development has been reviewed by a number of authors—Crawford (1928a, 1954), Daniel (1975), Deuel (1971) Downey (1980), and St Joseph (1951a)—so we need not here do more than point to some of the landmarks along the way.

The beginnings

The earliest air-photographs were taken from balloons, so it is appropriate that the first known air-photographs of an archaeological site in Britain were achieved by this means (1). These were the oblique and vertical photographs of Stonehenge taken by Lt P H Sharpe from an Army war-balloon in 1906 (Capper, 1907). But to realize the full potential of the technique required manœuvrable aircraft, while the incentive to develop the appropriate skills was in due course provided by the needs of military intelligence in the 1914–18 War. On some fronts military resources were in fact devoted to the photography of archaeological sites, notably by the Germans. In Britain air-photography remained a significant element of Royal Air Force training after the War, and it was the interest aroused in serving RAF officers by some of the earthworks which they saw around them that laid the foundations of British archaeological air-photography.

This interest was focussed by O G S Crawford, the first Archaeological Officer of the Ordnance Survey. He was quick to perceive the value of this technique to archaeological fieldwork. Of crucial importance was his recognition on routine RAF photographs taken in 1921 of crop-marks of the Stonehenge Avenue, continuing the line of the earthworks recorded by William Stukeley in 1723. Excavations undertaken with A D Passmore in September 1923 at three points along the lines seen on the photographs proved the existence of buried ditches at each place, despite the fact that no surface relief had been visible for at least two centuries (Crawford 1924). This was the beginning of a completely new method of archaeological exploration, by which buried archaeological features could be traced through the differential growth of surface vegetation, most readily seen and recorded from the air. (Crop-marks as such were not entirely unknown before this from ground observation and had even prompted excavations; but these were rare and isolated instances that had not prompted any general conclusion leading to a search for other examples.)

Earlier in the same year Crawford had made a first essay in applying the evidence from air-photography to what we should now call 'landscape archaeology', by observing the layout of systems of Celtic fields and their relationship to other earthworks (Crawford 1923). In 1924, with the aid of A Keiller, he himself undertook a programme of air-photography in Wessex almost wholly devoted to recording earthworks. Despite un-

1 *Stonehenge, Wiltshire, photographed from a balloon, summer, 1906*
The ditches of the main circular enclosure and of the Avenue show as ribbons of darker unparched grass. Some of the sarsen uprights on the right have had to be shored up with wooden props.

favourable weather and other setbacks this programme was outstandingly successful and demonstrated how the aerial view, even of remains surviving in considerable relief, could bring new understanding, sometimes indeed elucidating an important structural sequence (Crawford & Keiller 1928).

Crawford's photographs, like most RAF ones, were taken with a vertical camera mounted on the aircraft, but the new discoveries being made by Sq Ldr G S M Insall and other officers were mostly recorded with a hand-held camera pointed at an oblique angle to the ground. Insall's discovery of Woodhenge in 1925–6 showed what a wealth of unsuspected detail could be revealed by this means, as well as demonstrating how much soil-marks and crop-marks of the same site could differ from each other (2, 3). Crop-marks began to be observed not only on shallow chalk soils, but over oolitic limestone and plateau gravels. It was nevertheless another milestone when Fl/Lts W E Purdin and B T Hood photographed crop-marks of the Big Rings at Dorchester-on-Thames (Oxfordshire) in June 1927, for this was the first time that such marks were to be tested by excavation anywhere but on the chalk. Excavation by Crawford and R G Collingwood in October of that year found the ditches of the henge cut in sand and buried beneath two feet (0·6m) of ploughsoil (Crawford 1928b). Crop-marks immediately began to be seen in other river valleys: those of the Roman town at Caistor St Edmund, which inspired a major programme of excavations, drew attention to the effect on crops of underlying stonework and metalling, which was the reverse of that produced by pits and ditches. Photography of

2 *Soil-marks of Woodhenge, Wiltshire, looking west, 16 December 1925*
Near the centre of the photograph a disc of chalky soil shows the site of a ploughed-down earthwork, thought by earlier antiquaries to be a barrow. A broad ditch with single entrance is just visible as a band of darker soil within the disc (cf fig 3).

3 *Crop-marks of Woodhenge, Wiltshire, looking north, 30 June 1926*
The same site as in fig 2 is now seen in a cereal crop. The ditch is clearly visible, and inside it six circles of post-pits have come into view. The resemblance to nearby Stonehenge soon inspired the name 'Woodhenge'. Several ring ditches are visible in the foreground, unlike the bank of the henge which is conspicuous by its non-appearance (p 70).

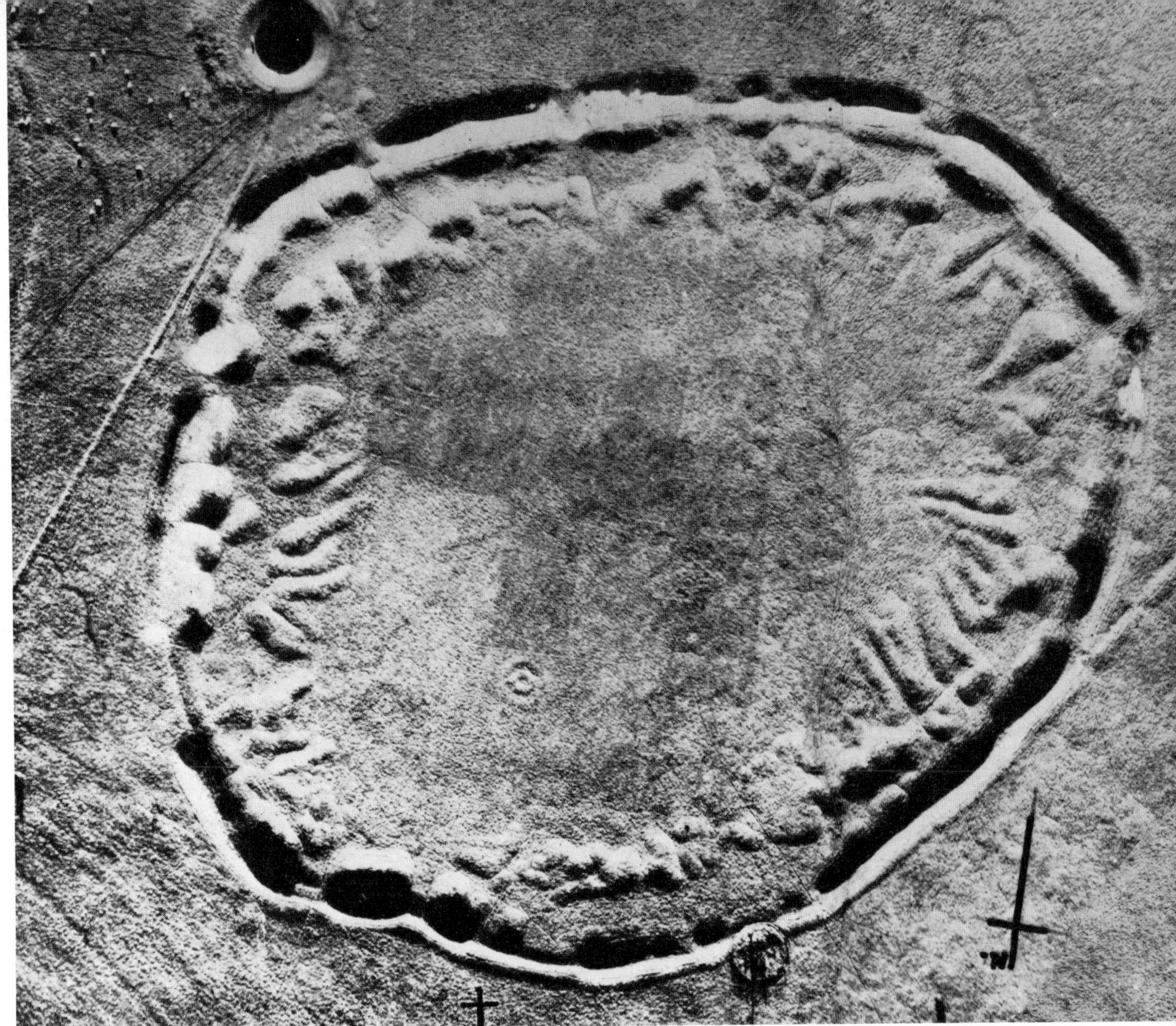

4 *Ladle Hill, Hampshire, 19 December 1929* Favourable lighting throws into relief the remains of an unfinished hillfort. Only in an aerial view can the eye make sense of these jumbled heaps of spoil and uncompleted lengths of ditch (Piggott 1931).

major earthworks was not neglected and was especially beneficial in making sense of hitherto puzzling remains like the unfinished hillfort on Ladle Hill (4).

Many of these early photographs were published in *Antiquity*, the journal founded by Crawford in 1927. So too were the photographs of Maj G W G Allen, who from 1932 to 1939 flew over an area extending from the Fens to Wessex. Allen worked principally in the Oxford region, the first time that an area so rewarding had been observed at all seasons over a period of several years. He sought not only to discover and illustrate archaeological sites of all kinds (5), but also to understand the processes that brought them into view, photographing the same site at different seasons to demonstrate its varying appearance, and taking a closer look at crop-marks by examining them on the ground (6).

In 1939–45 military needs again promoted technical development and greatly intensified activity in air-photography. Many archaeologists served as photo-interpreters, a few more as actual photographers; but there was little leisure for archaeological reconnaissance. Fl/Lt D N Riley was fortunate in finding the opportunity to continue to work of

5 *Crop-marks of a cursus, Benson, Oxfordshire, 9 July 1933*
On the future site of the wartime and modern airfield can be seen most of the outline of a cursus of exceptionally regular shape.

Allen in the Oxford region and the Fens. At the end of the War Dr J K St Joseph began his series of reconnaissance flights on behalf of Cambridge University which reached over all parts of Great Britain, and later of Ireland, and were devoted to study of all aspects of the landscape, of which archaeology is only one. The photographs obtained formed the basis of what is now one of the country's major specialist collections of air-photographs (p 25). Most parts of the country had never been studied in detail from the air before and the first years naturally brought many spectacular discoveries. The fact St Joseph went on to make such discoveries over a period of 35 years is both a tribute to his flair for this kind of work and also testimony of the great fund of archaeological information which changing patterns of agriculture have continued to bring to light (Whimster, forthcoming).

Other pioneer fliers whose long experience of archaeological reconnaissance has made a major contribution to knowledge are W A Baker, who has worked in the West Midlands since the late 1950s, and J Pickering, whose flights in the East Midlands and elsewhere began a few years later.

The present situation

The first official involvement in archaeological air-photography by a national body came with the establishment in 1965 of an Air Photographs Unit within the English National Monuments Record. This provided for the first time a distinct national archive in which all archaeological air-photographers were invited to deposit prints or negatives. The Unit, under J N Hampton, has also since 1967 made its own photographic flights throughout England, and it provides a cartographic service, transcribing data from air-photographs to maps, in response to requests from the Department of the Environment and other official bodies.

The numbers of local fliers engaged in archaeological reconnaissance of often quite limited areas greatly increased in the 1970s. The NMR Air Photographs Unit has played an invaluable liaison role in relation to these, furnishing advice and practical assistance, encouraging the deposit of photographs in the national archive, and providing an annual forum for fliers and users of air-photographs to discuss common problems. In 1974 the Council for British Archaeology added an Air Photography Committee to its list of research committees, and this in turn fostered the creation of a network of informal regional committees for the coordination of local flying, archives and plotting of results. Much local flying has been funded from the 'rescue' budget of the Directorate of Ancient Monuments and Historic Buildings, but to ensure that the resulting information is genuinely available for official and other uses a growing proportion of the money has been earmarked for transcribing the data on to maps.

In England the responsibility for local archaeological archives, in which the work of plotting from air-photographs is generally done, as well as for much of the local flying, rests today with county planning offices and archaeological Units or their equivalents, though before the introduction of the Unit system in 1973–4 much more of the local archives were in the hands of county museums. Programmes of plotting have been undertaken over the years to varying standards of accuracy and with even more variable degrees of understanding, this task having been delegated too often in the past to a junior or temporary member of staff with little experience. In Wales such responsibilities lie with the county Archaeological Trusts, which, being newer in the field, have been able to achieve a more consistent standard of photo-interpretation. Arrangements in Scotland are broadly similar though less easily categorized, local responsibilities being handled at Regional or District level. Since 1976 the Royal Commission on the Ancient and Historical Monuments of Scotland has made reconnaissance flights with the support of the Scottish Development Department, mainly in lowland areas.

PUTTING THE PHOTOGRAPHS TO USE

There is nothing magical or scientifically very advanced about air-photography. The aerial observer does not see, nor does the aerial camera normally record, what cannot already be seen on the ground—except in the obvious sense that roofs and tree-tops are better seen from above than from below. The aerial view is nevertheless of the greatest value because for many purposes an elevated viewpoint allows the best appreciation of the ground sur-

6 *Burcot Pit, Oxfordshire, 7 July 1933*
A small ditch can be seen in section in the face of a disused gravel pit. Above it cereal plants are growing appreciably taller and greener than to either side. The difference is slight, but is readily detectable from the air following the same line as the ditch beneath.

7 *A football pitch south of King's Lynn, Norfolk, 3 January 1970*
Vertical photograph (scale 1:1200). The incorrect angles, curves and distances incorporated in the layout of this pitch were evidently far from obvious on the ground, yet from the air they are painfully apparent.

face and its features. A ground observer is often too close to what he is studying to see it entire, or else too distant to discern enough detail, while the awkward angle of view seriously hampers recognition of what lies in front of him. The truth of this is apparent from fig 7, which is a vertical photograph of a football pitch. This is by no means the worst example of marking out to have been seen from the air, but it is reasonable to conclude that, if the groundsman or the players had been aware of the skewed right angles, non-parallel lines and untrue curves, they would have had something done about them. Yet, when seen from overhead, these mistakes are all perfectly obvious.

Similar considerations apply to archaeological sites. The comprehensive view obtained from the air aids the perception of significant pattern and the appreciation of relationships between one feature and another. It is the pattern made by earthworks, soil-marks or crop-marks that identifies them as belonging to archaeological remains as opposed to a variety of geological, agricultural and other phenomena and in many cases allows them to be attributed to a given type of site. Crop-marks in particular are often so subtle in expression, and almost always so difficult to scan from any place on the ground that is ordinarily accessible, that they are virtually undetectable except when seen from the air. It is not that they are actually invisible on the ground, but rather that they are undecipherable unless the pattern can be examined as a whole.

a First among the archaeological uses of air-photographs, therefore, is that of *illustration*.

This function, although simple, is important. There is no other way, for instance, that major earthworks like hillforts can be comprehended in a single glance, while individual details of their layout can be studied in context as parts of the larger whole. This is particularly valuable on sites such as castles where many parts of the masonry structure may still survive, making appreciation of the ground-plan difficult because the view is so often blocked by standing walls. Drawn plans can partly meet this need, but do not have the immediacy of an actual photograph. Plans are not always easy to understand or to relate to a given viewpoint because they conventionalize and because they portray only selected detail, whereas a photograph shows its subject in a form easily recognisable as similar to that already familiar to the eye. When earthworks are only slight, on the other hand, they are difficult to trace on the ground and it may take the overall view of an air-photograph to make them comprehensible. This is even more true of soil-marks and crop-marks. Indeed, there is no way that most crop-marks *can* be illustrated except by air-photographs or by plans derived from air-photographs.

A somewhat different approach is involved

when air-photographs are used to illustrate the modern appearance of a piece of ground pictured in historical documents. An Elizabethan village plan showing strips in the open fields can then be compared with the layout of visible ridge-and-furrow, or a seventeenth-century engraving of a formal garden largely swept away in later improvements may furnish the key to understanding some sparse and disconnected fragments of a once elaborate layout, still discernible on some air-photographs.

At the same time as displaying one or more sites, of whatever character, the photograph will also record something of the setting. This, indeed, is the modern setting at the time of photography, something which is important in its own right in relation to the history of each site (cf fig 1), but which also forms the basis for inferring the ancient setting in which it originally stood. Where the archaeological remains have survived intact, apart from superficial damage such as ploughing, the topographical situation cannot usually have been drastically transformed; but the photographs may yet provide evidence for the former presence of marshy ground, for the abandoned course of a river or for the occurrence of landslips, all of which mark significant changes between the ancient and the modern.

b The qualities which make air-photographs of value for purposes of illustration are equally rewarding for *research*. To study the mutual relationships of a complex series of earthworks it is desirable above all to be able to see them to advantage. Similarly, analysis of the plan of a group of crop-marks or soil-marks can hardly begin without examining the relevant air-photographs or transcriptions from them.

What air-photography is best and rightly known for, however, is the discovery of sites previously unknown. This is especially valuable, as well as being most spectacular, in those areas where centuries of ploughing have removed all surface traces, yet the remnants below ground can still make their presence known through the medium of crop-marks. Complementary to the rediscovery of sites apparently destroyed is the recording of those that still survive. There is an urgent need for detailed reconnaissance of areas where the destruction of archaeological sites by cultivation and other means has not yet become widespread. Newly discovered earthworks may not have previously been recorded out of sheer remoteness and inaccessibility. Others may have escaped notice for one of two contrasted reasons; either they were so slight that they had no perceptible meaning until observed together as a single group, or they were so substantial that they remained incomprehensible because of their size. In both cases it is the view from above that makes sense of the remains, by presenting a recognizable plan.

The accumulation of new discoveries results in revised and extended distributions. This affects our understanding both of individual types of site and of settlement as a whole. Notable extensions of knowledge due to the photography of crop-marks have taken place on the sands and gravels of the major river valleys, on the chalk of the Lincolnshire and Yorkshire Wolds and the Hampshire Downs, on the outcrops of the Corallian and Magnesian Limestones in Yorkshire, and on glacial outwash sands and gravels in many parts of Britain. The most dramatic of these has been in the river valleys, whose importance for early settlement, although great, should not now be over-emphasized. It has to be understood that the evidence from crop-marks is virtually limited to those soils which are favourable to their appearance, whereas the evidence for settlement derived from fieldwalking and excavation is not limited to those soils but extends onto the heavier land that often separates the rivers, especially in Midland England. The new distribution-pattern created by air-photography, though fuller than before, is little more representative of prehistoric settlement than the old.

Changes in the known distributions of individual types of site have sometimes been revolutionary: well-known examples are cursuses (pp 77–8) and Neolithic causewayed enclosures (pp 73–4), both once apparently limited to the chalk downland of southern England, but now extending to the Trent and beyond. With types of site that are already known all over the country, however, like henges (p 75), the addition of new examples has a less spectacular effect and, despite a number of valuable local studies, the evidence of air-photography has so far been comparatively neglected.

Continuing discovery can achieve even more revolutionary results, making it possible to identify completely new types of site, previously unrecognized because known examples were too few. The existence of a definite class of Roman military base with an area of about 10ha was scarcely suspected until 1962, yet there are now a dozen or more examples known or reasonably conjectured, mostly from the evidence of air-photography. The photographs sometimes draw attention to a special feature not previously regarded as being particularly significant. Some early Celtic monastic sites in Ireland had long been known to have been placed inside ancient cashels, but it took a programme of air-photography to show up the presence of circular earthworks around many other of the known sites, and of similar enclosures surrounding ancient churches not previously known to be monastic at all.

Current research on archaeological data from air-photographs has two main objectives apart from the investigation of individual sites.

One is to construct a soundly based taxonomy, especially of crop-mark sites. The first analysis must be from the crop-marks themselves, for not all types of site commonly seen as crop-marks have clear analogues among surviving earthworks, and only few are ever likely to be excavated. The obvious comparisons and identifications have already been made, and these can be found in Chapter 3 of this book; what is needed now is to classify the more ordinary sites, to catalogue their associations, and to plot their individual distributions. Such work has been undertaken or is in hand in a number of regions (eg Palmer, forthcoming), but a national synthesis will take many years to complete. Until then we shall still not know accurately the full distribution of even the commonest types of prehistoric settlement known from crop-marks, still less those of the many different classes of enclosure.

The second objective is to trace the development of the man-made landscape from prehistoric times to the present day. The same data are now analysed in relation to topography and mutual association. Instead of isolating an individual type of site and documenting its presence across the landscape, attention is concentrated on a particular area, which is then examined in its entirety. Every feature is related as precisely as the evidence allows to its neighbours, and from this a provisional sequence of development is constructed.

These two approaches are complementary and interdependent, each providing in some sense a framework for the other. Both are also dependent on excavation for the provision of outside control, by furnishing evidence of dating and function, and by testing the reliability of air-photographs as a guide to the detailed planning and general character of buried archaeological remains.

c Air-photographs in their turn give much assistance to *excavation and fieldwork*.

By revealing many new sites and providing a convenient means of comparison air-photographs contribute much to the selection of a suitable excavation site. Gone are the days when it was justifiable to excavate a site simply 'because it was there', even if threatened by some form of destruction. Excavation is undertaken because the site is a good typical example, or is interestingly atypical, or because of its key position in the development of the local landscape. Evaluation of such matters is one of the main archaeological uses of air-photographs, as we have seen. When there is a particular problem to be solved, the information gleaned from air-photographs can be remarkably specific, pointing to the exact spot where excavation might yield a satisfactory answer. In Scotland north of the Antonine Wall there are two long-known series of Roman marching-camps with areas of about 25ha and 52ha respectively; only at Ardoch (Perthshire) do members of the two series overlap; and of the two points where their ditches cross one lies inconveniently beneath a modern farm-track. Excavation of the other crossing-point established which of the camps had preceded the other (St Joseph 1970b).

When a site is known from crop-marks, these provide a framework for the excavation by revealing in advance the main elements of the plan. It should not be supposed that there is nothing else of importance to be discovered, however. Many items of major interest may be revealed by excavation which are rarely if ever seen in terms of crop-marks; these would include circular houses, many other post-built structures, cremation burials and much more (Jones 1980; Miles forthcoming). But much time will still be saved by not having to trace laboriously with spade and trowel what can already be seen on the photograph, and some valid questions can already be posed before the excavation begins.

Photogrammetry, or the science of obtaining accurate measurements from a photographic record, has been used on a number of excavations to supplement, or largely replace, the time-consuming chore of detailed planning in the field. Suitable photographs for this purpose need to be at a scale which is more easily achieved from scaffolding and similar contrivances than by means of an airborne camera. There is nevertheless scope for aerial survey on large and scattered excavations, especially where these have to be related to complex earthworks or ruins, though this is more often a necessity in the Middle East or North Africa than it is in Britain. And, whether under excavation or not, extensive and complicated groups of earthworks can be surveyed more economically by use of photogrammetric methods in conjunction with ground control than they can by ground survey alone (Johnson forthcoming).

The use of air-photographs is particularly helpful to archaeological fieldwork in remote, little-known, or poorly mapped regions. Vertical surveys are used, especially in North America, for terrain analysis, as a means of predicting where archaeological sites might reasonably be expected to have existed. When the photography is at a large enough scale to show actual sites, it may be possible to define areas that are void of visible remains and thereby save much time-consuming exploration simply to prove a negative. By showing the character and placing of natural and man-made obstacles air-photographs can aid the planning and execution of a fieldwork programme, and in poorly mapped or featureless terrain such photographs may, with all their incidental detail such as bushes and boulders, prove more useful for navigation and for field recording than any maps that are available.

d A fourth area in which air-photographs play a vital part is that of *conservation*. Air-photographs provide the evidence for many of the archaeological sites that are included on Planning Constraint Maps. When surface remains have been totally obliterated, a pattern of crop-marks on a photograph is probably the only thing that will persuade a Planning Committee that there really is something there. This is a dangerous weapon to use, however, for once a layman has been educated to understand that crop-marks indicate an archaeological site, he is almost bound to believe that the absence of crop-marks indicates the absence of an archaeological site, which is very far from the truth but is much less easily explained.

In framing a conservation policy for a given area it is often the information furnished by air-photographs that gives the clearest picture of the character and extent of archaeological sites, even at our present stage of interpretative skill. The picture will not be a complete one, of course, nor necessarily very representative, but without it little might be known at all. This turns out to be as true for upland areas in terms of stone walls and earthworks as it is, more obviously, for lowland areas in terms of crop-marks (Johnson forthcoming).

Finally, air-photography provides a means of monitoring the current condition of scheduled monuments, which are not always easily accessible on the ground, being sometimes in remote places or deep within jealously guarded private estates.

PHOTO-INTERPRETATION

Previous work

The first systematic description of archaeological air-photography as a guide to photo-interpretation was made by O G S Crawford (1929). He introduced the now familiar division into shadow-sites, soil-sites and crop-sites and illustrated the varying amount of information to be derived from each in different conditions. In crops he noted both the lusher growth over buried ditches and the poorer growth in shallow stony soil, as well as patterns made by cornfield weeds which were so much more familiar to him than they are to us today. Attempts to assess the relative merits of various crops as a medium for archaeological discovery, both in this paper and in an earlier one in the same series (1928b), neglected the critical part played by the timing of photography; the sensitivity of a crop for this purpose is related to the stage of growth, so the superiority of horse-beans or barley is liable to change as the season progresses. Crawford clearly recognized the importance of understanding the non-archaeological elements in the landscape: his final illustration, although ostensibly of the hillfort at Hambledon Hill (Dorset), was used principally to show the appearance on an air-photograph of a hayfield.

In a later publication (1938) Crawford assembled a representative selection of air-photographs of archaeological sites in Britain, using many that had been taken by G W G Allen. In an introductory essay he included his own photographs of a carpet seen from the height of a cat and from that of a man. The cat's eye view of the carpet is like that of a man on the ground looking at a field of crop-marks; he can see that there is a pattern, but he cannot make sense of it. The human view of the carpet is like a vertical photograph of the same field, with its pattern clearly displayed to view. It is a pity that the same portion of the carpet does not appear in both photographs, but the message is nevertheless clear and vivid and makes an excellent analogy. Crawford also drew attention to some of the rarer manifestations of archaeological features, such as damp-marks in bare soil and differential melting of frost and snow. Again he included a photograph of a non-archaeological pattern, this time of frost-mound hollows in the Pang valley in Berkshire picked out by crop-marks.

In 1944 D N Riley presented the first comprehensive account of what he termed 'the technique of air-archaeology'. This well-organized and lucid essay has remained the best treatment of its subject for a generation. Diagrams showing the sunlight falling on earthworks, soil-marks being created by ploughing, and crop-marks produced by buried ditches and wall-foundations have been reproduced or copied by other writers ever since. Of particular value has been his coinage of the terms *positive* and *negative* crop-marks to describe the two latter effects. Riley placed much emphasis on the importance of surface geology as a limiting factor on the appearance of crop-marks, which were only to be expected on the lighter, free-draining soils. He also took care to describe a number of misleading non-archaeological features such as frost-cracks, jointing in limestone, fungus-rings, and tree-holes.

Subsequent authors have elaborated on some of Riley's themes: J Bradford (1957) contributed his wide experience of aerial archaeology on the Continent and in Mediterranean lands, while I Scollar (1964), working in Germany, provided a more detailed analysis of the development of crop-marks through the growing season.

Reference should be made to the *Manual of Photographic Interpretation* of the American Society of Photogrammetry (Colwell 1960).

Remote-sensing techniques including air-photography are used in North America principally for ecological analysis of the terrain as a guide to predicting the occurrence of archaeological sites, which may then be sought on the ground, rather than as a means of detecting such sites by direct observation (cf Ebert & Lyons 1980). By contrast, the Royal Commission on Historical Monuments (England) published in the same year (1960) a study of the occurrence of archaeological sites on the river gravels of England as directly revealed by their crop-marks. As that time it was still possible to discuss the morphology, associations and distribution of all known crop-marks in England and to collate them with the results of excavation, though the dry summer of 1959 marked the beginning of an information explosion that has ensured that such an overall review has never been attempted again.

International conferences devoted in whole or in part to aerial archaeology were held at Ravenna in 1961, at Delft in 1962 and in Paris in 1963. These were important in allowing comparison between the results obtained in different areas and in showing the different ways in which air-photographs were used to study archaeological problems, but apart from Scollar's paper already cited they did little to explore or explain the physical processes which caused the appearance of archaeological sites on photographs. This, however, was precisely the subject of a paper by R J A Jones and R Evans (1975) given to the conference held in London in 1974; and the same authors have collaborated in relating the changing appearance of particular archaeological sites over the years to the local meteorological records (Evans & Jones 1977). The proceedings of the London conference also contained a description of the photographic techniques found essential by the Cambridge University team for successful pictures of archaeological sites, in terms as relevant to photo-interpretation as to actual photography (Wilson 1975a), as well as a collection of misleading photographs showing features that simulated genuine sites but proved on close examination to be spurious (Wilson 1975b).

One of the most significant events for aerial archaeology in recent years has been the publication of a journal devoted specifically to that discipline under the name *Aerial Archaeology*, which has appeared at least once a year since 1977. Amongst much else this has featured reports on recent flying, notes on the major photographic collections, articles on a variety of topics including photo-interpretation, regional gazetteer-bibliographies of published air-photographs, and some provocative statements of opinion about the role of air-photography in archaeological research and administration.

A final reference should be made to the conference organized by the Council for British Archaeology at Nottingham in 1980 on 'the impact of aerial reconnaissance on archaeology'. Publication of the proceedings is expected in 1983 (Maxwell forthcoming). This was a valuable assessment of how archaeology and air-photography can work together, and a number of the papers are cited here.

Scope of the present book

It is on these foundations that the present book has been constructed.

An essential first step is to understand what is happening on or below the ground to produce the patterns which we see on air-photographs (Chapter 2). This is particularly important in relation to soil-marks and crop-marks, for although these are displayed in the form of a two-dimensional pattern, they are the result of processes acting in three dimensions. If we are not to make mistakes, especially in comparing one photograph with another, we must be able in imagination to look below the surface. At the same time we must also be aware of the atmosphere filling the space between the camera and the ground, taking account of local conditions of haze and lighting and of their varying importance in relation to the angle of the camera. All these factors affect the quality of the photographic image which we are seeking to interpret.

Archaeological and non-archaeological features are distinguished by the differences in their characteristic patterns. It is convenient to describe the archaeological features first (Chapter 3) because they are the principal subject of the book and because it is in terms of accidental resemblances to archaeological features that the non-archaeological features have most often to be considered. The principal types of archaeological site at present recognizable on air-photographs are described in terms of their layout and dimensions. They are for the most part grouped into functional categories (ritual sites, forts, settlements, etc.) rather than on the basis of shape, because there is no overall morphological classification at present available and it would be misleading to imply that there was as yet sufficient information in the right form to construct one. It is to be hoped that in this book's successor, perhaps in ten years' time, it will be possible to look up 'an isolated double-ditched oval enclosure of maximum diameter 200m with a single plain entrance, sited on a ridge-top in Berwickshire', and to learn not merely that it is a prehistoric settlement but also its probable date and cultural associations and the distribution of the type. For the time being we must be content to set down for the first time what is so far known in fairly broad outline. The diagnostic features of individual types of site are emphasized and very full cross-references are given to features both archaeological and non-archaeological with which they might possibly be confused.

Considerable importance is attached to the succeeding chapter describing a wide range of non-archaeological features (Chapter 4). The identification of any pattern on an air-photograph as being probably of archaeological origin is always to a significant degree dependent on a process of elimination. No normal agricultural process or other modern activity or geological feature appears to be involved, therefore there is a good chance that we are looking at an archaeological site. And if a good representative range of archaeological sites has never been systematically described before as an aid to photo-interpretation, still less have the non-archaeological features. Some of the geological patterns described are not to be found in any geological textbook, and the only general description of soil-patterns seen on air-photographs of lowland Britain is hidden away in a photogrammetrical journal (R Evans 1972). The normal appearance from the air of healthy crop-plants is not something which takes up appreciable space in the agricultural literature, though the effects of pests and disease are often well illustrated with air-photographs. And few of the more miscellaneous items (disused airfields, fairgrounds, gas-pipe trenches) have previously been described. Space will not permit every feature of the landscape to be included, so attention is concentrated on those which bear some resemblance to archaeological sites or have relevance to their interpretation.

The contents of these three chapters are essential to successful photo-interpretation, but they are only a beginning. Guidance is still required on how best to set about it and how to avoid jumping to false conclusions (Chapter 5). This is regarded as being a practical matter to which the theoretical analysis of interpretation (eg in Lueder 1959) contributes little; but there is one fundamental division which it is vital never to abandon, between the *recognition* of archaeological features on a photograph (eg ditches forming a four-sided enclosure with four entrances) and their *archaeological interpretation* (a Roman camp, probably of the third quarter of the first century AD). The inferences made in the process of recognition, in this sense of the word, may require some correction in the light of later photography but may generally be expected to stand, if competently done in the first place; but the subsequent archaeological interpretation is always subject to revision as a result of widening knowledge or more detailed analysis. Archaeological interpretation is in its nature provisional, even when made with justifiable confidence, and room should always be left for reinterpretation at a later date.

Two further topics call for consideration, though necessarily in summary form. These concern the recording of interpretations, especially by means of drawing accurate outlines on a map or plan, and the subsequent retrieval of the information contained by means of some kind of systematic index (Chapter 6). Detailed instructions on how to achieve these aims must be sought in appropriate handbooks elsewhere, but the general strategies to be adopted are given a critical appraisal.

DIFFERENT TYPES OF PHOTOGRAPH AND WHERE TO FIND THEM

Vertical and oblique photographs

Vertical photographs are those taken with the camera pointing straight down at the ground. Nowadays the camera is fitted inside the aircraft, fixed in a mount on the floor over an opening constructed specially for the purpose. The vertical view is an unfamiliar one and for many subjects difficult at first to understand, but for archaeological sites with little or no relief this scarcely applies and is indeed counterbalanced by the resemblance to an archaeological plan. The lens of a survey camera is designed so that, if the ground is perfectly flat and the axis of the lens is perpendicular to it, every feature will be represented on the photograph in its correct plan position. In practice, of course, this seldom occurs, because of sloping or uneven ground or of camera tilts. It is normal to use a wide-angle lens for survey photography, so although the view is truly vertical at the centre of the frame, making an angle of 90° with the horizontal, this angle is reduced nearly to 53° at the centre of each side and to less than 45° at the extreme corners of the format. Any irregularity of the ground will thus produce geometrical distortions in the photographic image identical to those we see on oblique photographs (p 196), and it is foolhardy to suppose that a single vertical photograph is equivalent to a scale-plan in the sense that accurate measurements can be taken off it directly without a good deal of geometrical analysis.

Vertical photography does not normally consist of single photographs, however. It is a survey technique in which strips of overlapping photographs of identical scale are used to cover a given area. Successive frames are normally made to overlap by 60 per cent, ensuring that every part of the subject is covered by at least two photographs taken from slightly different positions. When the two images are combined in a stereoscope, a three-dimensional picture or *model* is seen, and when this model is adjusted to the coordinates of a small number of corresponding ground control points, accurate plans and measurements can then be directly obtained. This is the science of photogrammetry (Kilford 1979, with references there cited).

Relatively little vertical photography has been carried out by specialist archaeological air-photographers. This is principally because it is only a professional air-survey organization that will have an appropriate camera or an aircraft specially modified to carry it. There are, however, other reasons also. The procedures for vertical photography are time-consuming compared with simply flying round a site and taking oblique photographs of it through the window opening, while flying-time is expensive and good photographic conditions often transitory. Furthermore, as will be seen in Chapter 2, oblique photographs offer a clearer rendering of most types of archaeological site and may record details that cannot be sufficiently well discerned on an equivalent vertical view.

Vertical surveys having been usually made for non-archaeological purposes, it is very much a matter of luck whether the lighting or the season was favourable to detecting archaeological sites. It is nevertheless worthwhile to make systematic searches of the available cover, and many important discoveries have been made in this way. Suggested sources of photographs are discussed below (p 25).

With oblique photographs there is no

temptation to regard them as virtual plans, since the effects of perspective are obvious. They are not in fact useless for cartographic purposes, though the methods required are often laborious and the results usually a little less than perfect (see Chapter 6). But they do have the advantage of being deliberate portraits of the archaeological sites concerned, taken (one should hope) from the most rewarding angles. When a specialist air-photographer records an archaeological site in this way, the most important elements in the interpretation have taken place before he presses the button on the camera. He has already decided that the site is worthy of photography and he has chosen a viewpoint to emphasise its character. Unlike vertical photographs which are non-selective, the specialist oblique is very selective indeed, and although it is sometimes possible to find important details in the photograph that were not appreciated at the time it was being taken, when a complete site remains unnoticed it remains unphotographed also.

Panchromatic, colour and infra-red emulsions

The standard emulsion for air-photography is monochrome panchromatic, used with a deep-yellow filter to exclude all blue light. This is despite the fact that for photo-interpretation, other things being equal, colour photographs must always be regarded as being preferable to black-and-white. It is absurd, for example, ever to be in doubt whether a particular field is in bare soil or under crop because the grey tones of the photograph are not sufficiently distinctive. Other things, however, are not in fact equal. Colour films and colour processing are costly of both time and money, at least if you aim higher than the routine processing by the manufacturer of a non-professional miniature film. Furthermore, colour films have less exposure latitude than monochrome, and incorrect exposure besides resulting in too little or too much colour saturation also upsets the colour balance. When colour is used in poor photographic conditions, the results are therefore disappointing. We can accept a less than perfect monochrome photograph as being adequate for a working record, but less than perfect colour no longer serves the purpose of using colour film, which is to have a true rendering of the colours seen. In serious archaeological reconnaissance, therefore, colour is used only sparingly and then in optimum conditions.

Emulsions sensitive to the near infra-red portion of the spectrum are specially useful for the study of vegetation. Monochrome infra-red gives a wider range of grey tones in rendering the foliage of different species than panchromatic film, and 'false-colour' infra-red has the further advantage of picking out very clearly dead or diseased vegetation. False-colour infra-red is available in the 35mm format and has a certain vogue, especially in France, for archaeological work. In reality its advantages are very slight. Infra-red films have better haze penetration than true colour or panchromatic; against that must be set the comparatively slow film speed of false-colour film, which makes it difficult to use in those conditions when haze is most troublesome, ie when the sun is low in the sky and the strength of the light is beginning to fail (p 31). Experiments have shown that false-colour film can on occasion reveal some crop-mark detail not recorded by other emulsions (Hampton 1974), but for the most part it shows the same marks as true colour and panchromatic film, in a less readily intelligible form.

One of the most useful characteristics of false-colour film for archaeological research is that it is possible to obtain from it black-and-white prints of exceptionally high contrast, by making them through a red or a green filter. This can be of value in studying crop-marks, the red filter being appropriate to isolating positive marks during their phase of maximum greenness (pp 56–8), while the green filter will emphasize the corresponding negative marks. Another method of enhancing the photographic image is to process it through a computer (Scollar 1979), supposing suitable hardware of sufficient capacity to be available. Numerous manipulations of the image are possible, for example to enhance the sharpness and the contrast and to minimize the effect of cloud shadow. It may be noted that 'density-slicing', i.e. the technique of isolating that part of the image that lies within a given range of density, whether done by computer or by special film designed for the purpose, is of doubtful value for tracing archaeological crop-marks on air-photographs. The times when an aid of this kind would most be of service are unfortunately just those when the crop-marks have furnished an image of very variable density.

Sources for obtaining air-photographs

Photographs are available from specialist archives catering specifically for archaeological research and from national and commercial sources of survey photography.

In Britain the principal specialist archives are those of the three National Monuments Records and of Cambridge University. The National Monuments Records form part of the respective Royal Commissions on Ancient and Historical Monuments, housed in London, Edinburgh and Aberystwyth. They hold photographs taken by numerous local fliers, supplemented in England and Scotland by those taken on behalf of the Commissions themselves, as well as historic photographs from the Crawford Collection and elsewhere. The photographs in the Cambridge University Collection have all been taken on behalf of the University since 1945 to assist teaching and research in a wide variety of subjects, amongst which archaeology has always been well to the fore. The areas visited include the whole of the British Isles, apart from certain of the Channel Islands, and the nearer parts of the European mainland. Honourable mention should also be made of the Allen Collection in the Ashmolean Museum, Oxford, which also holds D N Riley's wartime photographs.

At a local level it is worth consulting the county Sites and Monuments Record or equivalent, which will itself contain many relevant photographs of the area as well as details of others which are to be found in the larger collections already mentioned.

The main collections of general survey photography are in the Air Photographs Units of the Department of the Environment and the Scottish Development Department. These contain photographs of the National Air Survey taken by the RAF since 1946, covering the whole country, and Ordnance Survey photography up to 1966. In ordering copies it is wise, in addition to giving the National Grid Reference of the area required, to indicate any preferences or limitations of choice: eg the earliest available cover, scale not smaller than 1:10,000, summer photography only, not more than 5 per cent obscured by cloud. There is no guarantee that particular photographs will not contain cloud and this can be very frustrating. Each Unit also contains a Central Register of Air Photography which documents a great deal of the commercial cover that is available; copies of these photographs must be sought from the firms responsible. Recent Ordnance Survey photographs are available from the Survey itself. It is also worth consulting the Survey's regional offices, which are little used by the general public and are usually glad to respond to any enquiry. Another local source of information is the Regional, County or District Planning Office. There can be few of these which do not have one or more sets of photographs for their area, which can usually be consulted through their courtesy, though not, of course, removed. Copies are not directly available, but it should be possible to learn the name of the firm that did the original survey and to note the reference numbers of the relevant prints. Amongst the commercial firms only Aerofilms maintains a photographic library fully indexed to allow consultation in terms of subject as well as locality.

Addresses

ENGLAND

The Air Photographs Unit
National Monuments Record
Royal Commission on Historical Monuments (England)
Fortress House
23 Savile Row
London W1X 1AD

Cambridge University Collection of Aerial Photographs
The Mond Building
Free School Lane
Cambridge CB2 3RF

Department of Antiquities
Ashmolean Museum
Beaumont Street
Oxford OX1 2PH

The Air Photographs Unit
Department of the Environment
Prince Consort House
Albert Embankment
London SE1 7TF

Ordnance Survey
Romsey Road
Maybush
Southampton

Aerofilms Library
4 Albemarle Street
London W1X 4HR

SCOTLAND

National Monuments Record of Scotland
Royal Commission on the Ancient and Historical Monuments of Scotland
54 Melville Street
Edinburgh EH3 7HF

Air Photographs Unit
Scottish Development Department
New St Andrew's House
St James Centre
Edinburgh EH1 3SZ

WALES

National Monuments Record for Wales
Royal Commission on Ancient and Historical Monuments in Wales
Edleston House
Queen's Road
Aberystwyth
Dyfed SY23 2HP

Air Photographs Unit
Welsh Office
Room G-003
Crown Offices
Cathays Park
Cardiff CF1 3NQ

Other methods of remote sensing

This book is concerned only with low-altitude photographic imagery, but brief reference may be made to other forms of remote sensing. High-altitude and satellite photography have been found of little relevance as yet to archaeological reconnaissance. Important sites are often difficult enough to see from 1500ft (450m) above the ground in oblique view, let alone vertically from a height of 15 miles. And the higher up you go, the more often there will be cloud underneath you, masking what you want to see.

Radar has been successfully used for archaeological research in parts of the world where conventional photography is difficult or non-existent (Adams 1980), but it would seem to have little to offer in the countries of western Europe.

Infra-red linescan is more promising. This should not be confused with infra-red photography (described above): it is a thermal sensing technique which records differences of temperature at the ground surface. So far thermal imagery has only been used to show visible earthworks and soil-marks which can be better recorded by conventional photography (Baker 1975), but it should theoretically be possible also to detect thermal differences caused by buried (and invisible) archaeological remains. That such differences do in fact exist is shown by the differential melting of snow and frost over archaeological features (p 49). The difficulty is that, except when the ground is white with snow, the thermal effect of the sun's rays falling on its surface quite blankets out the feeble differences of temperature caused by buried ditches. The technique should be tried out when the sky is completely overcast for several hours; otherwise it would seem that thermal sensing for archaeology can only take place at night, which has too many disadvantages to be likely to be widely adopted.

2

The Nature of the Evidence

There are four principal guises in which archaeological sites make their appearance on air-photographs: as buildings, earthworks, soil-marks and crop-marks. To the last three of these, substantial sections of this chapter are devoted. Little space is given to upstanding buildings; this is because their remains are in general self-explanatory and require no special elucidation. An architectural historian has no reason to feel baffled or confused by the aerial view. With other forms of archaeological remains it is quite otherwise, and inadequate appreciation of the peculiarities of air-photography may lead to erroneous conclusions.

The first step is to consider the nature of the evidence on the ground, both above and below the surface, and the way in which it is rendered in the photographic image. This is not the place to describe photographic techniques as such, but it is important for the interpreter to have some understanding of the conditions in which photographs come to be taken. Many of the factors involved in obtaining a successful air-photograph (Wilson 1975a; Parsons 1980) are directly relevant in interpretation, not least for assessing the value of a particular print as a source of archaeological data.

FEATURES IN RELIEF

We are concerned first of all with places where men have shaped the surface of the ground, deliberately or accidentally making mounds and hollows, banks and ditches, terraces, lynchets and artificial platforms. It is convenient to refer to all of these simply as 'earthworks', but this term must be understood to include walls and tumbled stonework, whether or not the stones are covered with earth or overgrown. Ruins are to be equated either with buildings or with earthworks according to their state of preservation.

Sunshine and shadows

Earthworks may be picked out on air-photographs by vegetation, snow, or flood-water, but they are chiefly revealed by the pattern of sunlight and shadow on their surface. At midday in summer, when the sun is nearly overhead, the slighter earthworks cast no appreciable shadow and so remain virtually invisible (8). As the sun sinks towards the horizon, the shadows become longer and the lighting more dramatic (9). An hour before sunset, provided the sun itself stays free of cloud, the lighting may have become so harsh as to be photographically unpleasing, but even minute irregularities of the surface will then be displayed, as long as they are not obscured by shadow from another feature. Such extreme conditions are not favourable for photographing larger earthworks, since too much ground is effectively lost in areas of deep shadow.

Different parts of the same site may in fact need to be studied on photographs taken in widely differing conditions. In a major hill-fort, for example, the defences may be seen to best advantage if photographed in the late morning or early afternoon on a day when direct sunlight is filtered through a thin layer of high cloud. Such soft overhead lighting provides sufficient light and shade for appreciation of relief in major earthworks without at the same time creating impenetrable shadows. But in order to detect the slight traces of contemporary hut circles or of subsequent

8 *Kirkstead Abbey, Lincolnshire, 8 June 1951*
A view of the abbey ruins, looking NNW, about midday near the middle of summer. The site is dappled with cloud shadow, but the principal remains are in sun. Shadows in general are very short and, although earthworks are visible, they are virtually incomprehensible, apart from some water-filled hollows, which stand out more clearly. The lofty piece of surviving masonry marks the south end of the south transept of the abbey church. Compare fig. 9.

The vertical black line running across the trees on the left side of the photograph is caused by a scratch on the negative (p 180).

9 *Kirkstead Abbey, Lincolnshire, 2 February 1969*
The view is similar to that in fig 8, but the low winter sun of a February afternoon picks out the grass-covered ruins with breath-taking clarity. The difference in the length of the shadows is made especially evident by the tall fragment of the transept, which acts like the gnomon of a giant sundial. The church itself, on the near side of this 'gnomon', is the least informative part of the site, presumably because it has been heavily pillaged by stone-robbers. The excellent rendering of the remainder of the plan is partly due to the sun being in the south-west: its rays strike the remains of east-west and north-south walls at a similar angle, without emphasizing either set at the expense of the other.

cultivation within the defended area it will be necessary to have photographs taken with the sun low in the sky and unobstructed.

Shadows are affected by the direction of the sun as well as by its elevation. Different features on the same site may be more or less easy to see solely because of their position in relation to the sun. Linear features lying square to the sun throw good shadows along their entire length and their appearance on the photograph corresponds well with their disposition on the ground. But linear features aligned on the sun's rays cast very little shadow, and what shadow there is gives little idea of their principal dimension. A deeply sunk hollow way, for example, may virtually disappear from view when the sun is shining directly along it, despite it being one of the principal features of a deserted medieval village (10, 11). In studying any group of earthworks it is therefore essential to have photographs taken on several occasions, at different seasons or at different times of day, so as to have the benefit of shadows falling in more than one direction.

The local topography also plays its part. Earthworks on hill-slopes facing towards the sun have shorter shadows; those on slopes facing away from the sun have longer ones, provided they are in sun at all. When a site occupies ground with varied slopes, photographs of the earthworks may therefore give a misleading impression of the relative scale of the remains in different parts of the site. The relative lengths of shadow gradually change as the sun moves round and the angle of its rays is varied; so comparison of photographs taken with the sun in different positions should reveal any error.

On oblique photographs the relative strength with which highlights and shadows are rendered is altered to an appreciable extent by the direction of view. Photographs taken looking down sun show principally the sunlit side of earthworks and give little emphasis to shadows (12). Photographs taken looking into sun have just the opposite effect and give the shadows their maximum visual

10 *Deserted medieval village, North Marefield, Leicestershire, 30 March 1965*
North is to the right, and the sun is a little south of west. The ground slopes down to the brook on the north side and also inwards to the tributary stream which flows through the village. The site of the church is marked by a level platform in a prominent position above the confluence. The village streets are shown by hollow ways, but those running in an east-west direction in the foreground are difficult to see because their sides do not throw a shadow. Compare fig 11. Note also variations in width in the surrounding ridge-and-furrow (p 124).

11 *Deserted medieval village, North Marefield, Leicestershire, 9 February 1978*
The same site as in fig 10 is seen from the same angle, but under snow and with the sun about south-west. The different direction of the lighting allows many features in the foreground, such as streets, house remains, lynchets and hollows, to be seen clearly for the first time. All these features can be traced on the earlier photograph *once they have been seen on this one*. By contrast, the channels of the tributary stream have recently been filled in, leaving conspicuously blank strips across the centre of the site.

impact (13). In photographic terms the view into sun yields the greatest tonal contrast, or at least it *would* do so but for the complication of atmospheric haze.

Haze is a very important limiting factor in all air-photography. It is derived mostly from industrial smoke and varies in concentration from one area to another and from day to day. Haze particles in the atmosphere scatter the light rays between the camera and the ground, reducing clarity and tonal contrast in the photographic image. For someone standing on the ground and looking upwards the same effect transforms the sky from a clear blue to a shimmering silvery grey. The effect is something like having layers of gauze drawn between the aircraft and the ground. The amount of interference caused, as with actual gauze, depends upon the lighting and the direction of view. Unfortunately, the conditions that favour the recording of earthworks on air-photographs (oblique sunlight and a view into sun) are precisely those that make the effects of haze most noticeable (14). Most earthwork photography is thus a compromise in which the length of shadow and the degree of haze have to be nicely balanced (Wilson 1975a). The extreme conditions described above, when the sun is no more than 10° above the horizon, can only be exploited where there is unspoilt visibility of 50km or more. The combination of clear skies, perfect visibility and a trained photographer at the right place and time occurs only rarely and certainly cannot be expected for the majority of sites; yet it is the photographs taken on such occasions that set the standard by which all other work has to be judged.

Surface vegetation

In the absence of direct sunlight, or in addition to it, there are a number of other indicators that contribute to the recognition of earthworks. Superficial vegetation may be affected by the earthworks' own relief and drainage. Certain plant species have an ecological preference for the better-drained position on a raised bank, while others prefer the relative dampness of the accompanying ditch.

12 *Walton Hall, Warwickshire, looking north, 15 November 1974*
In the foreground, between the lawns and the river, sheep are grazing. The ground is uneven but shows no significant pattern, apart from the straight line of a drain running down to the river on the left (cf fig 13).

13 *Walton Hall, Warwickshire, looking south-west, 15 November 1974*
This photograph was taken on the same occasion as fig 12, but looks towards the sun so as to emphasize the shadows. It is now possible to recognise the remains of a small deserted village with a broad hollow way, bordered by rows of crofts, leading down to a road-junction by the river.

A Roman camp on moorland, for example, may be outlined by rushes growing in its ditch (57a). Such differences of vegetation may be made visible by taller, darker or more luxuriant growth, or the reverse; and the effect may be compounded by the effects of preferential grazing by cattle, sheep or rabbits. On occasions there may be a striking contrast of colour. The earthworks of a deserted medieval village for example, may be picked out by yellow lines of buttercups growing along the banks. Such effects can be recorded satisfactorily on monochrome film, but are even more telling when photographed in colour.

In conditions of drought these variations in the local drainage may become critical for the survival in that spot of a particular species. They also have a marked effect on the vegetation in general, whatever its specific composition. Plants growing on the sun-baked surface of a mound or bank will be more likely to wilt than similar plants growing in the shelter of a moist ditch. The first to show signs of parching will be those rooted in shallow soil over an impenetrable layer such as road metalling, masonry or solid rock. On many earthwork sites the visible grassy banks cover the stumps of masonry walls, long ruined; lines of parching develop above the stonework and plainly mark out the banks, quite independently of sun and shadow (15). Conversely, in a prolonged heat-wave, when whole fields of grass turn brown under the scorching sun, lines of green may continue to pick out the ditches of archaeological features until eventually they too dry out and no green remains at all.

Another aspect of the ecology of earthworks may be mentioned here, though unlikely to be encountered on recent photographs. Before the spread of myxomatosis rabbits used to be numerous on chalk downland. Prehistoric and later earthworks were so attractive to the rabbit population for their burrows that in some areas the lines of earthworks could be traced on air-photographs by means of the white patches of chalky soil exposed in rabbit scrapes.

14 *The Wrekin, Shropshire, 30 January 1966*
The view is south-west, almost directly into the winter sun. The inner and outer north-east gateways into the hillfort are clearly seen in the foreground, but all background detail is lost in haze.

Snow, frost and flood

Snow and hoarfrost contribute to the photography of earthworks by a variety of special effects. They are both very reflective: even a light dusting of snow or frost provides an excellent background for recording stone-walled settlements on moor and fell and may enable photographs to be taken when conditions would otherwise be too dull. Even in the absence of shadows the dark lines of tumbled stonework show up against the white expanse where snow has settled. In direct sunlight all varieties of earthworks are displayed with brilliant clarity, as much by the shining highlights as by the shadows. Every change in

slope is signalled by a corresponding change of tone, and subtle effects of light and shade reveal significant shapes normally too indistinct for the eye to perceive (16). Light snow cover is a particularly sensitive medium for rendering surface texture, lying in a continuous sheet on smooth areas of mown or close-grazed turf but broken over rough grass and scrub. The outstanding example is found on golf courses, where the greens and fairways are seen as vivid splashes of gleaming white, while the 'rough', by contrast, seems merely to have been stippled with the same brush. With a greater depth of snow some blurring of the finest detail is bound to occur: the textural differences are smoothed away, leaving

15 *Deserted medieval village, North Marefield, Leicestershire, 2 July 1976*
The same site as that illustrated in figs 10 and 11 is seen here in conditions of summer drought. The time is near midday and the earthworks throw no shadows. Hollow ways are still visible as ribbons of unparched grass, but the bed of the moat has dried out completely round half its circuit. Beside the village streets there are rectangular outlines marking the positions of about three dozen cottages, where the stone foundations have caused extreme parching in the grass above. Although many of these cottages are detectable from surface indications in relief (figs 10, 11), the parch-marks provide more precise and unambiguous data.

16 *Roman camps north of Grindon, Northumberland, 2 February 1970*
Three small camps are visible under a thin mantling of snow. The best preserved, at the top of the picture, has three entrances with protecting traverses, of which the clearest is on the north side, towards the right. The south rampart has been damaged by ridge-and-furrow ploughing, and the whole camp is scored by field drains. The camp in the foreground was discovered from the air in 1930 and appears to have entrances in the east and west sides; faint traces of the traverses can still be seen. The third camp lies inside the first but seems not till now to have been recognised: winter sunlight reveals a small square enclosure bounded by a very low bank with slight external ditch; internal *claviculae* may also be visible, though this is not certain.

The camps are presumably 'practice works' built by troops serving on Hadrian's Wall (p 100).

17 *Medieval fort south of Ors, Nord, France, March 1970*
The outline of a thirteenth-century fort on the west bank of the Sambre is preserved in the modern field boundaries; the double moat only comes into view when filled with water by persistent rain.

nothing to distract the eye from the essential shape of the ground. The glistening surface now makes a perfect screen on which to view the pattern of highlight and shadow (71), and the shadows themselves, although crisply defined, are not so dark as to limit detailed scrutiny.

In windy conditions snow accumulates in some places more than others. The more exposed areas such as the Pennine moors may be swept virtually bare by high winds, while the intervening dales are blocked with massive drifts. Farmland often shows varied but unpredictable patterns where the wind has eddied round trees or driven through gaps in hedges, scouring a broad track across all or part of a field (119). Ditches and hollows are soon filled with deeper snow whose smooth surface contrasts with their windswept surroundings. Banks collect the snow variously on the upwind or downwind side, either acting as an obstacle against which drifts are piled, or as a windbreak behind which the flakes can sink to a sheltered resting-place. Only features lying across the path of the wind will generate these effects. When the snow eventually melts, the deepest drifts survive the longest, and these may compose photogenic patterns in which many of the banks and lynchets in a complex site are picked out by lines of white (Wilson 1975a, fig 8). Similarly, snow may survive where it lies on the icy surface of water-filled ditches (59).

Standing water is another useful indicator. Moats and fishponds, for example, are much easier to see when water-filled (8). The smooth surface of the water is reflective and contrasts well with surrounding grassland. Water standing in the fields because of heavy rain, melted snow or floods finds its way quickly into hollows, possibly including some not previously noticed (Chouquer 1977). Thus, the gentle depressions left by a filled-in ditch-system may be virtually invisible on the ground or from the air, yet leap into view when holding a centimetre or two of water (17). Flood-waters can draw attention to individual earthworks by cutting them off from dry land; but the exact height of the water is critical, and the discovery of previously unrecorded earthworks by this means must certainly be rare. Major floods have more importance for the insight they afford into topography and into the conditions that would exist in the absence of flood banks, sea defences and artificial drainage channels. When the River Great Ouse burst its eastern bank below St Ives in March 1947 and flooded part of the Fens near Cambridge, its waters halted on a line that bounded the known distribution of Romano-British settlement. Survey photographs taken by the RAF to record the extent of the flooding were found to be of considerable value in subsequent archaeological investigation of the area (Bromwich 1970, 114–15).

Photographic conditions and the timing of photography

It should be clear from these comments that there is no one time of year at which photography of earthworks should be generally undertaken. On the contrary, the most reliable interpretations are those based on photographs of the same site obtained at several different times. More important are the conditions in which the photographs themselves are taken. For pictures of good quality the requirements are visibility of not less than 20km, and bright sunlight with the sun no more than 20° above the horizon. During the winter months (November–February) the sun in Britain scarcely climbs any higher, even at midday. At midsummer, by contrast, similar lighting only occurs in the south of the country in the early morning, before 0700, and in the evening, after 1900 (British Summer Time). Photographs taken in less favourable conditions, eg with the sun higher in the sky, are far from being worthless, but there is a significant reduction in the amount of detailed information to be gained from them (8). No credence should be given, for example, to a statement that visible earthworks are wholly absent from a given site, if the conclusion is derived solely from inspection of photographs taken at 1530 on a July afternoon.

While summer and winter photography are equally desirable, there are seasonal differences that make winter photographs of special interest. Good photographic weather is, of course, limited, but it can be very rewarding when it does occur. There are long shadows when the sun shines, and their appearance may be enhanced by snow. There are some earthwork sites which can be effectively photographed at no other time of year, because in summer they are smothered in bracken or screened from view by trees (18). Commercial surveys are seldom planned for the winter months, as opportunities for completing the work are too unpredictable; and relatively little archaeological reconnaissance has been done in winter either, for broadly similar reasons. Winter photographs are therefore prized for their rarity as well as for their quality and scientific value.

It sometimes happens that a site is so awkwardly placed, at the foot of a steep hillside for example, that it is only seldom reached by the sun at low elevation. In theory, suitable oblique lighting occurs both in the early morning and in the evening, but early-morning photography has found favour with few practitioners since Crawford and Keiller in 1924. Quite apart from the practical difficulties of getting into the air and reaching the relevant area in time, visibility is often reduced during this part of the day by a temporary moisture haze, as the sun warms the earth's surface and the dew evaporates.

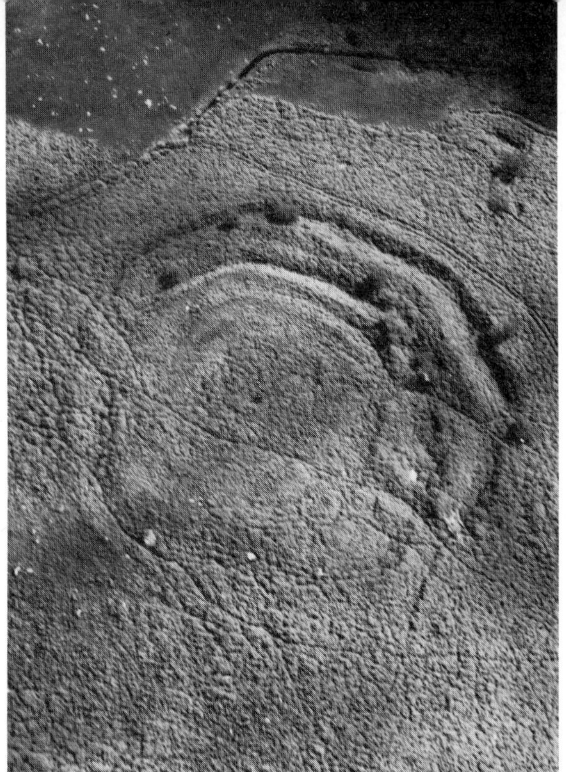

18 *Beanley Moor, Northumberland: (a) 26 July 1972, (b) 31 January 1969*
The photographs show the same small hillfort in summer and winter conditions. In July the earthworks are smothered in bracken, preventing detailed interpretation, but in January they are clearly displayed in the slanting winter sunlight.

Earthwork photography is thus effectively restricted to the evenings for most of the year, though in winter suitable lighting is also available in the middle of the day.

There is considerable variation in the direction of sunset from one season to another, and this means that a given site may come into evening sun at one season only. In southern Britain the sun at midsummer sets to north of west-north-west (about 305°); at midwinter, to south of west-south-west (about 235°). Photography may go on until 90 minutes before sunset, but not much longer unless conditions are exceptional; by then the midsummer sun will have reached 285° or a little more. This is the most northerly position of the sun likely to be of use for earthwork photography. The equivalent position in midwinter is about 215°. In winter, photography in similar conditions is also possible in the middle of the day when the sun is in the south. To catch the sun further to the east involves flying in the early morning, which is subject to the practical limitations mentioned in the preceding paragraph. At the beginning or end of winter, photography can begin at 1000, when the sun is at around 150°. If we take that as the extreme position for most practical purposes, there is a total range of useful illumination of about 135°. This is sufficient to cover the majority of sites, but would still miss one overlooked by a steep slope facing north-east. To obtain suitable photographs of that would entail making special arrangements for an early morning flight in summer. It should not be forgotten that overlapping vertical photographs of a sufficiently large scale, say 1:3000 or larger, could make an acceptable record even in the absence of favourable lighting (see below).

Verticals or obliques?

The relative merits of vertical and oblique photographs for archaeological research have already been summarized in Chapter 1 (p 23), but certain characteristics are specially pertinent to the interpretation of earthworks. For studying relief there is no adequate substitute for the three-dimensional image afforded by overlapping vertical photographs viewed with a stereoscope. The stereoscopic effect is independent of lighting, vegetation and other effects described above, but in practice the eye is aided by them so much that they become virtually indispensable. Most available vertical photography is at scales that are relatively small for the study of archaeological earthworks, being at 1:10 000 or smaller. Unless the earthworks are emphasized in some way, their image is so inconspicuous as to be likely to escape notice altogether. At larger scales, the combination of effective lighting with stereoscopic viewing provides a realistic and unambiguous image from which detailed interpretations can be made with confidence.

Oblique photographs, on the other hand, have the advantage of being able to exploit the most telling point of view. When the remains are very slight or poorly preserved, the extra emphasis and increased contrast obtained from one particular camera angle may make all the difference in recognising some significant feature, which may in turn transform the interpretation of a whole site (19).

MARKS IN BARE SOIL

How soil-marks are made

When a field containing earthworks (20) is brought into cultivation, the uneven surface usually needs to be prepared for ploughing by some degree of preliminary levelling. The tops of the earthworks are scraped off and the spoil is dumped in the deeper hollows. The characteristic raw scars left by the bulldozer blade are conspicuous against the otherwise unbroken turf, especially when the soil is

19 *Roman camp, Ystradfellte, Powys, 8 June 1956*

Although the view is westwards, looking directly into sun, the slight ramparts of the camp (arrowed) are not particularly easy to recognise. The north-west angle is crossed by a system of drains, and parts of the east side cannot now be traced. At the centre of the east side, however, can be seen the characteristic curve of an internal *clavicula*, putting beyond doubt that the earthworks belong to a Roman military camp (p 98). Other photographs taken from different angles on the same occasion do not show the *clavicula* with sufficient clarity to permit a positive identification.

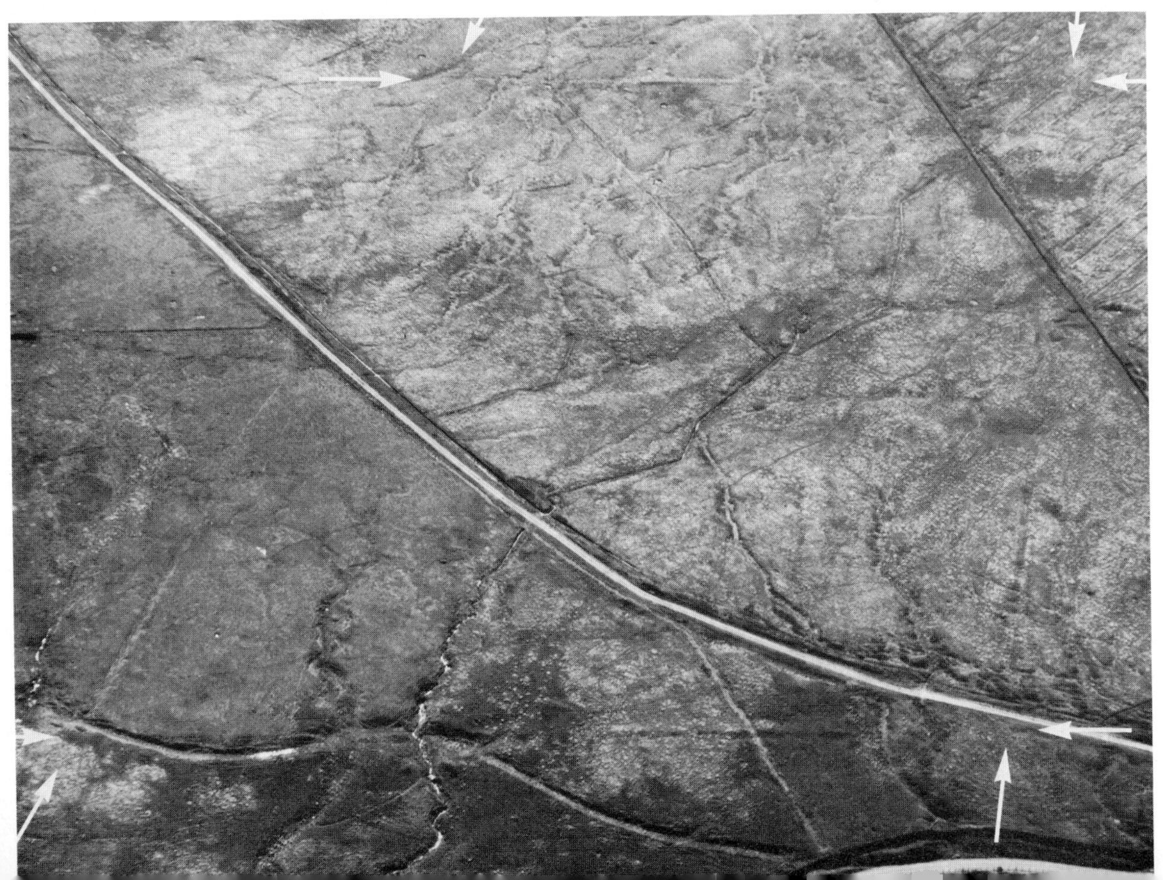

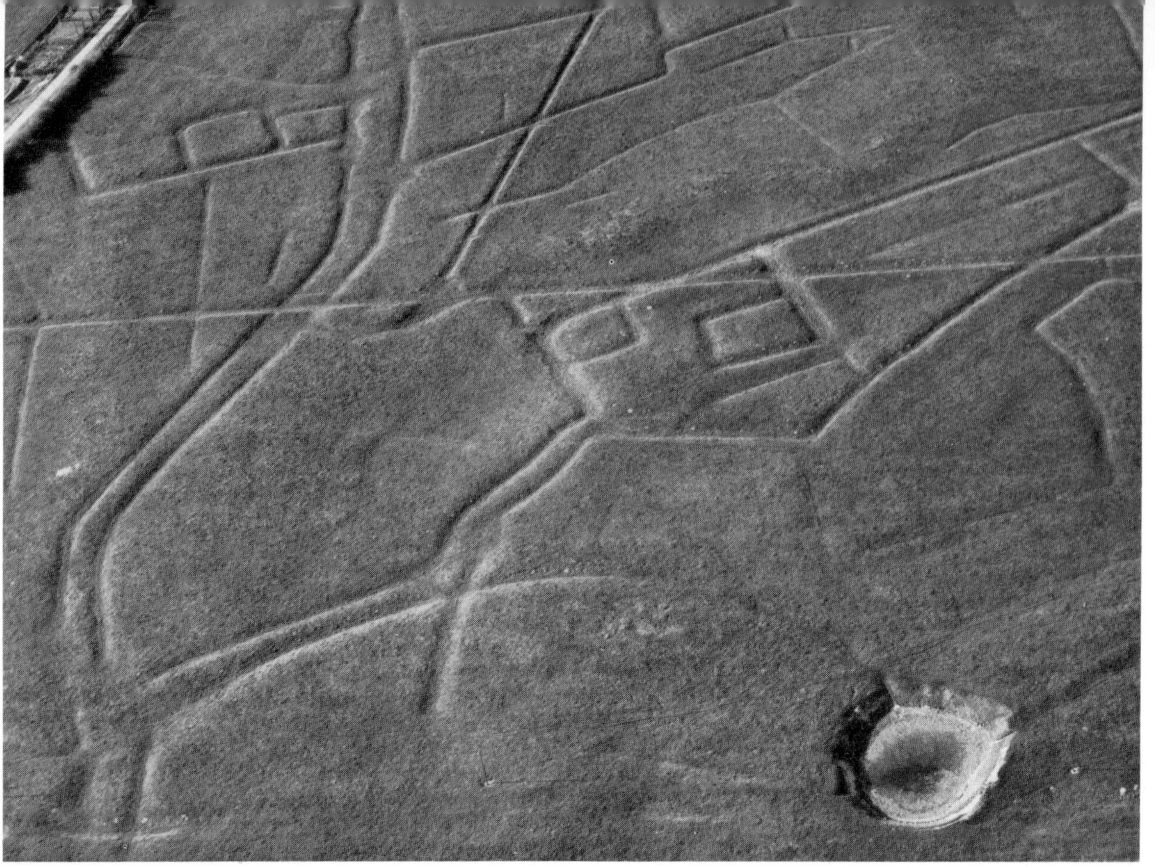

20 *Shell Bridge, south-west of Holbeach, Lincolnshire, 21 April 1960*
This group of earthworks is typical of the remains of Roman exploitation of the Fens. Two small enclosures are sited either side of a cross-country lane; the lanes, fields and enclosures are all bounded by drainage ditches. Two straight ditches in the upper half of the picture cut across everything else and are evidently post-Roman, as is the pond in the foreground. Slight ridging of the surface of the field, including the Roman lane, shows that there has been some post-Roman cultivation. Compare fig 21.

21 *Shell Bridge, south-west of Holbeach, Lincolnshire, 14 March 1961*
The earthworks recorded in fig 20 are seen again less than twelve months later. Most of the site has been ploughed, but work was halted on the two enclosures during preliminary levelling in order to allow archaeological excavation. Comparison of the two photographs shows that a new system of drains has also been inserted. Some new archaeological details are visible as soil-marks, e.g. the narrow lines outside the ditches of the two lanes in the foreground, perhaps marking trenches to hold fences; but it has become more difficult to separate ancient from modern features.

light-coloured (21). Some sites, such as deserted medieval villages in the English Midlands, are composed principally of hollows, with few banks and mounds in proportion to hollow ways, moats and boundary ditches, and these require different treatment. Here soil is brought in from elsewhere and used to level off the surface. The site is then ready for its first ploughing.

The combination of bulldozing and ploughing quickly diminishes all except the most massive earthworks. After two or three years the ground may still be visibly uneven, but the original pattern of the earthworks is irrecoverable in any but the vaguest sense from their relief alone (St Joseph 1971). Thereafter, the remains may survive in this reduced condition for a surprisingly long time. Once all serious obstacles to ploughing have been cleared out of the way, the plough itself tends to maintain the smoothed profile, as it bites down into the softer filling of ditches and rides over the more compact material at the base of artificial banks.

Once earthworks have been ploughed up, there is generally more to be learnt from the resulting marks in the plough-soil than there is from any residual relief. Each time that the plough passes across the site, it brings to the surface a series of samples sliced from the underlying archaeological features. Each sample may be only a centimetre thick on the very bottom of the sod, but as the sod is turned by the plough, this lowest layer is the one that is displayed to view (22). The result is a continuous and systematic 'demonstration' (in the scientific sense) of the character of what lies beneath. Since archaeological layers differ from the natural soil, and from the plough-soil that succeeds it, a pattern of marks is produced in the field that corresponds to that of the former earthworks (20, 21). Pits and ditches, for example, unless deliberately filled with other material, often contain a dark filling comparatively rich in organic matter. This contrasts with the remainder of the field, making distinctive spots and bands of darker tone. Banks, on the other

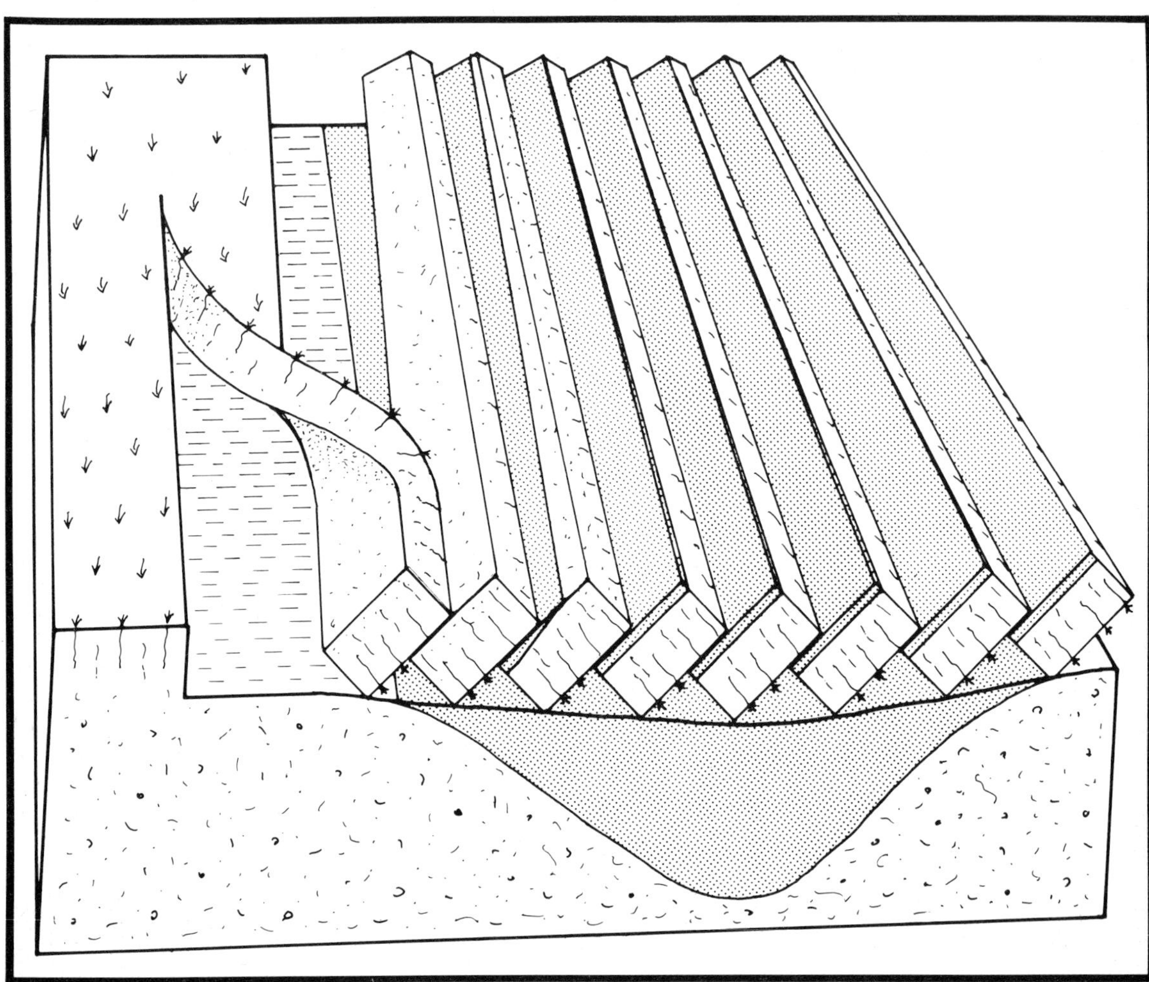

22 *Diagram showing the effect of ploughing over a buried archaeological ditch* (based on Bowen 1961, fig 1).

hand, are mostly made of the local subsoil or of materials specially brought in, such as clay, turf and gravel: in each case the archaeological material is likely to be distinguishable by a difference in colour, tone or texture. Building debris may also be present in sufficient quantity to be visible from the air.

Soil-marks produced by ploughing are directly derived from the physical remains of archaeological features, but they do not mark the *precise* spot at which the features lie. During the time that the furrow-slice is cut, lifted, turned and dumped it is carried forwards by the plough. The distance varies according to local conditions and the actual machinery used, but it is large enough to be appreciated on air-photographs. When ploughing takes place in alternate directions, the marks have a characteristically ragged edge, as the archaeological layers have been pulled first one way and then the other (21, 82). The same effect is very clearly seen in photographs of Roman villas and other buildings taken by Mr R. Agache in northern France, where deep ploughing has brought up chalk blocks from the wall foundations and disposed them alternately in two parallel rows (28). When the field has been ploughed in 'lands' (p 156), dislocation of the soil-marks by changes in the direction of ploughing is less frequent but often more dramatic. The effect can be so vivid as to give the impression that the earthworks themselves have in some way been displaced (23), but this is a misunderstanding of the nature of soil-marks. The marks are entirely superficial, capable of being displaced by plough and harrow and eventually scattered and lost; the archaeological features from which they are taken remain in position to supply further soil-marks until they are eventually obliterated. As long as soil-marks continue to make their appearance, two archaeological conclusions can be drawn: first, there are still some physical remains beneath the surface, however slight; but second, they are being subjected to repeated erosion in the course of ploughing.

Soil-marks are generally at their brightest and clearest the first time that earthworks are ploughed. The ploughshare cuts deeply into material that has long been protected by a covering of turf and is little weathered, creating marks that look outstandingly fresh. This freshness fades gradually with successive ploughings, as the archaeological layers become more deeply weathered and disturbed and the amount brought up to the surface grows less. A change to deeper ploughing may rejuvenate the marks, signalling an increase in the severity of plough damage, but care is needed in drawing this conclusion from the evidence of photographs, since brightness is also affected by soil moisture, clod size and

23 *Ridge-and-furrow, Bittesby, Leicestershire, 28 March 1956*
Soil-marks reveal the complex interlocking pattern of ridge-and-furrow in one of the open fields of a vanished medieval village. The subsoil is Keuper Marl, and the view directly down sun emphasizes contrasts in the red soil. Two tractors are at work harrowing. The marks are brightest where the ground is still unharrowed and the modern plough-furrows are aligned on the sun's rays. They are least clear during the first hour after harrowing, when the clods are newly broken and there has been little time for the surface to dry out. The medieval ridges are in several widths, and many of them have a narrow dark line along the crest; these narrow lines are either obscured or obliterated in the course of harrowing. Dramatic discontinuities resembling geological fault-lines occur between the 'lands' in which ploughing and harrowing have been carried out; these affect only the surface soil and are quite ephemeral. Photographs taken in a later year show no sign of permanent displacement.

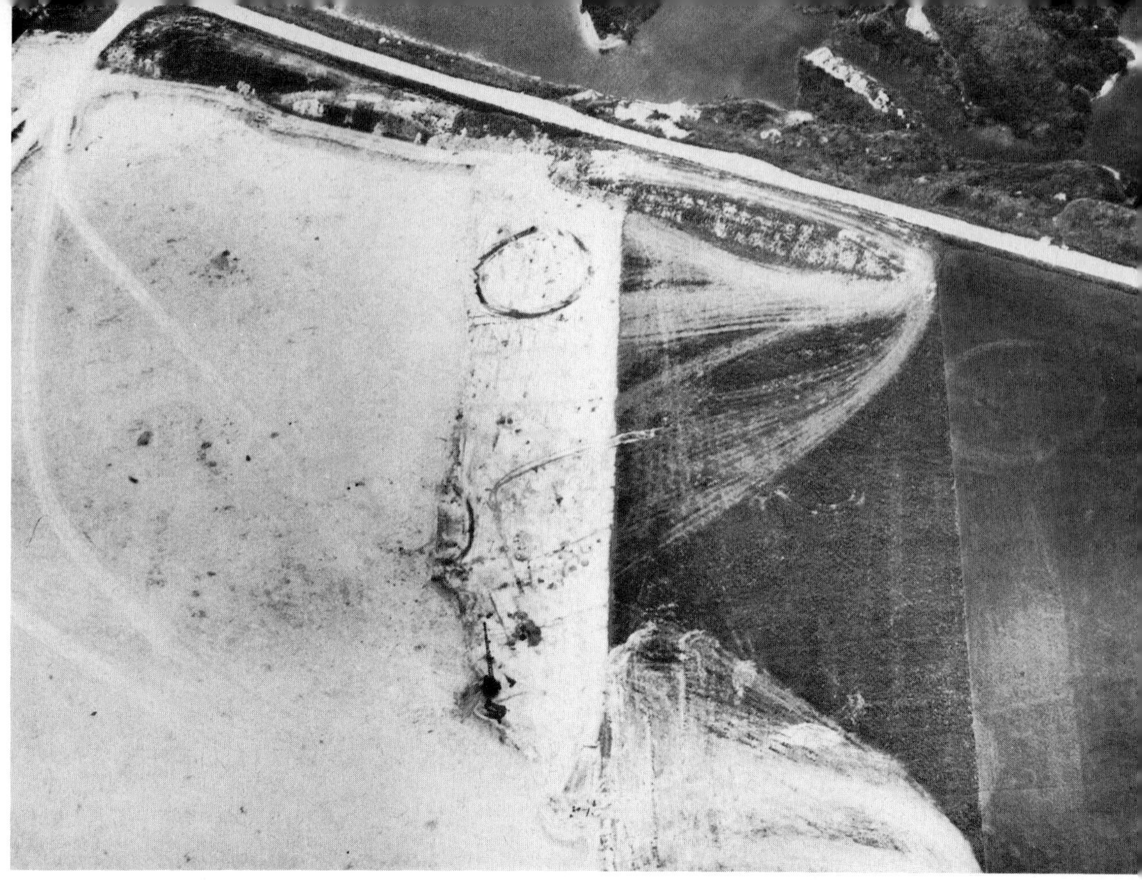

24 *Vicarage Field, Stanton Harcourt, Oxfordshire, 23 June 1952*
Gravel extraction is in progress on an archaeological site: the dragline excavator can be seen (bottom centre) above the quarry face. To the left, emergency archaeological excavations in 1945 and 1951 found remains of Neolithic to Roman date. In the central strip, removal of topsoil has uncovered a ring ditch 24m in diameter, with part of a second, and much of a rectangular ditched enclosure containing pits. Both ring ditches are somewhat irregular and have a palisade-trench immediately inside the ditch; a circle of pits near the centre of the further ring ditch probably marks the site of an Iron-Age or Roman-British house. On the right, where the ground is still in cultivation, a large ring ditch and other crop-marks can be seen; these were subsequently destroyed without archaeological excavation.

direction of view (p 45), not to mention the tonal contrast of the lens, film and photographic paper.

The most persistent soil-marks are those of major earthworks with substantial ditches, such as moats, fishponds, henges and hillforts. Medieval ridge-and-furrow produces a comparable effect when brought back into cultivation, as the soil exposed on the ridges is comparatively little weathered and contrasts with the dark, organically rich, surface soil accumulated in the former furrows. The strength of this contrast will depend very largely on the colour of the subsoil, being most pronounced when this is very pale or bright (23).

Soil-marks in pits and quarries

An entirely different source of soil-marks is the stripping of topsoil from areas intended for quarrying or gravel-working. No upstanding remains can survive this process, but features cut into the subsoil are exposed to view as in the floor of an archaeological excavation (24). Features revealed in this way are under immediate threat of total destruction and, in the absence of emergency excavation or survey, the air-photographs may well prove to be the only existing records of the site. It is important in interpretation to make a clear distinction between marks in pits and quarries

25 *Spalding Common, Lincolnshire, 10 March 1954*
Part of the Romano-British landscape is revealed by soil-marks in the silt-fen. An organised pattern of lanes, fields and farmsteads bounded by straight lengths of drainage ditch has been superimposed on a natural pattern of wandering creeks most of which were evidently dry in Roman times. In the bottom right-hand corner one of the modern fields is being harrowed; this produces a marked change of tone, but does not obscure the soil-marks.

and marks in fields: soil-marks in a quarry show archaeological features actually *in situ*, whereas those in a ploughed field are already at one remove from their original context. Marks in fields are in the majority, however, and the comments in this book refer to them unless soil-marks in quarries are specifically mentioned.

Variations in contrast due to geology, soil moisture and cultivation

Soil-marks can occur in some form on most soil-types found in Britain, but they are most easily seen when the subsoil is brightly coloured or reflective.

Chalky soils are outstanding as a source of clear and detailed archaeological information, yielding distinct marks with a broad tonal range, the palish plough-soil contrasting equally well with the brown filling of pits and ditches and with the brilliant white of unmixed chalk incorporated in banks and barrows (48). Given that the chalk downs of southern England and the chalk wolds of Lincolnshire and Yorkshire were attractive to early settlement, the wealth of detail discernible in soil-marks in shallow chalk soils has peculiar importance. The very high tonal contrast presents photographic problems, however. Unless the exposure, development and printing of the film have been carefully controlled to give maximum definition to marks in bare soil, much of the archaeological detail is liable to be lost. Photographs derived from routine surveys carried out for non-archaeological purposes may sometimes be disappointing for this reason, with some fields appearing as uniformly white when more sympathetic printing would have revealed the presence of archaeological features.

Soil-marks of notable clarity but less intense contrast are found in the silt-fen of south Lincolnshire and north Cambridgeshire, where the dark soil, filling drainage ditches and extinct natural watercourses, shows up boldly against the light-toned silt through which they are cut (25). In the adjoining peat-fen the colours of the natural drainage pattern are reversed (p 154); archaeological features on the silt roddons show clearly, but on the black peat soil, marks do not survive with any clarity after the first year or two of ploughing. Red soils, e.g. on sandstone or Keuper Marl, are capable of furnishing vivid results if photographed on standard panchromatic film. Panchromatic emulsions render the colour red in a relatively light tone, extending the tonal range of the soil-marks to a sometimes surprising degree (23). On other subsoils there is less difference of colour between the soil and its parent material and results are therefore less spectacular, being limited mostly to large or newly ploughed earthworks.

In any particular soil, colour differences are most apparent when the surface is fairly dry and well weathered, but they disappear if it becomes wet or dries out completely. With shallow soils over chalk, for example, it has been found that there is a stronger tonal contrast when the moisture content of surface clods is 5–6 per cent than when it is either 1–2 per cent or 19–22 per cent (Jones & Evans 1975). These figures refer principally to the interior of the clod and its weathered outer skin will be distinctly drier. Cultivation of the surface by rolling and harrowing breaks open the clods, exposing damper soil in the breaks, which therefore show a darker tone. How long this change of tone survives, and how far it affects the visibility of archaeological marks, will depend on the character of the individual soil and on its existing moisture content, as well as the weather conditions prevailing at the time. In some places, where the ground is very dry, harrowing might for a time actually enhance the appearance of soil-marks. Over chalk, however, it will often transform a field of complex soil-marks into a uniform expanse of pale-brown, which may take a day or more to regain its former varied tones. Fig 23 shows harrowing taking place over Keuper Marl: the immediate effect is to blot out all differences in tone, but recovery is very rapid, the tonal range being restored before the tractor can pass five times across a large field. In fig 25 on the other hand, harrowing in the silt-fen is making no difference to the visibility of soil-marks of a number of broad ditches, though there is a marked general change of tone.

The purpose of harrowing and rolling is to break down the clods to give a more even tilth for the seed bed. Although soil-marks do survive, as we have already seen, they are far from being unaltered. Mixing of the surface soil causes a reduction of tonal contrast, obliterates most of the finer detail and increases blurring of the outlines (26). The final effect almost gives the impression that this part of the photograph has been taken in soft focus.

Tonal contrast is also affected by the relative positions of sun and camera and by the direction of ploughing. Soil-marks will normally yield the brightest image in an oblique view looking directly down sun, though damp-marks (p 48) will often appear most clearly when viewed from the opposite direction (Agache 1978, 265; 1979, figs 22–30). On sites where the maximum definition is required, oblique photography is thus to be preferred. The same effect can be seen on vertical photographs taken through a wide-angle lens, since the view to the edge of the format is noticeably oblique (*c* 45°). Soil-marks recorded near the edge of the photograph on the side away from the sun appear brighter than similar marks on the opposite side. If the same soil-marks can be studied on two or three consecutive frames of an overlapping series, the differences of contrast due to the change in angle become very evident. Another tonal effect that has been observed on vertical photographs is that, if the direction of ploughing is east-west, the contrast is reduced, as much light is then reflected away from the camera (Jones & Evans 1975). This comment takes

for granted that the photography was carried out in the middle of the day when the sun was in the south. But the same effect is to be seen when the sun is in other positions, if not too low; and it also occurs on oblique photographs. Thus, in fig 23 the sun is nearly south-west; there is an appreciable difference between the brightness of soil-marks in the centre of the picture, where the sun is shining down the furrows, and that of similar marks on the right, where it is shining across them.

26 *Iron Age settlement, north of Itchen Abbas, Hampshire, 23 January 1976*
An enclosed settlement of polygonal outline straddles the boundary between two fields on the Hampshire Downs. The subsoil is chalk and the nearer field has been harrowed. The soil-marks in the foreground are soft and blurred; those beyond the fence, brighter and more distinct. Other soil-marks in the photograph are of a round barrow, enclosures, and various boundary ditches. In the background, a third field has been ploughed in lands, causing a number of dislocations in soil-marks of a long line of ditch.

Ephemeral marks appearing after rain, snow or frost

In the ordinary way, despite the effects of weathering and cultivation, soil-marks will persist for a matter of months. In certain special conditions, however, marks may appear very briefly in places where no soil-mark is otherwise to be seen. These conditions occur after rain while the ground is drying out, and after snow or frost during the following thaw.

At the end of a spell of rain the surface of a field in bare soil is virtually waterlogged. If the soil is light, the surface dries out quickly; if it is heavier, the process takes longer. The visible change in tone from the waterlogged state to the merely moist is quite marked, and this draws attention to variations in the rate of drying between one part of the field and another. Such variations may be due to differences in the drainage or to differences in the composition of the soil itself. Patterns of field drains, for example, are revealed briefly at this stage by the appearance of paler lines of drier soil. Less expectedly, in ploughed-out systems of ridge-and-furrow the position of the

27 *Oplinter, Brabant Province, Belgium, 28 October 1968*
A field in bare soil in drying out in the late afternoon sun after a shower. Among various irregular patches of drier soil, shown by lighter tone, is a circular mark about 30m in diameter. Similar circles elsewhere in Belgium have been found to overlie buried ditches of Neolithic and Bronze-Age date. A mark of this kind lasts only for as long as it takes the rest of the field to dry.

furrows is also marked by rapidly drying soil. While field drains are designed to carry away excessive ground water, medieval furrows have a very localized drainage effect and in fact normally contain additional moisture because of their deep, organically rich soil. We must distinguish here between what is visible at the surface and what happens lower down. Rainwater percolates downwards from the surface into the bottom of the furrow, allowing the surface soil to dry out relatively quickly despite the reservoir of moisture beneath, whereas water in the shallower soil above the ridges can only seep away sideways over a more protracted period. Other archaeological features are capable of producing a similar effect: all that is needed is a substantial pit or ditch acting as a sump into which rainwater can quickly drain.

These short-lived marks caused by differences of drainage have received little attention in Britain, where other forms of soil-marks are relatively abundant. In Belgium and northern France, however, large areas are covered with *limon* (brickearth), in which there is scarcely any colour difference between the plough-soil and the normal filling of ditches. It is only by deliberately flying between showers in search of damp-marks, in unsettled conditions that the British aerial archaeologist would almost certainly shun, that his French and Belgian counterparts can obtain archaeological results from bare soil in these areas (27). There is no reason to believe that similar methods would fail to produce similar results in Britain, at least on shallow well-drained soils. Observation of ploughed-down ridge-and-furrow would soon establish in which areas the appropriate conditions existed.

Besides their effect on local drainage, archaeological sites are also capable of altering the permeability of the soil. On sandy or loamy soil, for example, the collapse or demolition of buildings with clay walls produces a local increase in the clay content of the soil, which will become visible in drying conditions as an area of damper, and therefore darker, soil. The effect is very transient, and in other conditions there may be no trace of archaeological features on the site. Roman villas and settlements on the fertile plains of Picardy, where the soil is *limon*, are unusual in having clay-walled buildings with footings of chalk, whose white outline in the soil immediately betrays the nature of the remains (28). It is rare to obtain such precise information from the study of photographs alone; elsewhere positive identification of archaeological sites from damp-marks of this kind will usually depend on careful field-walking and documentary research.

Melting snow and frost provide another special context in which archaeological sites may make a brief appearance. The rapidity of melting is affected by a variety of factors including soil temperature: provided the other factors (eg depth of snow, air temperature and

direct sunshine) are operating evenly, variations in the soil temperature can determine which parts of a field start melting first. Since archaeological features are liable to contain abrupt changes in many soil characters, such as depth, moisture, particle size and compactness, their effect on the soil temperature can be sufficient to cause significant patterns in the melting snow. The resulting marks are vivid (44b), but are seldom seen and recorded.

Temperature differences in the soil are not constant, since they derive from the varied response of different materials to changes in exposure. A familiar analogy is provided by the way in which the sea, which is cooler than the land during most of the day, stays warmer than the land during most of the night. It is slower to warm up under the sun, and it is slower to cool down by night. Similar, if smaller, variations occur within the soil, where differences of composition cause heat or cold to be absorbed more or less quickly at different places. The resulting temperature fluctuations are themselves complex. Immediate response to the current weather is superimposed on a seasonal rhythm: as gardeners

28 *Roman villa at l'Epinette, Coullemelle, Somme, France, March 1967*
Deep ploughing has brought to the surface material from the chalk foundations of a simple Roman farmhouse with six rooms. Each of the shorter walls appears to be marked by a double broken line, but close inspection shows that this is really a single line staggered every few furrows in response to the passage of the plough in alternate directions. An area of damp ground round the house is caused by the presence of clay derived from its ruined walls. Similar damp areas extending to the right of the picture show where outbuildings with no perceptible foundations once flanked a trapezoidal courtyard 200m long (as marked by the arrows). Another damp area behind the farmhouse (marked *i*), if not the site of another building, may have been a pond.

will know, the soil as a whole is warmer in the autumn than in the early spring. For all these reasons it is impossible to state as a general rule that the filling of buried ditches will always be cooler or warmer than the undisturbed subsoil. Experience has shown that in winter conditions, when frost and snow occur, buried ditches have been revealed by lines of unmelted snow on a variety of subsoils (44b, cf

Léva & Hus 1975, 88); but elsewhere the reverse effect has been seen, with snow melting first over the darker filling of the ditch. An important factor may be the amount of moisture contained within the ditch at the time.

Differential melting can even occur when archaeological features are covered by the turf of a mown lawn. The buried foundations of demolished buildings, eg on the site of a medieval abbey, form lines of persistent coldness which tend to conserve any overlying snow and produce lines of white on the grass. In this way the plan may become visible from the bedroom windows of a succeeding mansion, as well as from an aircraft. The contrary effect was observed from the air at Kirkham Priory in February 1970, when hoarfrost melted first along the line of the walls of some long-vanished buildings north of the church (Wilson 1975a, fig 10). It was suggested that this melting was caused by the presence of robber-trenches from which all stonework had been removed. This conjecture was confirmed by further observations made after the summer drought of 1975, when the same pattern emerged as lines of unparched grass implying a greater depth of soil and an absence of substantial masonry (see below, pp 60–1).

Anomalies in soil temperature caused by buried archaeological features might be expected to produce visible effects only in the most favourable conditions. These would include thin snow, a slow thaw, and a minimum depth of topsoil. Yet an unmetalled Roman road in Belgium, detected by Mr C. Léva in February 1969 from a line of unmelted snow, was found to lie at a depth of 1.40m below the surface (Léva & Hus 1975, fig 6). Someone unfamiliar with the *limon* soil and with the full severity of a Continental winter can only report such an observation with awe.

Photographic conditions and the timing of photography

Soil-marks can be seen at all seasons of the year, but are most abundant in the spring when there is most land in bare soil. They remain visible from the time of ploughing until after the young seedlings have appeared, but are clearer before being harrowed. Some weathering of the soil after ploughing is usually an advantage, especially on stony ground, where stone-free areas are more easily discerned after surface stones have been washed clean by rain.

The soil, at the time of photography, should be neither soaking wet nor bone dry: the ideal condition varies from one soil-type to another. In the silt-fen, experience shows that soil-marks are clearest in drying conditions a day or two after a period of rain. On chalk, the soil needs to be relatively dry, since chalk loses its full brilliance when wet (cf the figures quoted on p 46). The special effects described on pp 47–50 can only be obtained in the particular conditions appropriate to each and are unlikely to be encountered on routine survey photographs. Specialist archaeological photographers will need to seize the opportunity of drying ground or melting snow as it occurs, if they are to win new information by these means.

The photographic conditions required for recording soil-marks are not so exacting as those demanded by earthworks. Photography is no longer restricted to periods of low sun and to areas free of cloud, but can take place in most conditions when the general light-level is sufficient. Haze is still a limitation, but the ability to work in the middle of the day even in summer, when the sun is high and the effects of haze less obtrusive, means that a greater degree of haze can be tolerated. Visibility of 10km, while less than could be wished, is still adequate to obtain photographs for a working record. Photographs of really good quality would need visibility of 20km or more. Sunshine is also an advantage, since sunny pictures look more pleasing and have stronger contrast; but satisfactory results can be obtained in shadow. Indeed, on chalk soils sunless conditions might even be preferable in view of the brightness of most of the soil-marks to be found there. What is less satisfactory is when a particular site lies partly in sun and partly in shadow. This presents photographic problems in exposure and subsequent printing, if all parts of the site are to be rendered with equal clarity. In addition, the patchy lighting is distracting to the eye of an interpreter. At their most misleading tonal variations due to cloud shadow can be confused with those due to colour differences in the soil. If the original negative is available, it will be helpful to have two differently exposed prints made from it, one produced specifically for the sunlit areas, the other for the shadows. Both prints should be used in any interpretation.

How good is the archaeological information?

It is important to be clear about the limitations of evidence derived from soil-marks.

In the first place, it was optimistically assumed on pp 41–2 above that archaeological layers can be easily distinguished from subsoil and plough-soil. In practice, as the experienced excavator knows, the filling of some archaeological features so closely resembles its surroundings that a great deal of skill and persistence is needed in excavation to identify the features with any certainty. This may be because the feature in question has been deliberately filled with the material originally dug from it. A post-pit dug in gravel and packed with similar gravel can only be detected, if at all, by slight differences in compactness and humic content. Natural silting can lead to a similar result. A ditch cut through an easily eroded subsoil such as sand or marl will rapidly fill with material that may be scarcely distinguishable from the undisturbed subsoil. The filling need not be homogeneous to cause difficulty: collapse of the sides of a half-filled pit over the top of its filling will successfully conceal the pit's existence until the lower levels have been reached. It would be unrealistic to suppose that features so elusive in excavation could be recognized from the air in terms of soil-marks.

Secondly, when soil-marks do appear, they refer specifically to the level at which erosion of the remains is currently taking place. In a quarry this is self-evident: marks seen in the area stripped for quarrying reveal archaeological features present at that level, but features more deeply buried remain invisible. The same applies to soil-marks seen in a ploughed field; they provide information about archaeological features at the depth to which the plough has reached. If the plough passes over the top of a feature, nothing will be seen. These propositions are elementary but important. Fig. 28, for example, is of a Gallo-Roman villa whose extent is shown by areas of damp ground: these are caused by the clay from the walls of its buildings. At the head of the courtyard the site of the farmhouse is boldly marked by lines of chalk foundations, but no foundations are visible along the sides of the courtyard where other buildings must have stood. This is a discrepancy for which there are three possible interpretations, each one postulating a different depth of ploughing in relation to the foundations of the buildings.

1 Ploughing below foundation-level: perhaps the outhouse foundations, being shallower than those of the farmhouse, have already been ploughed away, leaving no surviving trace.

2 Ploughing at foundation-level: the outbuildings in this modestly appointed villa may have been constructed from the first without chalk foundations, and therefore there are none to be revealed.

3 Ploughing above foundation-level: all the real foundations may be at a lower level, still to be reached by the plough. The farmhouse, however, could have had walls in which the lowest courses were also of chalk, and it may be these which are now being disturbed.

Any supporter of the third interpretation must also account for the accumulation of soil in post-Roman times by which the Roman features are said to be buried. Explanation no. 2 is the most plausible, but no. 1 remains a possibility. All three interpretations require to be considered, but only excavation will yield a definitive answer.

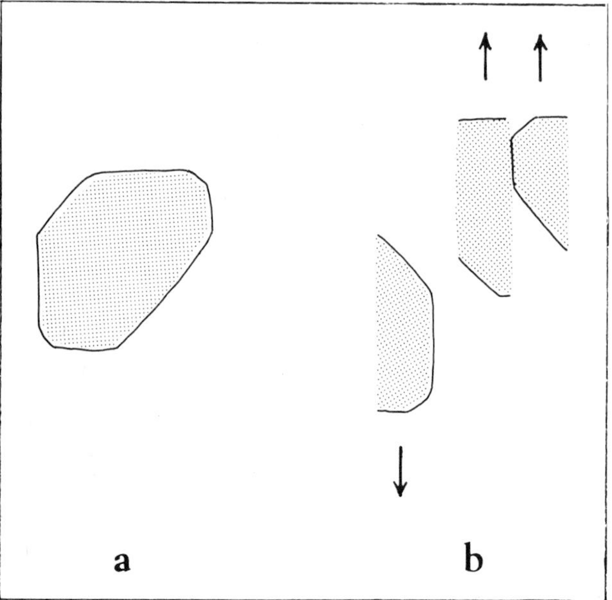

29 *Displacement of soil-marks by the plough*
(*a*) Plan of an archaeological feature below the plough-soil. (*b*) Plan of soil-marks derived from the same feature. The direction of ploughing is indicated by arrows.

Thirdly, the picture of archaeological remains presented by soil-marks on ploughed land is subject to a number of distortions. These have been described above, but can usefully be restated. The actual 'picture' is made up of a series of narrow parallel strips; these are the furrow-slices, 200–400mm wide. These strips are seen in their correct sequence, but each one has been reversed to give what is in effect a mirror image. At many sites groups of strips are pulled out of register with their neighbours, either in a regular succession of small bundles of 2–4 furrows, typical of 'one-way' ploughing, or in larger blocks, when ploughing has been done in 'lands' (p 156).

These distortions are individually slight, but their cumulative effect can be quite significant. The total effect can be likened to looking at a scene through textured glass; the stronger and more definite elements in the pattern can be read without much difficulty, but fine details are liable to get lost. A small mark divided between two furrows, for example, is physically split into two distinct portions, which may be further separated if the plough has reversed its direction (29). If the double mark is still read as one, it will appear larger than it should; but if not, it is unlikely to be intelligible at all. Linear marks are more easily picked out, but much may depend on the angle at which they cross the furrows.

Soil-marks in pits and quarries present their own problems. While they can appear with notable clarity (24), they are also liable to be obscured by the tracks of earth-moving machinery. Minor features may disappear, and at worst the archaeological pattern is so disrupted that interpretation in any detail becomes virtually impossible.

The fineness of detail possible in soil-marks may be estimated from selected photographs of the more exceptional sites. At Allington Hill in Cambridgeshire soil-marks photographed in 1964 showed the post-pits of two aisled houses (Wilson 1974b, pl 24 B; cf RCHM 1972, fig 22). The pits for the main uprights of each house appear to be somewhat less than a metre across, while those for the corresponding posts in the side walls appear to be less than half of that, ie no more than 0·4m. It is probably significant that side posts cannot be recognised at all the relevant positions; this suggests that marks of this size are at about the threshold of perception in ploughed land on chalk. We may compare soil-marks in a gravel pit recorded at Vicarage Field, Stanton Harcourt in Oxfordshire (24 above; cf Sturdy 1973, fig 2). Palisade-trenches inside two of the ring-ditches are estimated to be no more than 0·15m wide.

The ultimate test in assessing the archaeological reliability of soil-marks is excavation. So little detailed information has as yet been published on this question that the observations of Mr R W Mackey quoted below are of particular value. The site is a Roman villa at Welton Wold, where soil-marks revealed only certain of the features (30).

The soil marks ... simply reflect the chalk-soil proportion in each fill. Many early features were

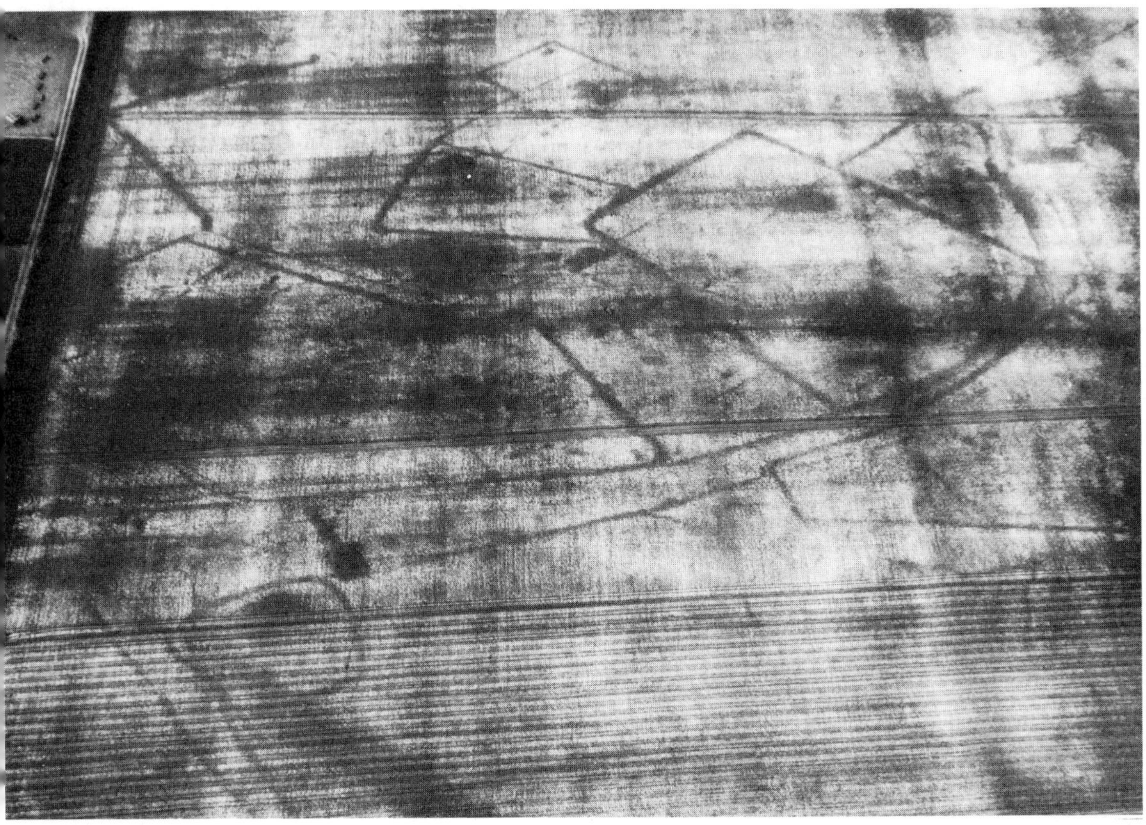

deliberately backfilled while most later ones accumulated more soil by silting slowly. This difference is reinforced by the fact that later soils are darker, due to increased organic content after three centuries of stock-rearing. The corridor-house is not visible because its foundation-trenches were cut in chalk and filled with chalk. Similarly the aisled barns [of which two fall within fig 30] are not clear because they mainly survive as post holes, which in some cases were backfilled. The only buildings which do show clearly are the oblong grubenhaus/workshops each with a corndrier at one end. . . . The floors are cut between 6 and 18 inches [150–450mm] below the natural chalk. . . . Some of the more amorphous areas . . . are around animal shelters and feeding points where the surface of the natural chalk has been eroded by trampling. (R.W.M. to D.R.W. 13 Nov. 1973)

30 *Welton Wold, N. Humberside, 28 March 1956*
Soil-marks reveal the site of an Iron Age and Roman farm on the Yorkshire Wolds, later excavated in advance of quarrying. A number of important excavated features are virtually invisible on the photograph. Slightly to left of centre was a small Roman house; its chalk foundations had been laid in trenches cut in the solid chalk. A square ditched enclosure surrounding the house was later modified. Parts of the circuit were deliberately filled with chalky soil and can scarcely be seen; other parts remained open and accumulated a dark soil enriched by dung from livestock. Major timber buildings represented solely by post-holes and beam-slots have not yielded visible soil-marks, but insubstantial animal shelters are marked by dark areas where the surface of the chalk has been worn away by trampling hoofs.

A comparison between soil-marks and crop-marks occupies the fourth section of this chapter (p 69).

CROP-MARKS

Causes of differential growth

Crop-marks are visible differences of growth

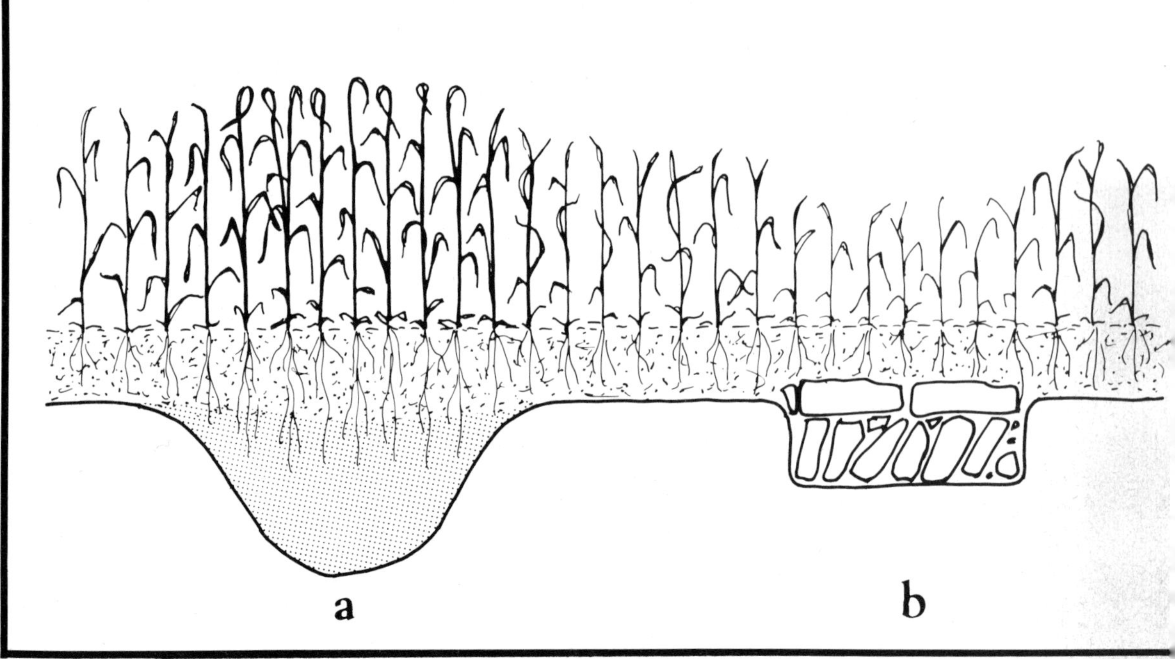

31 *The effect of buried archaeological features on the growth of crops.*
(*a*) Positive marks over a ditch; (*b*) negative marks over wall foundations.

caused by buried archaeological remains. If the effect on the crop is favourable, the plants grow taller and more luxuriantly over the archaeological features (positive crop-marks); if unfavourable, growth is checked and plants may become stunted (negative crop-marks). In either case there are differences of hue, tone or plant size discernible in the crop, closely following the line of buried features and tracing out their plan.

Positive crop-marks are mainly caused by *negative* archaeological features, ie those that have been formed by cutting into and removing the subsoil. Most of the surviving buried remains in arable land are of this kind: they include ditches for drainage or defence, foundation-trenches and postholes of timber buildings, cellars, cisterns, wells and cesspits, graves, quarries, and pits of all kinds. Archaeological features of this kind favour plant growth in two ways. When the soil is waterlogged, inhibiting growth, they provide improved drainage; and when there is a shortage of water, the greater depth of soil allows roots to penetrate further and affords a reserve of moisture and nutrients when upper levels have been exhausted. In either case growth is maintained locally despite the prevailing unfavourable conditions (6, 31). Conversely, negative crop-marks occur where the root-system is impeded by an impenetrable layer such as a buried street or metalled yard, stone wall-foundations or solid floors (31). These features only survive below plough level, and in shallow soils they cause relatively little difference to the actual depth of soil. Negative marks may thus develop later or in more severe conditions than positive marks.

Ploughed-down mounds and banks may give rise to crop-marks of either type, provided there is a strong enough contrast between the plough-soil and the materials of which they are made. A cairn or gravel bank, for example, may be sufficiently stony to bring about negative marks (44a, 46), just as the turf-built rampart of a Roman fort will sometimes produce positive ones (38). Most remains of this kind, however, have no visible effect on the growing crop.

When crop-marks first appear, they are faint and blurred. They are difficult to record satisfactorily and unrewarding to interpret.

As they develop, the marks become bolder and more sharply defined, as if being gradually brought into focus. The speed at which this happens is greatly influenced by the type of soil. Where the particle size is coarse (ie in sandy soils), all the water held in the soil is immediately available to sustain plant growth, until exhausted. The supply of moisture then ceases abruptly, inducing severe water-stress in the crop. Where the particle size is fine (ie in clayey soils), the water is held at progressively increasing tension as the amount available diminishes, and the rate of plant growth is gradually reduced over a much longer period (Jones & Evans, 1975, quoting May & Milthorpe, 1962). The visible effect of this difference is that crop-marks developing on light well-drained soils may achieve full definition in a matter of 2–3 days, whereas on heavy clay soils they may take as many weeks.

A fall of rain in the meantime will interrupt this process, reviving wilting plants and either halting or reversing the development of crop-marks. If dry conditions continue, however, even slight buried features may become visible for a time; but minor differences in soil moisture are soon eliminated, and the corresponding marks are likely to be short-lived. In a prolonged drought the entire range of crop-marks eventually fades as the whole of the field becomes parched, though a faint residual pattern may survive.

Shallow soils over chalk constitute a special case. Although chalk is well known for its capacity to store water, this is not available immediately there is a soil-moisture deficit, but only after it has reached a certain degree of severity. The development of crop-marks over chalk goes through two distinct stages. The first stage resembles what happens over gravel: positive marks occur where plants growing over pits and ditches are able to draw on the moisture contained within them. In the second stage, which is only reached if the drought continues sufficiently long, the tonal values are suddenly reversed, as all the plants in close contact with the chalk bedrock take up water from there, whereas those over the ditches, having now exhausted their reserves, have no further resource (65, 94).

The crop-marks so far described all occur in conditions when there is a shortage of moisture in the soil. Marks can also occur when there is a *surplus* of moisture. Waterlogging of the rooting zone caused by an impermeable layer or pan at shallow depth inhibits growth and leads to crop failure. The effect is alleviated by an increase in soil depth, and where this occurs above buried features, faint crop-marks may then result (Evans & Jones 1977). Indeed the presence of buried features may so far improve the local drainage that an impeding horizon never forms in the soil within or above them, leading to crop-marks of nearly normal strength.

Water is important because it carries the nutrients essential for plant growth; yet excessive water leaches those nutrients away, and actual waterlogging causes additional denitrification. The most significant nutrients in this context are nitrogen and calcium. Nitrogen is responsible for most of the visible signs of healthy vigorous growth, ie plant size, leaf area, and greenness, as well as a lengthy growing period. Nitrogen is a major constituent of natural and artificial fertilizers, so that a top dressing in the spring masks all potential crop-marks until its effect has been nearly exhausted. A correct balance of calcium is essential to enable other nutrients to be utilized; so crop-marks may result from local differences in the pH value (acid-alkali scale) in the soil. At low pH, for example, when the soil is relatively acid, phosphorus ceases to be available, causing thin growth and poor colour in the crop. Lime in the mortar of buried wall-foundations will correct calcium deficiency in a very acid soil, leading to improved plant-growth there and revealing the plan of the vanished buildings. At high pH, on the other hand, there is liable to be a deficiency of manganese and copper and, in certain conditions, of nitrogen also (Jones & Evans 1975, quoting Russell 1961). In calcareous soils the filling of buried ditches commonly has a lower pH value than the surrounding soil, and this may improve the availability of nutrients in such soils. This effect could contribute to the clarity of crop-marks on shallow chalk soils and in the silt-fen.

Type of crop

The degree to which a particular crop responds to differences in soil moisture depends on the species and variety and on the stage of growth it has reached at the time. Few herbaceous crops can be so unaffected by dry conditions that they never develop crop-marks, but deeply rooting plants are the most sensitive to archaeological features. In other countries crop-marks have been recorded in sisal and lavender, and even in vineyards, tea plantations and paddy fields (Bradford 1957, Monguilan 1977). In Britain cereal crops are the most rewarding for archaeological purposes; sugar-beet and grass are also important, and most fodder crops will yield satisfactory crop-marks in favourable conditions. Weeds and other wild plants also play a part and should not be forgotten.

a *Cereals*. The principal cereal crops grown in Britain are barley, oats, rye and wheat. Maize is beginning to be more widely grown as a fodder crop, but its value for archaeological purposes is still to be assessed and it is not included in the following discussion.

Cereal crops are pre-eminent as a source of crop-marks because they are so widely grown, responsive to variation in soil moisture, and sensitive to detail in buried archaeological remains. Their growing season coincides with a period of uncertain rainfall (April–July); it is rare for a dry spell not to produce crop-marks at some stage, though there is great variation from one year to another. The main rooting zone of cereal plants is only 300–400mm deep, but there is normally at least one long root that will penetrate, if need be, to depths of 1·2m or more in search of water. In addition, the close spacing of the plants permits a very precise rendering of archaeological detail. Any growing crop can be considered as if it were a medium of graphic reproduction and its performance analysed in those terms. From this viewpoint the individual plant is equivalent to a single dot in a newspaper photograph printed by the half-tone process. When a field of corn is drilled in rows 175–250mm apart this virtually acts in the manner of a half-tone screen with a fineness of 4–6 lines to the metre. A closer spacing of 100mm between rows achieves a standard of 10 lines to the metre. Both these figures compare favourably with the corresponding figure for root crops (p 64).

Particular species and varieties have individual characteristics which make them more or less suitable for a given district, field or farming programme, but none is *generally* superior as a medium for showing crop-marks. When adjoining fields in different crops show crop-marks of unequal quality, it is just as likely to be due to a difference in soil depth or in time of sowing as it is to simple specific characters. Particular instances cited to show the superiority of one crop over another are valid only for the local conditions at the time of photography; a week or two later and the relative merits of the crops might appear to be reversed.

The appearance of crop-marks in cereals varies with the stage of growth. Positive marks may be seen at virtually any stage, from the first appearance of the seedlings until the corn is fully ripe. When fields display soil-marks of strong contrast, principally on chalk and in the silt-fen, seedlings tend to come up earlier and in greater numbers in the darker areas which absorb more heat from the sun. Buried ditches and similar features filled with dark soil are then picked out by bands of green isolated in an otherwise bare field. This pattern continues to be visible after the remaining seedlings have appeared; the original plants now form a relatively dense stand of even colour, whereas the latecomers are thin and sparse, leaving most of the ground surface still in view (100, 101). When the ground cover is complete, crop-marks mostly disappear, though visible differences may some-

32 *Crop-marks near Store Darum, Ribe* amt, *Denmark, 5 July 1970*
The photograph was taken about 1800 on a July evening. Slanting sunlight picks out differences of stem height in the crop, revealing a series of ditched enclosures. The complex pattern suggests that several of the ditches have been re-cut (cf fig 33).

33 *Crop-marks near Store Darum, Ribe* amt, *Denmark, 8 July 1970*
The site is the same as in fig 32, photographed on a dull morning three days later, about 1115. Much of a circular enclosure on the right is still fairly visible, but in the absence of suitable lighting there are virtually no other crop-marks to be seen.

34 *Prehistoric settlement at Butterwick, near Foxholes, N. Humberside, 2 August 1970*
Marks in a ripe cereal crop receive additional emphasis from shadows cast by the evening sun. The viewpoint is chosen to get the best possible contrast without losing the effect of the shadows. The settlement is made up of a group of oval or subrectangular enclosures whose ditches have been many times re-cut (p 113).

The crop also shows a number of dark linear marks caused by the cultivation pattern (p 158) and by a track across the centre of the field (p 167). In addition the photograph is crossed by narrow light-toned lines derived from scratches on the negative; these are especially obvious where they cross the road and are caused by mishandling in the darkroom (p 180).

times survive until the spring dressing of fertilizer masks most other effects.

For a time after top dressing the appearance of the crop will be dominated by fertilizer marks. The next marks to appear, on the heavier soils, will usually be of field-drains; it is not until they have carried away all surplus water from the plough-soil that archaeological features at greater depth will have occasion to come into view. The first archaeological marks are shown by greater stem height, without any change of colour. The height differences can be detected only in oblique lighting, when the taller plants cast a perceptible shadow (St Joseph 1969a, Wilson 1975a, fig 17); they are visible from a limited angle, looking almost directly into sun, and can only be recorded by oblique photography (32, 33). This phase is short-lived; the taller plants soon begin to display a difference of tone visible at all times of day in sunshine. This is caused by variations in reflectance of the crop-plants at different stages of growth; in particular, the more advanced and vigorous plants have a greater leaf area and may also have a greater number of stems, through more active 'tillering' (Jones & Evans 1975, quoting Rackham 1972). Positive marks usually appear darker than the remainder of the crop at this stage, but this can vary with the direction of view, the same marks appearing as light or dark lines from different angles. In due course this tonal difference is reinforced by a change of colour to a darker shade of green, which contrasts well with the rest of the crop and can be observed in shadow as well as in sun. When the other plants turn yellow, these darker plants stay green as they complete their growth. The tonal contrast is now very good, but there is usually some coarsening of detail, and as individual plants change colour, the pattern of positive marks temporarily disintegrates. By the time that all plants are yellow, the remainder of the crop has darkened appreciably, so that positive marks are seen as pale yellow lines against a background of darker, slightly brownish or sometimes pinkish, colour. Much archaeological detail may still be visible, though not easy to see because of reduced contrast. Photography in oblique lighting comes into its own again here, using the shadows of taller plants to improve the definition and emphasis of the marks (34). Even after harvest, positive marks may remain in stubble because of the thicker and more abundant stems.

The taller plants making up positive crop-marks are peculiarly susceptible to being lodged, or laid by wind and rain, once they are in ear. A storm-damaged crop yields poor crop-marks, since the lodging is erratic and only partly related to the archaeological features. The lines of laid corn are ragged and usually obscured in part by larger areas of battered crop, but archaeological information of value may nevertheless remain (35).

Negative crop-marks are composed of plants with short stems, scant leaf area, poor colour and a short growing period. They go

35 *Crop-marks south-west of Eynsham, Oxfordshire, 26 July 1973*

A field of ripening corn has been buffeted by storms. Crop-marks of ring-ditches and of a prehistoric settlement are visible either as lines of taller growth, picked out by the late afternoon sun, or as lines of laid crop, where the taller plants have caught the wind. Part of the archaeological pattern is obscured by broader swathes of storm damage.

Parallel lines of slightly shorter plants, crossing from top to bottom of the photograph, represent the 'open furrows' between 'lands' (p 156).

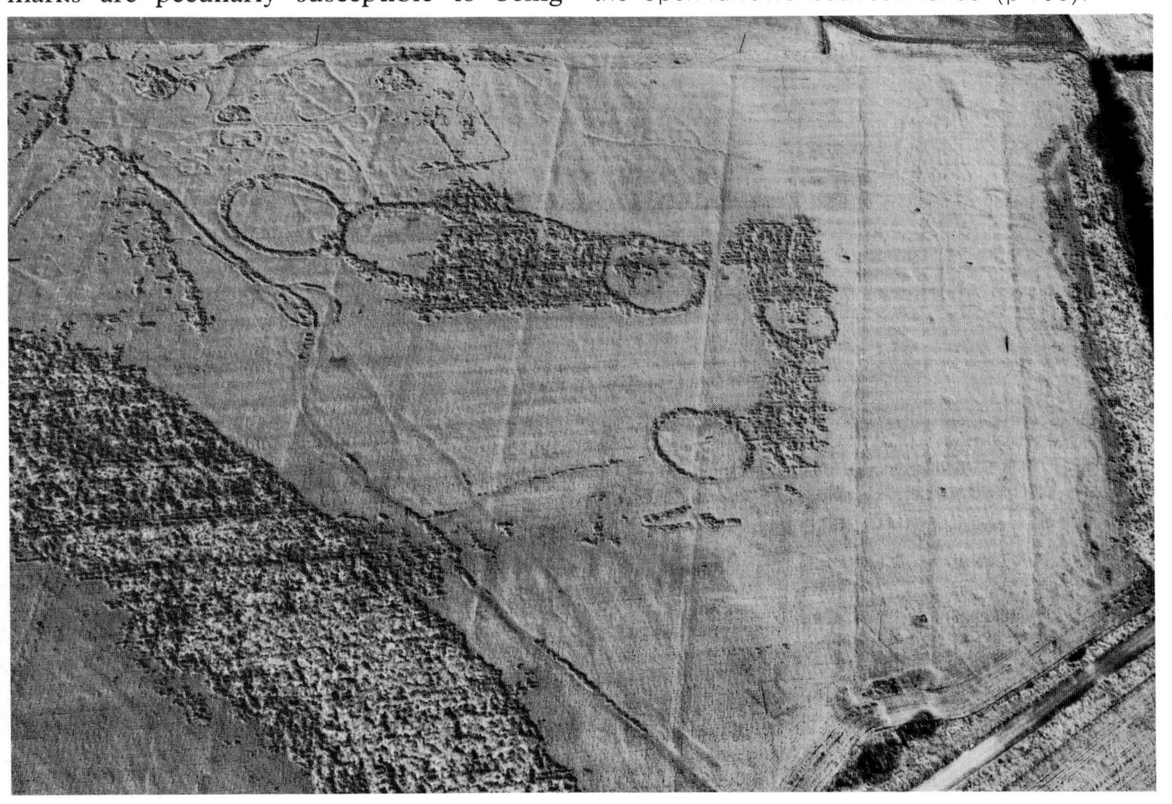

36 *Part of the Roman town at Chesterton, Cambridgeshire, 21 June 1966*
Streets and buildings in the Roman town of *Durobrivae* are marked by lines of retarded growth over gravel metalling and stone foundations. The Roman high street (Ermine Street) is at the top of the picture. Below it, on the right-hand side, is a large public building with central courtyard. One of side streets (bottom right) has had much of the metalling deliberately removed. Compare fig 37.

through a similar development to positive marks, appearing first as lines of retarded growth recessed below the surface of the crop (36). A loss of greenness soon follows, the colour turning wan and yellowish (62). In severe conditions the plants may fail altogether, leaving bare patches which are quickly colonized by weeds. If the plants survive, they fail to achieve full growth and ripen early, turning colour before the remainder of the crop. By the time that the whole field is yellow, negative marks are seen as lines of darker, almost brownish, colour (37).

b *Grass*. Grassland on air-photographs mostly falls into three categories: permanent pasture, ley (ie temporary pasture or hay on arable land), and lawns. In all three categories grass is slower than cereals to show the effects of soil moisture deficit, and crop-marks do not normally appear in grass except in drought conditions (cf Evans & Jones 1977). In most years such marks are rare, but in times of severe drought they are abundant and yield important information, much of which is otherwise inaccessible.

Crop-marks in hay are particularly rare, since the crop is mostly cut early in the season, about the time that crop-marks in cereals are only just coming into view. They are most likely to be seen if the crop is allowed to mature, when positive marks appear as lighter lines against a brownish background. These marks have good definition, and better contrast than in ripe cereals.

Crop-marks in pasture and lawns (including playing-fields) are produced by parching of the turf. This effect, which has been described above in relation to sites with earthworks still surviving in some relief, also occurs where the remains have been levelled. Negative marks appear first, as the grass fails over buried streets, floors and wall-foundations

37 *Part of the Roman town at Chesterton, Cambridgeshire, 4 August 1970*
The same area of *Durobrivae* as in fig 36, seen in ripe corn in another year. The marks of streets and buildings now appear as dark lines, having turned colour first, but the pattern is the same. Some details are clearer in this photograph; others are clearer in fig 36.

(69, 79). In a prolonged drought the effects of parching become more extensive, and positive marks begin to be seen as lines of green surviving in tracts of otherwise brown turf (38, 106). Positive marks only become at all widespread in a drought of national importance like those of 1949 or 1975–6. At such a time marks become visible in places like football fields and riverside pastures where they would normally never be seen (39). While negative marks are seen more often, they too are most frequent and mostly clearly defined in severe conditions. The period of maximum information is, however, limited. As drought continues, there comes a time when all reserves of moisture are exhausted and every plant succumbs, regardless of the presence of buried archaeological features. Parch-marks then disappear again in a uniform sea of brown.

c *Roots*. Root-crops are easily recognized on air-photographs by the rougher 'texture' of the surface of the crop as compared with cereals and many green fodder crops (78). For archaeological purposes they can be divided into those with a deep tap-root, like beets, and those whose root-systems are shallow, like swedes, turnips and potatoes. The latter group are little affected by archaeological features below the plough-soil, though they may respond to soil differences caused by the remains of an earthen rampart (Richmond 1943).

Beets, by contrast, are sensitive to differences in soil moisture, having roots capable of penetrating to depths of at least 1·6m. The field-beet or mangel is no longer much grown, but sugar-beet is an important source of crop-marks in southern Britain. The growing season is later than that of cereals, maximum leaf area being attained at the end of July and harvest taking place about three months later. In a normal season crop-marks will have ample opportunity to develop during the dry summer months. Sugar-beet is sown in rows

38 *Part of the Roman legionary fortress, Inchtuthil, Perthshire, 3 July 1949*
An area of parkland shows the effects of severe drought. Narrow lines of unparched grass follow the foundation-trenches of vanished timber buildings, tracing out part of the plan of the quarters of one cohort. Larger patches of green grass mark the position of rubbish-pits in use during the occupation of the fortress or dug when it was demolished. The south defences of the fortress, which survive in some relief, run obliquely across the left side of the photograph; the grass remains green both in the ditch and over the remains of the rampart.

39 *The University Parks, Oxford, 7 September 1976*
Marks seen in grass at the culmination of the drought of 1975–6 show a complex series of overlapping enclosures, witnessing to a long period of prehistoric occupation on the banks of the R. Cherwell. Two of the large rings in the foreground appear to be truly circular, the middle one not; all have broad entrances but no visible internal features. Most of the smaller enclosures are likely to belong to a settlement of Iron-Age or Roman date. Many of the dots with which the turf is stippled seem to form lines, but they are best regarded as having a geological origin.

The modern use of the ground is for sport and recreation. Two hockey pitches are just discernible in the foreground, and the boundary of the University's cricket field appears to the right.

40 *Crop-marks south of Easington, Oxfordshire, 18 May 1977*
Faint marks in a yellow field of oil-seed rape pick out a large oval ditched enclosure with annexe, perhaps a lowland 'hillfort'. Narrower lines seem to show an outer ditch surrounding both parts of the site and also a ring-ditch in the interior. The marks result from a number of plants growing along the ditches not yet having come into full flower. This effect is seldom seen and is probably very transient.

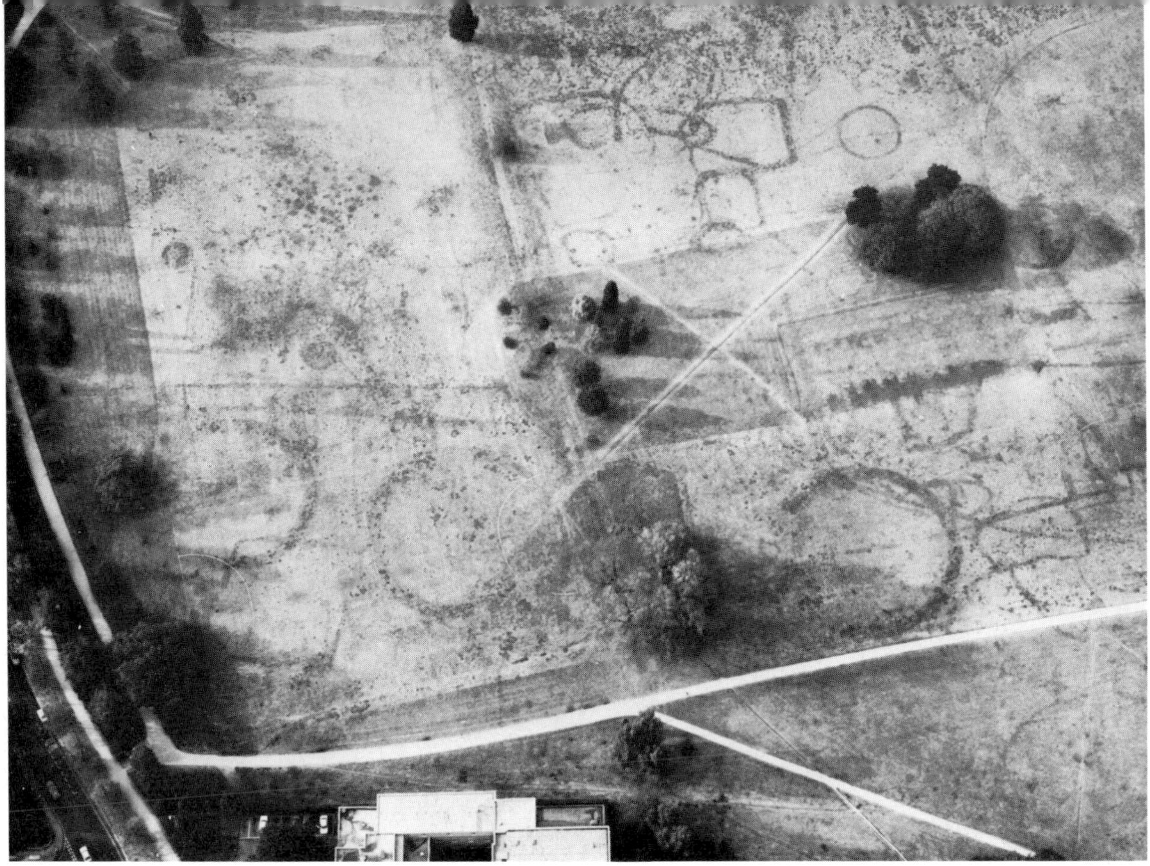

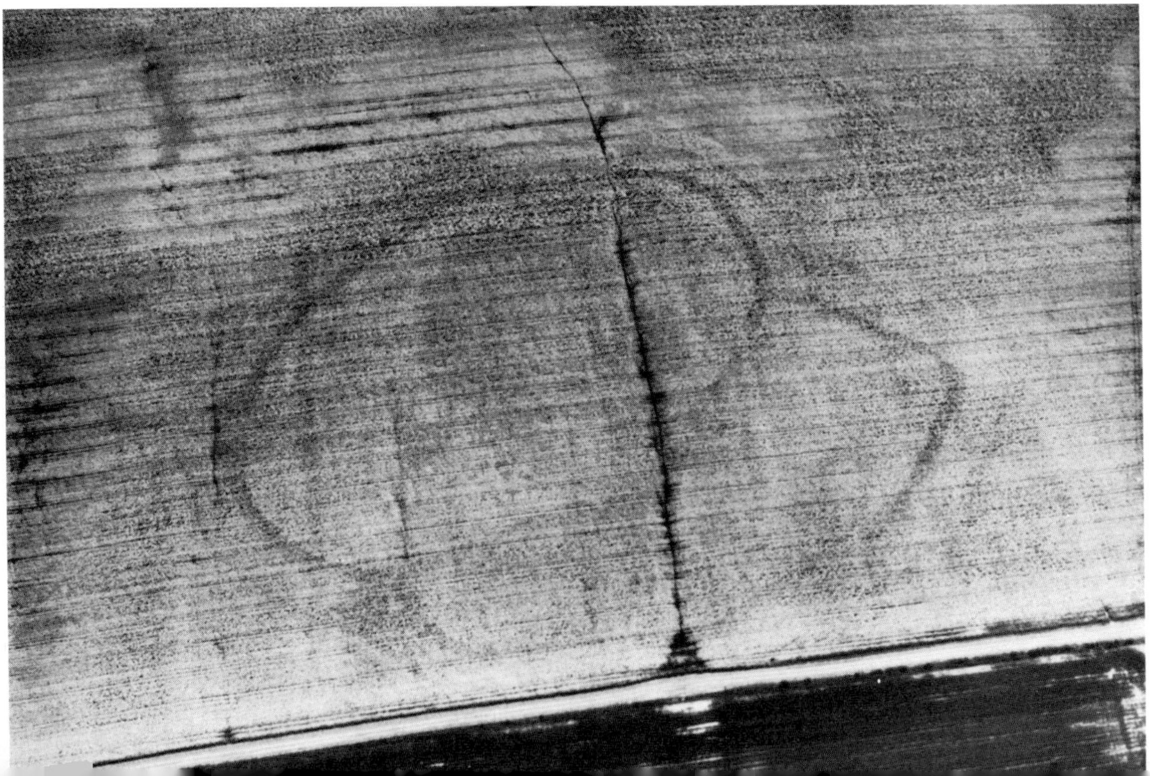

450–550mm apart, which corresponds to a 'reprographical' standard of two lines to the metre. This figure can be compared with those given above for cereals (p 56). Plants within the row are normally spaced 130–180mm apart. Fine archaeological detail cannot be expected, but the wide spacing makes for maximum contrast of appearance between adjacent plants: those subject to water-stress turn yellow, the unaffected plants stay green, and there are virtually no intermediate tones (78).

d *Green fodder crops, etc.* Good crop-marks have been recorded in beans, clover and lucerne, all of which have well-developed tap-roots. They may appear at several stages: in young growth of an undersown crop as it comes up through the cereal stubble; in re-growth of a ley crop after it has been cut; and in the grown crop when subject to water-stress.

Crop-marks are seldom seen in *Brassica* species, whether grown for fodder (kale, rape, cabbage) or for seeds (oilseed rape, mustard). Positive marks in rape and mustard can occur at the time of flowering but have poor contrast; in the brilliant yellow fields the more vigorous plants growing over archaeological features come into flower late and show up dark (40).

e *Weeds and other wild plants.* Cornfield weeds with tall stems and bright flowers used once to bring a touch of colour to growing crops, but today 85 per cent of land producing cereals in Britain is treated with chemical herbicides to control weeds (Eddowes 1976). In untreated areas it is only the red of the poppy that is still at all commonly seen from the air. Poppies enhance the appearance of positive marks in cereals, usually growing around the marks but not through them, so that the green line over a buried ditch is bordered by splashes of red. This may mean that poppy seedlings within the crop-marks have been smothered by the denser and more vigorous growth of the cereals, or more probably that poppies growing over a buried ditch come into flower later than the rest. The contrast between red and green is very vivid but can only be appreciated on photographs taken in colour. On panchromatic film the difference in tone is barely adequate to record the marks and gives no hint of their colourful appearance. On rare occasions the complementary effect is seen, when cornfield weeds with long tap-roots (poppy, charlock, wild radish) themselves form the crop-marks, picking out a buried ditch with a line of red, yellow or white respectively. This time photography has taken place when only the later-flowering plants are still in bloom.

Wild oats can also form positive crop-marks, responding to greater soil depth with taller growth, easily out-topping the cultivated cereal crop in which they are growing. These very prominent plants can sometimes be detected as pale lines with a shimmery quality that is related to the form of the ear in this species (information from R Evans).

Areas of poor growth in any crop are liable to be invaded by weeds better suited to the local conditions. If the crop has failed because of some underlying archaeological feature, weeds growing in its place may come to form 'crop-marks' of their own, as described above (p 60). The reverse effect is also known, with the original crop surviving only along the lines of crop-marks (Jones 1980, pl 65).

Weeds growing in level pasture have so far provided little archaeological information on British sites, though the importance of flowering plants in Mediterranean pastures may be noted (Bradford 1957). Where pasture contains earthworks surviving in relief, these provide a variety of micro-climates favouring the growth of particular species or subspecies at definite positions on banks or level ground or in the ditches. Buttercups are well known to botanists for having such detailed preferences: as many as three subspecies may be present at different levels on the undulating surface of ridge-and-furrow, for example. These distributions can only be observed from the air when the plants are actually in flower. Yellow lines of buttercups have sometimes been photographed following the banks of deserted medieval villages, as remarked above; at other times they have drawn attention to such banks by physically avoiding them. In each case only those plants growing in archaeologically significant positions were in flower at the time that the photographs were taken.

Direction of view

The direction of view is of great importance in the photography of crop-marks. It is not something that lies within the control of the photo-interpreter, but the principles involved have to be understood if competent interpretations are to be made.

When crop-marks are at their best, they are wonderfully clear and it makes little difference from what angle they are photographed. With the great majority of crop-marks more trouble has to be taken. There is a perceptible increase in tonal contrast when the marks are viewed from one particular direction, and this appreciably enhances their definition. In addition, a substantial minority of crop-marks cannot be seen or photographed at all except from a single limited angle. These observations are confirmed by the appearance of crop-marks on overlapping vertical photographs taken with a wide-angle lens. Marks that are quite clear when seen near the edge of the first photograph (where the view is, of course, oblique) may become too indistinct for exact measurement when they lie at the centre of the second photograph and then disappear completely when sought near the opposite edge of the third photograph. Vertical photography is only of use for crop-marks when there is a strong difference of tone or colour present, and even then a properly angled oblique will often yield a crisper rendering of detail.

The optimum direction of view is normally related to the position of the sun. When stem height is the most important factor, the most telling photographs are taken looking into sun, to emphasize shadows thrown by the taller plants. When differences of colour are more important, the best contrast is usually obtained with the sun behind the camera; but there are also differences of tone related to the texture of the surface of the crop for which the opposite direction of view is more effective. These variations are subtle; crop-marks which appear to have reached the same stage of development may need to be photographed from opposite directions in adjacent fields, perhaps because of a difference in the time of sowing or in the depth of soil. Similarly, crop-marks in wheat may look best from one direction, those in barley from the other, either because sown at different times or because of generic differences in the growth of the plants. Even within a single field, sown with the same crop on a single occasion, archaeological features of different character may produce crop-marks that are only clearly visible from opposite directions (41, 42). Effects such as these are somewhat exceptional and are soon modified by further development of the marks, but even the more bizarre examples are not so uncommon that they can be safely ignored.

Another factor of special relevance to cereals is the strength and direction of the wind, which will ripple the surface of the crop in its later stages of growth. Light is reflected many ways from the rippled surface, making a dappled pattern against which archaeological marks are less easily seen. The crop-marks themselves may also be distorted by the waving of the crop. If the marks are reasonably distinct, a view looking up or down wind will foreshorten the rippling effect and give a clearer rendering. But if they are faint, it is only in photographs angled in relation to the sun that the marks will be visible at all.

Photographic conditions and the timing of photography

In general, the conditions suitable for photography of crop-marks are similar to those for soil-marks (p 50), but there are more occasions on which sunshine is a necessity. Marks revealed solely by their shadows cannot be seen or recorded except in oblique sunlight, and even when marks are faintly visible as a

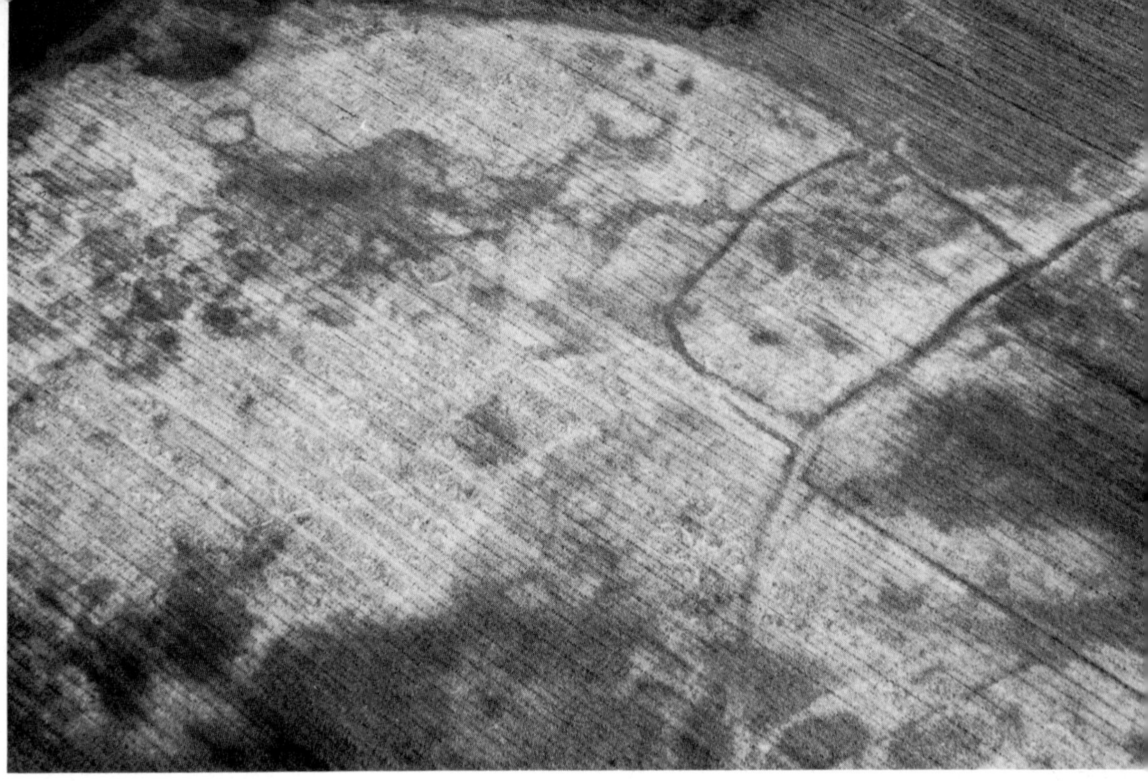

41 *Crop-marks SSE of Burton Agnes, N. Humberside, 24 July 1974*
The view is looking ESE, across sun. On the right an irregular enclosure occupies the angle between two ditches; on the left is the clear outline of a square barrow. Other square barrows are just visible as vague shapes, but could not be adequately identified from this photograph alone (cf fig 42).

difference of colour they are unlikely to be observed unless they are brightly lit. The lower the sun in the sky, the better the chance of perceiving height differences in the crop, but the greater the need also for good visibility, as in the photography of earthworks (p 37).

The appearance of crop-marks is seasonal, being controlled by the growing periods of the relevant crops. Only cereals and sugar-beet produce marks in sufficient abundance to provide a basis for planning a programme of photography. In cereal crops growth is checked by water-stress with greatest severity in the period immediately before the emergence of the ear. In a normal British year this would mean that the best crop-marks could be expected in the period from late May to early July. Once the crop has ripened, no new marks are formed, though existing crop-marks continue to be seen with diminishing clarity until harvest in August–September. The cereal harvest is a poor time for air-photography because of smoke from straw-burning in the fields, but September and October give the opportunity to record crop-marks in sugar-beet.

Experience shows that few years are in fact 'normal', and the season may be early or late for a variety of reasons. Thus in 1966 spring-sown cereal crops were late because of the wet spring, during which farmers could not get onto the land to drill the seed, and crop-marks did not appear in any quantity until July. In 1974 spring-sown cereals were also late, this time because the spring was dry; the seed was drilled early, but little growth was made because of the lack of rain. In 1970–1 the mild winter brought on autumn-sown cereals abnormally fast and the first crop-marks were being seen in winter wheat before the end of March. The same summer saw the wettest June of the century, with flooding in some river valleys; crop-marks in spring cereals came late and never achieved much contrast. Sugar-beet in the meantime had benefitted from the exceptional rainfall to make unac-

customed growth and by late July was showing better crop-marks than the cereal crops.

With so much variation in the season, anyone planning a future photographic programme, or evaluating a past one, needs some guidance when crop-marks are most likely to appear. A simple rule of thumb is that when the first hay is cut, crop-marks will be beginning to be seen; but the main crop-mark season will still lie some way ahead. Contact with farmers or the agricultural press will provide information whether the season as a whole is earlier or later than usual, and contact with active aerial archaeologists (eg through the bulletins sponsored by the Council for British Archaeology) will bring news of the actual appearance of crop-marks.

Conditions favourable to the development of crop-marks can also be monitored by calculating the 'potential soil moisture deficit'. This figure is derived from local rainfall data and an estimate of 'potential transpiration' and is less laborious to work out then the actual soil moisture deficit for a particular site. The figure is accurate enough to use as a generalized datum for the timing of photography, crop-marks beginnning to appear when the potential soil moisture deficit exceeds 50mm and occurring in some abundance when it climbs to 100mm (Riley 1980a). The method of calculation is summarily described by Jones and Evans (1975), drawing on Penman (1948) and Smith (1967); the same authors give examples of potential soil moisture deficit at actual sites in Evans and Jones (1977). An equivalent calculation, combining data for rain, temperature and wind, is described by Dassié (1978).

42 *Crop-marks SSE of Burton Agnes, N. Humberside, 24 July 1974*
The site is the same as in fig 41, now seen from the north-east, looking into sun. Tonal contrast is much reduced and some tonal values are reversed, but differences in stem height are emphasized by shadow. The enclosure, now on the left, is still visible, but only with some difficulty, whereas nearly a dozen square barrows have come into view, several of them showing a central grave-pit. Both photographs were taken in the same conditions, the only difference being in the direction of view.

Current soil moisture data for Great Britain are also available from the *Hydrometeorological Bulletin* issued fortnightly by the Meteorological Office. A short commentary on the rainfall pattern is accompanied by maps showing the soil moisture deficits for virtually the whole country divided into 190 separate units each 40km square.

How good is the archaeological information?

In evaluating crop-marks a fundamental rule is not to rely on negative evidence. When crop-marks are present, their probable causes can be inferred and used as a basis for interpretation. When crop-marks are absent, there is simply no inference to be made.

The factors contributing to the appearance of crop-marks in a given place are complex. The ground must be 'in good heart' agriculturally and the crop healthy. The variety grown should be suited to the local climate and soil, as well as being capable of responding to buried archaeological features. The weather pattern in the growing season needs to turn out opportunely in relation to the time of sowing and the rate of growth so as to bring the roots of the crop within reach of archaeological features at a time of moisture shortage. Not least, if crop-marks are to provide usable information, an air-photographer has to see and photograph the site during the time that the marks are visible. The difference between missing and achieving an acceptable record of crop-marks on a specific site can be as little as a few hours. Thus, while the absence of archaeological features would be a fundamental cause of the absence of crop-marks in the available photographic coverage of a site, it is only one possible cause among many.

Similarly, the fact that *some* crop-marks have been recorded on a site, even in apparently favourable conditions, is no guarantee that other marks may not be seen there another time. A noteworthy instance was provided by the Roman site at Ythan Wells (Aberdeenshire), where the known marching-camp had been inspected from the air at an appropriate season by an experienced aerial archaeologist not less than once a year for 23 years before the slender ditch of a second camp produced crop-marks clear enough for recognition (St Joseph 1970b).

Many features will never give rise to crop-marks, being too slight, too deeply buried, or cut into other features. Crop-marks cannot reproduce the full complexity of a multi-period site, only the total extent of archaeological disturbance. There can be few excavations of crop-mark sites that do not uncover much that is unexpected. This does not detract from the usefulness of crop-marks as a guide to excavation, as long as the excavator is not deceived into thinking that they have told him the whole story.

There are times nevertheless when the roots of crop-plants form a more sensitive instrument for detecting archaeological features than the excavator's trowel. Examples were given above (p 51) of features difficult to identify in excavation because the filling and the matrix were virtually identical. These examples were chosen precisely because they were features which have been traced by means of crop-marks. Plant roots in search of moisture can feel the difference between marl or sand or gravel that is undisturbed and the same material redeposited: the disturbed material is unconsolidated and holds more water. The resulting crop-marks, when recorded on air-photographs, reassure the excavator that the feature in question really does exist and assist in its eventual identification.

Marks produced in a growing crop by water-stress are related to features at the depth to which roots have reached. As the roots penetrate further, crop-marks may change. For instance, marks photographed by Mr A Baker at Wroxeter showed one of the streets in the Roman town crossing a pair of ditches. The first time he photographed them the pale mark of the street was clearly interrupted by the dark lines of the ditches; the second time, just over a week later, the street appeared to be continuous and the ditches interrupted. These conflicting observations were vital to an assessment of the relative age of the features; but how could they be reconciled? Mr Baker's solution took into account the growth of the crop between the two dates of photography. He suggested that when the street was originally laid out the ditches were already in existence, but had been ignored, so that it eventually sank into their softer filling. In the earlier photographs the plants were drawing on moisture in the top of the ditch filling and their roots had not yet encountered the road metalling where it had subsided, thus producing a continuous dark mark along the line of each ditch. By the time that the later photographs were taken the roots had penetrated to the bottoms of the ditches, except where they were prevented by the solid remains of the street, which was now shown as being continuous. The archaeological information from both sets of photographs was therefore sound, but each related to a particular depth below the surface. Interpretations based on the gradual development of crop-marks, as opposed to their appearance on a single occasion, acquire in this way a new dimension.

The degree of detail in crop-marks is controlled by the spacing of the plants in the crop concerned. Comparative figures were given above (pp 56, 64) for the distance between rows in cereals and sugar-beet. Spacing of plants within the row is appreciably less, but too variable to form a satisfactory basis of comparison. The finest marks undoubtedly occur in grass and cereals, and actual dimensions have been recorded for excavated examples. In the Neolithic causewayed enclosure at Orsett (St Joseph 1973b), for instance, the palisade-trench accompanying the outer ditches was only 0·7–0·8m wide. Some of the narrowest lines to be seen on air-photographs are those produced by the foundation-trenches of timber buildings inside Roman forts: these trenches are regularly 0·25–0·35m wide. The ease with which such narrow marks can be discerned is affected by their orientation relative to the rows of plants. A very fine line running exactly along the rows is almost certain to be lost among the normal cultivation patterns, whereas another running at right angles to the first would cut across the 'grain' of the crop and would be more readily picked out. Points or dots of significant tone are more difficult to recognise with any certainty, and so the relevant dimensions tend to be coarser than for linear marks. The smallest of the post-pits at Woodhenge, for example, were found to measure 0·6–0·9m in diameter (3).

The definition of crop-marks is not only dependent on tonal contrast and close spacing in the crop; it also involves the quality of edge-sharpness. When an archaeological feature has gently sloping sides, the depth of soil increases only slowly and the corresponding change of tone in the crop is gradual. The resulting photographic image has a soft blurred edge from which it is difficult to take a precise measurement. If the dry spell is protracted, the width of the mark is liable to shrink as the outer plants become parched, but the softness of the outline will continue. The opposite effect is seen over filled-in quarries and other features with vertical sides, such as huts with sunk floors (*Grubenhäuser*). There the edges of crop-marks are sharply defined and unchanging (52, 64). Most ditches cut in soft materials have sides that are of moderate slope, nearer to 45° than to the extremes already cited; their crop-marks are fairly well-defined, though lacking the exceptional precision of those just mentioned. There is likely to be little change in the width of these marks during their life, since the roots of the outer plants will be guided inwards by the sloping sides of the ditch, reaching down virtually as far as those of plants growing in the middle.

SOIL-MARKS AND CROP-MARKS COMPARED

Many archaeological sites produce both soil-marks and crop-marks. Both sets of marks are derived from the same features and look superficially similar, but there are essential differences between them which it is important to grasp. We conclude this chapter with a critical comparison of their character and archaeological potential, as well as some hints on telling them apart.

Soil-marks present a picture of archaeological features at the level to which ploughing has reached. They can tell nothing about features that lie more deeply buried, nor can they indicate to what depth the visible features still survive. Crop-marks show what is present at a lower level. Given favourable conditions, they can distinguish between features of different depth, and even between those with vertical and sloping sides. Features that are deeply buried will not often be seen, but may still be revealed in extreme conditions.

Soil-marks and crop-marks do not show all kinds of archaeological remains equally well, and to some extent the information which they provide is complementary. The exceptional clarity of soil-marks on chalk should not obscure the fact that in most soils the traces of pits and ditches are difficult to see and only show up well when the features are of massive dimensions. The remains of banks and mounds, on the other hand, are often more obvious. Crop-marks, for their part, reproduce the plans of pits and ditches particularly well, but only seldom give any sign of a surviving mound or bank. Thus it may happen at a particular site that an earth bank is known from soil-marks (2), while the corresponding ditch and other features are attested by crop-marks (3).

The advantage of crop-marks in tracing archaeological features filled with material similar to that in which they are cut has already been noted (p 68).

On a monochrome print there may be a problem in deciding whether the marks it displays are actually seen in a crop or in bare soil. On certain soils and for certain states of crop the grey tones on the print do not sufficiently distinguish between the alternatives, and to rely on the probabilities of the calendar (soil-marks in March, crop-marks in June) is inconclusive and unreliable. Close inspection of the marks and of the field as a whole should provide the answer. Soil-marks produced by ploughing have a distinctively ragged outline which is particularly noticeable in marks that cross the line of ploughing. After harrowing and rolling the marks are even more blurred. Crop-marks look, by comparison, precise and well-defined. There may also be hints in other parts of the field, or in adjoining fields of identical appearance. The crop may throw a slight shadow on one or two sides; or part of it may have been cut, or damaged by animals or storms, revealing its true character. It is also helpful to be able to find an unambiguous example of a field of bare soil in the same locality, to compare with the field in question.

A more perplexing problem, in one sense at least, is posed by *composite* marks formed partly of differences in soil colour and partly of the pattern made by emerging seedlings. Both soil and crop are involved, but at this early stage of growth the crop-marks have nothing to do with length of root and reserves of soil moisture; as we have already seen (p 56), they are related to differences in germination of seeds caused by temperature differences in soil of different colours. More seeds germinate in dark-coloured, warmer soils and the seedlings come up earlier. Composite marks may therefore be considered as an extension of simple soil-marks and they should be interpreted according to the same principles.

3

Identification of Archaeological Features

The identification of particular types of archaeological site on air-photographs is very largely a question of morphology; that is to say, it involves the recognition of certain recurring shapes or patterns. There are some kinds of evidence relevant to the evaluation of individual sites which are sometimes able to hint at a relative or absolute age but it is only criteria of general application that have a place in this chapter.

We shall be concerned principally with soil-marks and crop-marks, since these pose problems of identification in which some guidance is called for. Earthworks seen on air-photographs are pictured in a two-dimensional image but are themselves three-dimensional features capable of being identified and surveyed on the ground. Given suitable photographs, the interpreter can recreate the third dimension at his desk by using a stereoscope. Earthworks studied on air-photographs are directly comparable with those known from fieldwork, and while air-reconnaissance may have brought new discoveries, and air-photography may have contributed a new and valued perspective, the problems of identification are not significantly different from those in conventional field surveys.

Soil-marks and crop-marks, by contrast, are ephemeral and are virtually two-dimensional representations of archaeological sites. If prints of the photographs can be obtained soon enough, some ground control is possible; but access to most crop-marks and to some soil-marks is restricted by the need to avoid damage to growing crops. The archaeological features are in any case only to be traced in terms of their plan. The sort of plan produced by such means has limitations which we should not forget. It relates to features at a single specific level: in the case of soil-marks, immediately beneath the ploughsoil, and in the case of crop-marks, at the depth to which the roots of crop-plants have so far penetrated. The rendering is selective, in the sense that only features of a certain minimum breadth or depth or favourable consistency will appear, but it is also non-selective, in that there is no discrimination in respect of age or original function or archaeological significance. Features of non-archaeological origin are certainly likely to be present: these are discussed at greater length in Chapter 4. In the incomplete but often complex picture that results individual archaeological sites have to be picked out and classified by reference to the shape of their major features.

It soon becomes clear that there are many types of archaeological site already known from excavation and fieldwork which have recognizable equivalents in terms of soil-marks and crop-marks. The correspondence is not always perfect, and discrepancies have to be carefully evaluated: most of the time the obviously plausible correlation has been confirmed by excavation, but there have been some mistaken identifications that have had to be corrected (p 192). In what follows, the identifiable sites are arranged for convenience according to their known archaeological character instead of in a purely morphological arrangement. This has the advantage that it builds on the reader's existing archaeological knowledge, and it emphasizes that identification depends on more than a mechanical analysis of shape. Ample cross-reference is given between types of site that are morphologically similar, as well as to non-archaeological features with which they might be confused.

A second category of site is known only from crop-marks and soil-marks, not yet from excavation. Any conclusions about age and function can only be speculative, and analysis begins perforce from the shape alone. So too with a third category, exemplified by ring ditches, which are well enough known both on photographs and in excavation, but for which all too many alternative explanations are available: a circular ditch may be dug around anything from a castle to a henhouse. Sites in both these categories, therefore, are grouped in accordance with their shape.

The classification adopted is thus based on a mixed set of criteria, partly functional and partly morphological. Its justification lies not in strict logic but in practical convenience. It would not, in any case, be feasible to construct a true scientific key to crop-mark sites using rigorous morphological criteria; to this our material is not suited, since the shapes of archaeological sites are not genetically controlled like those of living creatures. Considerable regularity is nonetheless to be perceived, and certain features may be regarded as diagnostic, permitting identifications to be made with a fair degree of confidence.

As its title implies, this book is written for the reader who is already acquainted with archaeology. It is hardly possible in the course of a single chapter to review the whole of the settlement archaeology of the British Isles—not to mention ritual monuments, agricultural and industrial remains—and it is necessary to assume that the reader has a working knowledge of the relevant literature. References will normally be given only to works that discuss or make use of the evidence of air-photography. Probably the best general treatments of field monuments in Britain for the photo-interpreter are by the Ordnance Surve (1973) and by Wood (1979), both of whic include many of the miscellaneous items suc as windmill-mounds that occur more fre quently on air-photographs than in conven tional archaeology textbooks.

The range of archaeological and historica remains to be seen and photographed fro the air is so vast that some selection has bee required. The types of site chosen for discus sion are those that appear of greatest relev ance, either because they occur frequently o air-photographs, or because there may be dif ficulties of identification and interpretation or because air-photography is able to contri bute new details to their understanding There are, after all, many types of site capabl of illustration by air-photography, but not al of them require special comment. It is true for example, that Martello Towers can be re cognised from the air along the coasts o southern Britain and Ireland, and that som of them have fallen into ruins. It is also tru that in Scotland the remains of brochs ar often found on coastal sites, as well as else where. But it does not seem necessary to se out criteria here for telling them apart, seein that the distributions of the two types of sit are well enough known and do not overlap

PREHISTORIC RITUAL SITES OF CIRCULAR OR OVAL PLAN

Neolithic causewayed enclosures

These are some of the oldest archaeologica sites in Britain to be recognizable from the air More than half the known examples ar crop-mark sites discovered by aerial recon naissance, and at four of them the assume Neolithic date has been confirmed by excavation. Discoveries up to 1975 have bee reviewed by Wilson (1975c) and by Palme (1976a).

Typically, a more or less oval enclosur between 200m and 400m in maximum diameter is bounded by one, two or three lines o ditch, each of which is broken into a numbe of short lengths by causeways. The circuit i not always completed if natural features mak

t unnecessary. There may be one or two inner enclosures, more or less concentric with the first, and there may be external annexes. Where earthworks survive, the broken ditches are accompanied by discontinuous lengths of bank, while at Orsett (Essex) and at Freston (Suffolk) crop-marks have revealed also the narrow slot for a palisade. The palisade at Orsett (St Joseph 1973b) runs at the rear of the two outer ditches, whereas that at Freston is sited between them (43); the latter arrangement raises the question whether the two lines of ditch may have been successive rather than strictly contemporary (pp 191–2).

The characteristic feature of these sites is the use of numerous short lengths of ditch to enclose a relatively large area. Individually the lengths of ditch have an irregular outline which causes crop-marks that look blobby.

43 *Neolithic causewayed enclosure south of Freston, Suffolk, 24 June 1976*
The ditch-system shows three elements: an outer ditch with well-marked causeways, a narrow palisade-trench which continues across most of the openings, and an inner ditch broken into even shorter sections. Within the enclosure and parallel to the top of the photograph can be seen closely spaced post-pits outlining a timber hall 36m long (p 111). The linear marks on the right of the picture are caused by fossil ice-wedges (p 149).

This may help to identify those enclosures where the causeways are so narrow as to be nearly undetectable on air-photographs.

There are other types of site with interrupted ditches, but none is likely to be mistaken for a causewayed enclosure of the type described. It may be archaeologically

a

b

44 *Henge, Hutton Moor, North Yorkshire: (a) 25 July 1967, (b) 27 November 1969*
The earthworks, though ploughed, still exist in some relief; but here they are primarily traced by means of crop-marks (on the left) or by differential melting of a light covering of snow (on the right). Comparison of the two photographs shows that snow has melted first on the bank and has lasted longest over the ditches (not as described in Wilson, 1975a, fig 9, which is incorrect).

significant that the outer ditches of some of the Yorkshire henges (notably at Thornborough) are indistinguishable from those of causewayed enclosures (46), though each site as a whole is of different character. Of fairly similar appearance are simple lines of interrupted ditch, occasionally observed as crop-marks merely crossing a field without turning to enclose a particular area; none of these has been dug, and their age and function are unknown. Ditches associated with round barrows are sometimes broken into separate segments but are of quite modest diameter. Pit-alignments composed of rectangular pits yield crop-marks like those of a ditch with frequent causeways; but individual pits are very regular and the causeways extremely frequent (every 2–3m), while the alignments, though often erratic, once again do not form themselves into large oval enclosures.

There are two types of site which are more likely to give trouble to the interpreter. The first is a geological pattern, typically seen on hilltops, where stratification of the bedrock causes a series of concentric bands in soil or crop (p 143). This pattern, especially if somewhat blurred, could be mistaken for a causewayed enclosure or a hillfort. It is often irregular in detail, which might be suggestive of Neolithic work, but these irregularities commonly go beyond what is plausible in the context of human workmanship. The whole pattern is very closely related to local topography, and although Neolithic enclosures are often found on hills, they seldom clasp the true summit or follow the contours closely. Hillforts may also be confused with Neolithic enclosures, especially when the ditches are rregular and their crop-marks none too distinct. Apart from the presence or absence of numerous causeways, which may be difficult to establish from the photographs, the form of entrance may prove to be significant. Neolithic causewayed enclosures so far known in Britain (unlike some in France) have simple entrances, shown only by the greater width of the causeway. Hornworks, overlapping ditches or inturned ramparts are all signs of a Bronze Age or later date.

It is not impossible for a Neolithic enclosure to precede a hillfort on the same hilltop site, appearing as a smaller earthwork circuit within the Iron-Age defences. Several examples of such inner earthworks still surviving in slight relief have been recognized on air-photographs of hillforts in southern Britain, but whereas that at the Trundle (Sussex) was indeed Neolithic, those at Scratchbury (Wiltshire) and Yarnbury (Wiltshire) both proved on excavation to belong to an earlier phase of the Iron Age. This emphasizes the danger of extrapolating from a single excavated example to superficially similar sites, even when these occur in an identical context.

Henges

Henges are found over much of the British Isles and survive in considerable numbers; it is on these visible remains that their classification is based. Air-photography has made substantial additions to their distribution, extending it, for example, to East Anglia, to north Wales, and to Strathearn in Perthshire, while the discovery of internal timber structures has come very largely (though not entirely) from aerial observation (cf 3). There is no published distribution-map that takes full account of the aerial discoveries.

The essential feature is a circular or slightly elliptical enclosure bounded by a bank with internal ditch. The diameter, measured from crest to crest of the bank where this survives, ranges from 30m to over 250m. There may be either a single entrance (Class I) or a pair of opposed entrances sited on the longer axis (Class II). The ditch is often of notable breadth, having to supply material for a substantial bank of greater diameter; it is sometimes supplemented by a second ditch on the outside of the bank (Classes IA and IIA) (44). The inner ditch is usually cut to a very smooth outline and precise geometrical shape, whereas the outer ditch, if present, can be quite irregular, discontinuous, and even polygonal (46).

Comparable enclosures less than 30m in diameter have been termed 'hengi-form' earthworks. They have similar plans but proportionately slighter earthworks than full-size henges.

On sites that are ploughed, the remnants of the bank are most likely to be shown by soil-marks, whereas the ditch will appear more clearly in terms of crop-marks (2, 3). Where the bank has disappeared entirely, identification depends on the broad and regular character of the ditch or on the presence of associated features such as circles of pits (45c, d). In the absence of the latter, a henge with single entrance cannot be positively identified from crop-marks, though it may be suspected from the appearance of the ditch. When there are two opposed entrances, the plan becomes more distinctive, and examples with a broad ditch of large diameter can be identified with a fair degree of confidence.

The regular curves and smooth outline of the ditches of henges, though not invariable, generally present a strong contrast with the Neolithic ditches described in the previous section. In later periods, however, such regular curves can recur in a variety of contexts, and caution is required. A broad circular ditch with single entrance could have so many explanations that further comment becomes unprofitable; barrows, homesteads, castles, moats, windmills and searchlights are only some of the possibilities (pp 90–3). The ditches surrounding windmill-mounds are of special concern, being sometimes notably broad in proportion to their diameter and usually having one, two or three entrance causeways. When two such causeways are diametrically opposite (45e) and the base of the mill itself has left no trace, the crop-marks are indistinguishable from those of a hengi-form earthwork. Larger enclosures with two widely spaced ditches (54), although apparently domestic rather than ritual in function, could easily be mistaken for henges. Some non-archaeological marks may also cause confusion. The broad circles of large diameter visible after irrigation with a large rotary sprinkler or a 'rain gun' are of similar size and proportions to the ditch of a large henge, and they may overlap the field boundary into another field as if quite unconnected with modern agricultural activity (p 162). No entrance will be visible, but this could always be out of sight beneath the hedge.

The seating-bank of a Roman amphitheatre (pp 107–8) closely resembles the equivalent bank of a henge but is distinguished by the absence of a ditch, material for the bank being derived from the whole extent of the arena. Natural ramparts of geological origin must also be borne in mind, eg those remaining from collapsed frost-mounds (p 145), but they are unlikely to reproduce complete archaeological forms except imperfectly.

Circles of pits

Among the features sometimes associated with henges, the most readily discerned in terms of crop-marks are circles of pits. It is not clear from crop-marks alone whether such pits originally held timber uprights or not, though there is an obvious analogy with stone circles. The pits may form simple rings, either concentric with the henge ditch, sited internally (45d) or externally (45c), or else eccentric. When the pits form a ring encircling the ditch, they may possibly belong to a timber revetment for the bank. More complex arrangements, with several concentric rings of pits (3), have been found on excavation to belong to elaborate circular timber structures whose original form and function are still the subject of debate.

All of these variations, like stone circles, may also occur in isolation. Interpretation of their function from air-photographs is even more hazardous than it is from excavated remains. Simple rings of pits (45f) are especially enigmatic if the ring is of modest size no more than 15m in diameter: it could then derive from an ordinary circular house (p 96) or from a ritual structure, with or without a roof; or the pits might not have held posts at all.

More complex plans offer more scope for interpretation, though they are seldom self-explanatory. On the right side of fig 50 can be seen a circle of about 16 evenly spaced pits surrounding a dozen others that are apparently sited at random. Although the detailed interpretation of this arrangement remains obscure, it does not look domestic. Multiple pit-circles of larger diameter bear some resemblance to the excavated timber structures at Woodhenge (3) and elsewhere but there are significant differences which should not be overlooked. One of two such sites at Barton under Needwood (Staffordshire) has about 225 pits arranged in five closely spaced concentric circles, with the corresponding pits in different circles radially aligned; these surround a broad central space over 35m across which is seemingly empty apart from a single large pit at the centre. On the second site a ring ditch forms the hub of a wheel-like figure whose spokes and rim are composed of lines of pits (121). Plans such as these display a concern with geometrical patterns that appears to go well beyond what is demanded by simple structural necessity.

The distinctive feature of both simple and multiple pit-circles is their regularity. Unless the circle is reasonably true and the pits evenly spaced, there will be little to distinguish them from other marks around them. Conversely, a complete circle is unlikely to be produced by crop-marks of natural or agricultural origin, though the interpreter should beware his own readiness to complete a regular figure from unconnected fragments. In a field where small dark marks are abundant one soon seems to see circles everywhere; but critical scrutiny will usually reject these as spurious. Certainly, when the same group of marks have

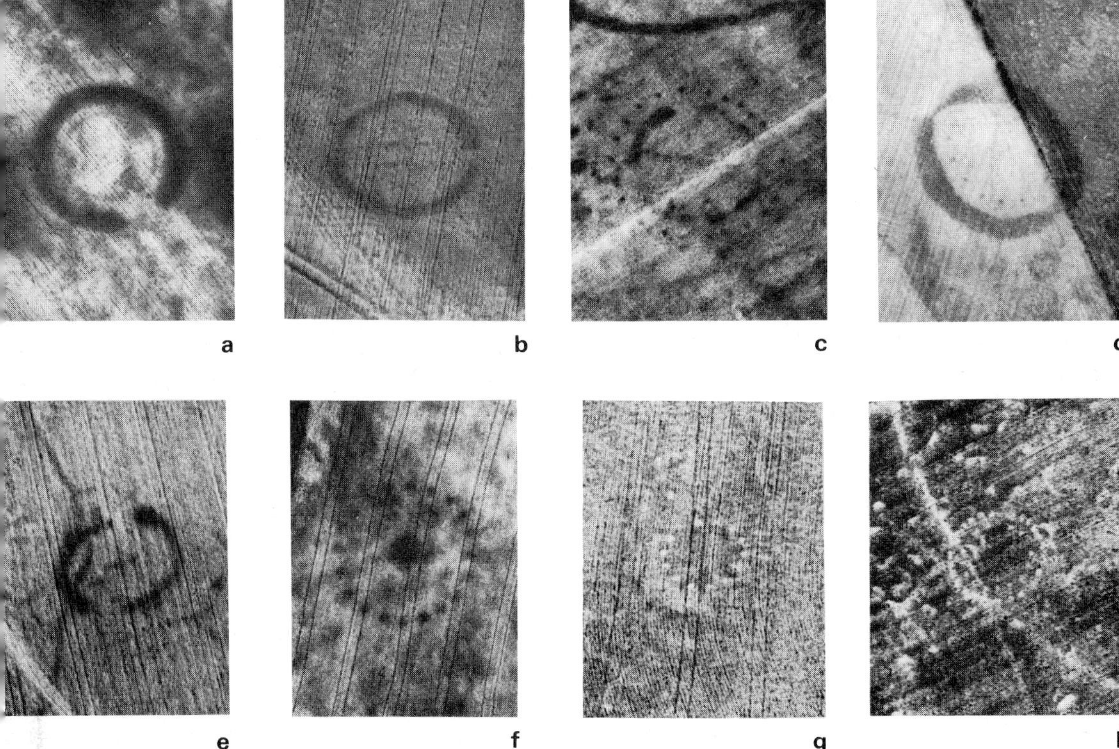

5 *Crop-marks of small circular enclosures*
a Circular house of late-prehistoric type, south of Thornhill, Dumfriesshire, 12 July 1949 (p 91)
b Roman watchtower at Roundlaw, on the Gask Ridge, Perthshire, 31 July 1979 (p 90)
c 'Hengiform' earthworks (?), with circle of 25 pits outside the ditch, south-west of West Ashby, Lincolnshire, 22 June 1970 (p 75)
d Henge with internal circle of about 15 pits, West Akeld Steads, Northumberland, 30 July 1976 (p 76)
e Site of windmill-mound, south of Knapton, Norfolk, 3 July 1976 (p 90)
f Circle of 20 pits surrounding a large square pit, south of Welshpool, Powys, 12 July 1975 (p 76)
g One of a group of circular houses north of Fochabers, Morayshire, 21 July 1976; the two outlying pits are inferred to lie at the terminals of an otherwise invisible palisade trench surrounding the house (p 97)
h Circular house or round barrow?—a circle of close-set postholes surrounds another more widely spaced, south of Boyton, Suffolk, 16 July 1974 (p 96)

been successively interpreted as forming part of two different circles curving in opposite directions, it is time to admit that they have no real significance!

When pit-circles are reliably identified, they will not always be ritual structures, nor even always prehistoric. Circular timber houses have already been mentioned: these are seldom more than 15m in diameter; some are distinguished by prominent porches, but most are not, and identification may depend on associated features such as surrounding enclosures or neighbouring houses (p 96). A near-modern example of multiple pit-circles is afforded by the 'round-house' at the base of a post-mill, when this is timber-built (pp 136–7). These could reach a diameter of more than 55m, but the spacing of the posts differs from that of comparable prehistoric structures, which all have a clear space at the centre as if 1–3 rings of a regular series had been omitted.

PREHISTORIC RITUAL SITES OF ELONGATED PLAN

Cursuses

Despite the fame of the Stonehenge and Dorset Cursuses, parts of which still survive as upstanding earthworks, most of what we know about the form and distribution of this class of monuments is derived from air-photography. The characteristic crop-marks were identified early (Leeds 1934, Crawford 1935a), and discoveries up to 1958 were summarized by the Royal Commission on Historical Monuments (England) (1960).

A long rectangular enclosure is bounded by a low bank and shallow ditch, each 1·5–4m wide. The sides are normally parallel and straight (5), 30–120m apart, though local diversions are possible to accommodate existing features such as round barrows (St Joseph 1966a, fig 1); nevertheless some Yorkshire examples, eg at Burton Fleming (Humberside), are less regularly set out. The ends may be either square (5) or rounded (RCHME 1960, pl 10*b*). Entrances occur most often near one end of a long side, but may also be found at its centre, or in one of the ends, or elsewhere. Typically the length is greater than 500m, and at least seven examples exceed 1500m. The Dorset Cursus consists of two such enclosures end to end, respectively 5·6km and 4·3km long. It is possible that similar juxtapositions exist elsewhere, but this cannot be inferred from a mere change of direction, since these

46 *Crop-marks of 'avenue' at Thornborough South Circle, North Yorkshire, 5 July 1975.*
On the right is part of the henge, with its bank and its broad regular inner ditch picked out by parching in pasture, and its causewayed polygonal outer ditch clearly visible in a cereal crop (p 75). On the left two parallel lines of pits about 11m apart are only just discernible as small dots except for five pairs of larger pits just below the centre of the photograph. At the far end of this avenue are two sets of parallel trenches, of unknown purpose; beyond these lie a ring-ditch and an isolated pair of pits. There is a scratch on the photograph close to the left margin (p 180).

occur in several examples without any visible sign of there being a junction at the angle (St Joseph 1964b, Dymond 1966). The supposed cursus at North Stoke (Oxfordshire) is anomalous both in its dimensions, 245m long and only 11m wide, and in having apparently open ends (51).

Smaller rectangular enclosures, less than 150m long, with straight sides and square ends, possibly stand in the same relationship to cursuses as hengi-form earthworks do to henges, but their date and function are as yet unknown.

The parallel sides of a cursus yield crop-marks similar to those of a variety of other features: these include Roman road ditches, modern field drains, and even the basic cultivation pattern of a field ploughed in 'lands' (p 155). For positive identification it is essential to recognize at least one of the ends as well as a substantial length of both long sides. Disused field and plantation boundaries sometimes display the parallel sides and square ends typical of a cursus, but are distinguished by their position in the modern field pattern, to which they are directly related.

Avenues

The Stonehenge Avenue (Wiltshire) has the distinction of yielding the first archaeological crop-marks in Britain to have been identified on an air-photograph and then authenticated by excavation (p 10). It has parallel banks, between ditches 23–34m apart, and runs for 2·5km from the river Avon to Stonehenge. It differs from the cursuses just described in that it leads to a specific and obvious monument, namely Stonehenge, and consequently does not have a closed end.

The term 'avenue' has also been used to describe parallel lines of standing stones leading similarly to some known monument, as the Kennet Avenue does to Avebury (Wiltshire). It is convenient to apply the same description to the parallel lines of pits detected by air-photography associated with the southernmost of the three Thornborough Circles (North Yorkshire) (St Joseph 1977a). These do not lead to the henge itself, however but to an enigmatic structure indicated by two sets of parallel trenches which presumably held some kind of foundation (46). The lines of pits may be supposed to have held uprights, probably of timber. The five pairs of pits nearest to the henge were of greater diameter than the rest, perhaps being intended for poles of greater height.

It is noteworthy that these larger pits were discovered first, before the remainder of the avenue was known. Seen thus in isolation they were interpreted as belonging to a Roman, Saxon or medieval timber hall. Similar arrangements of large pits have been photographed elsewhere, though not (apparently) forming part of longer avenues. They are shown not to be timber halls either by excessive size, or by close association with other possibly ritual structures, or by the poor correspondence between individual pairs of pits in the two facing rows (all illustrated in St Joseph 1977a, pl 20*c*). Explanation in terms of ritual use is hypothetical but plausible.

FUNERARY SITES

Long barrows and long mortuary enclosures

The identification of long barrows from the air has been relatively little studied. Most of the certain examples of crop-marks of long barrows have been seen in the areas already known to contain similar earthworks, but a few have been recorded in the river valleys (47a). Elsewhere, crop-mark enclosures have been tentatively identified as possible barrows or mortuary enclosures (Webster & Hobley 1965, Erith 1971), but without excavation this can be no more than a guess.

When undamaged, long barrows have mounds generally 25–120m long, rectangular or trapezoidal in plan. The trapezoidal form is the more distinctive, being higher at its broader end, when this remains intact. After prolonged ploughing, however, there is little surface relief, and even the corresponding soil-marks may be reduced to the point where a barrow can be recognized only with diffi-

47 *Long barrows and long mortuary enclosures*

a Crop-marks of long barrow north-east of Drayton, Oxfordshire, 25 June 1962

b Crop-marks of possible long barrow south of Ashwell, Hertfordshire, 1 July 1976

c Crop-marks of long mortuary enclosure, north-west of Burton Agnes, Humberside, 2 August 1971

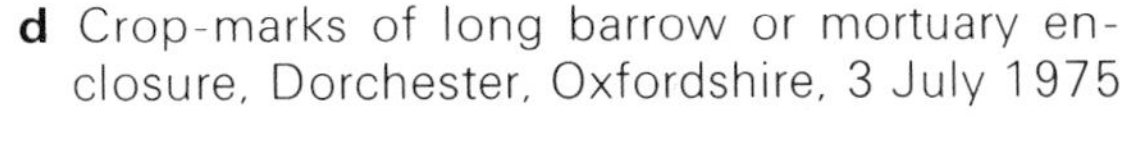

d Crop-marks of long barrow or mortuary enclosure, Dorchester, Oxfordshire, 3 July 1975

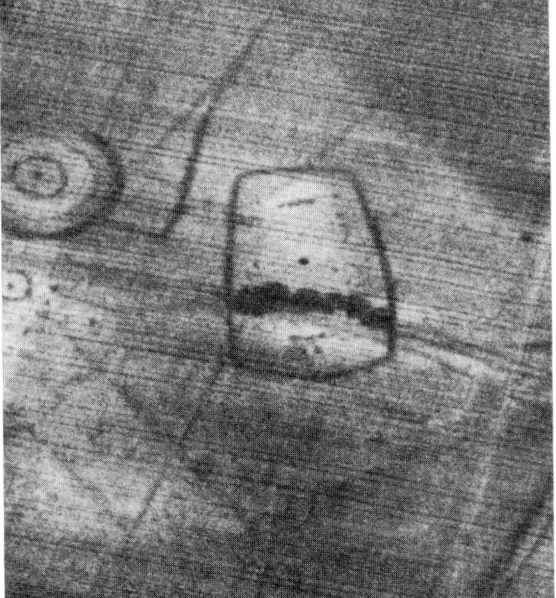

culty (RCHME 1979). Clearer indications may be given by crop-marks of the ditches, which are normally broad (up to 15m wide) and flank the mound on either side (47a). Some examples have a deeper and narrower ditch which encloses one or both ends of the barrow; the resulting oval or trapezoidal enclosure is not readily distinguished on air-photographs from the sort of mortuary enclosure to be described in the following paragraph. Crop-marks of parallel-sided enclosures with rounded ends, of a size appropriate for a long barrow, are not uncommon in crop-mark areas; but in default of any special features suggestive of a barrow their identification can only be tentative without ground investigation. The example illustrated (47b) is crossed by the ditches of a field-system conjectured to be of Roman date. A peculiarity is that while these ditches undoubtedly penetrate the enclosure, they dwindle away to nothing near its centre. This could be the result of their having been dug into the remains of a raised mound, thereby failing to penetrate the subsoil, so that when the mound was subsequently levelled, some parts of the ditches were totally removed. If this explanation is accepted, the site can be identified as that of a former long barrow (but see also below).

A number of excavated long barrows have been found to incorporate timber mortuary houses and other internal structures or to cover ditched mortuary enclosures. Internal features may also be revealed by crop-marks in favourable conditions (47a). Mortuary enclosures generally echo the plan of the overlying barrow, but they also occur independently (47c); it is often unclear whether a particular site seen in terms of crop-marks was once covered by a mound or not (47d).

Care is needed in distinguishing the denuded remains of a long barrow from other long banks of similar size. Attention should be paid to the ditch or ditches; the broad ditches most often found with long barrows can be regarded as diagnostic, and the berm or level space which sometimes separates the ditch from the mound is also characteristic, though not very common. Chambered long cairns, it may be noted, have the same trapezoidal plan as many earthen long barrows, but do not have the flanking ditch. Most long cairns are also distinguished, if well preserved, by a revetted façade at the broad end, often recessed for a forecourt or curving inwards to a portal. Most of the parallel-sided mounds which might be compared with long barrows also have no ditch: these include tip-heaps, isolated fragments of railway or tramroad embankments, and the firing points on disused rifle ranges (p 173). Pillow-mounds (p 140) are surrounded by a ditch with no berm; individually some examples are virtually indistinguishable from some long barrows, but pillow-mounds are mostly found in groups, whereas it is almost unknown for more than two long barrows to be found together.

Particularly deceptive are rows of confluent round barrows, where a line of up to five is enclosed by a single ditch. Ploughing blurs the individual shapes and runs them together so as to form an elongated mound. Several distinct summits may still be visible, but these are more readily recognized on the ground than from the air. Soil-marks that appear to show the mound of a long barrow should always be scrutinized for possible subdivision or a lobate outline. The ditch will sometimes betray its composite origin by skirting each of the barrows in turn, in a series of intersecting arcs, but a smoother line is also to be found (35). It is possible that the slightly waisted shape of the enclosure in fig 47b is due to this cause, indicating a pair of round barrows in place of the long barrow postulated above. This explanation is not likely to be correct, however, since it would bring the nearer of the two field-ditches across a low point between the two barrows, where it ought to be relatively well preserved, whereas this ditch actually appears to be the less well preserved of the two.

Round barrows

These are some of the commonest field monuments of lowland Britain. Individually their

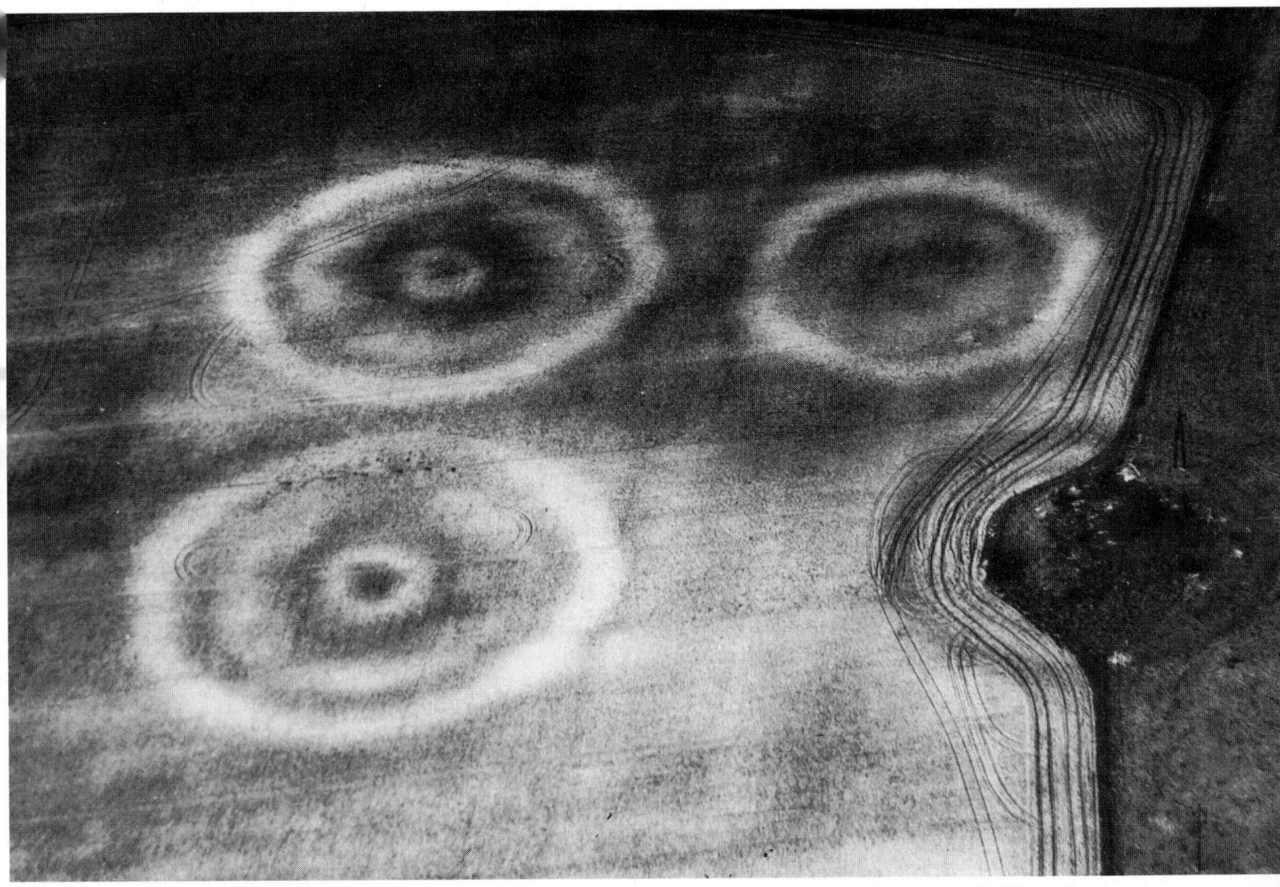

48 *Round barrows north-east of Winterbourne Stoke, Wiltshire, 27 March 1954*
A brilliant pattern of concentric circles, seen in bare soil on the chalk downs of Salisbury Plain, marks the site of three levelled disc barrows. The mound of a more substantial barrow has escaped the plough and protrudes into the field from the right, but soil-marks show that part of the surrounding ditch has been ploughed over. This barrow differs from the other three in having no outer bank.

remains are often ambiguous, but identification is assisted by their frequent occurrence together in groups.

Typically the mound is 5–45m in diameter and is surrounded by a ditch. There may or may not be a berm, large or small, inside the ditch or an upcast mound outside it. The ditch usually forms a continuous circle but may be interrupted by a single entrance causeway, or even occasionally be broken into a series of disconnected segments (p 93). The remains of the ditch may be inconspicuous through being partly filled and overgrown; not infrequently the ditch is ploughed over when the mound itself is carefully preserved (48). Sometimes, however, no ditch was ever present, as, of course, is normal with a cairn of stones. The material of an earthen barrow is seldom uniform, the central burial being usually covered by an inner mound of turf or loam, which was then enveloped in an outer layer derived from the local subsoil. These internal variations are most apparent in barrows that have been reduced by ploughing and are principally visible as soil-marks or crop-marks (48). The stone-free core of the barrow, when exposed by the plough, is shown by darker soil or by positive crop-marks. Such marks are very similar to traces of disturbance caused by casual barrow-digging, and this should be borne in mind by anyone trying to assess the modern

condition of barrows seen on air-photographs (Ashbee 1960, 28–9). Crop-marks are also capable of revealing underlying features formerly hidden by the barrow-mound, such as circles of post-pits (52) or a central burial-pit (50).

Some barrows have a complex history: when the mound has been enlarged to receive secondary interments, there may be two or three successive ditches, more or less concentric. As long as the mound survives, it conceals all except the last of these, but on a site levelled by ploughing crop-marks will display all phases simultaneously, in the form of a multiple ring ditch (47a, 50, 51).

When well preserved, the bermed varieties of round barrows (ie disc and bell barrows) are readily identified, especially if they have an upcast mound. Bowl barrows are not so distinctive and may be confused with other mounds of circular plan. A small medieval motte, for example, with no bailey attached, is scarcely distinguishable from a round barrow by aerial observation alone. It is true that mottes usually stand higher and have a steeper profile than the majority of barrows, but the same is also true of prehistoric cairns and Roman barrows containing burial chambers. Windmill-mounds (p 136) resemble a smaller size of barrow, but are normally distinguished by a cross-shaped depression at the centre; when this is poorly preserved, it may look more like the work of treasure-hunters (73). Spoil-heaps around mine-shafts also have a depression at the centre (p 135); spoil-heaps in other positions are less likely to be misleading as they are seldom truly circular. In addition it has to be remembered that circular

49 *Crop-marks near Burton Fleming, north Humberside 16 July 1975*

An Iron-Age square-barrow cemetery extends across a lane bordered by rectangular closes; it is not clear from the photograph which set of features is the earlier. The ring ditch near the top of the picture is presumably associated with the square barrows.

On the right the modern road follows one side of a narrow dry valley (p 155).

mounds, whether heaps of earth or (especially) cairns of stones, are erected on occasion for a variety of commemorative and miscellaneous practical purposes: the interpreter must be wary.

Round barrows more or less levelled by ploughing are most readily identified when some traces of the original mound can still be seen (26), though there is some possibility of confusion with certain ground markers of wartime bombing ranges (p 173). When evidence for a mound is lacking, however, the interpretation of a circular ditch on its own is far from straightforward in that there are so many alternative explanations to choose from. These alternatives are described below in a special section devoted to ring ditches and their variants (p 88). Some ring ditches are nevertheless known to belong definitely to vanished barrows, through excavation or from maps; examples are illustrated in figs 50 and 109.

Square barrows

Although observed in some numbers in east Yorkshire in the nineteenth century, few now survive above ground. Evidence for their distribution comes largely from air-photographs recording the crop-marks of their ditches and grave-pits. This confirms the concentration of Iron Age square barrows on the Yorkshire Wolds and adjacent areas (Whimster 1981, fig 31), but it also reveals the presence of square barrows, as yet undated, in eastern Scotland, from Fife to the Moray Firth (Maxwell 1979).

The following description applies principally to the Yorkshire and north Humberside examples. The barrow ditch, up to 3m broad, takes the form of a rather irregular square with blunt corners, 5–15m across. This surrounds a grave-pit 2m long, usually oblong but sometimes enlarged until nearly square. The largest barrows have the broadest ditches but the least obvious grave-pits; the body being deeply buried by spoil from the ditch needed only a shallow grave, yielding poor crop-marks or none at all. Conversely, the smallest barrows have very slight ditches, often too shallow to be visible from the air, but a deep grave-pit producing strong crop-marks (49). The barrows sometimes cluster together, looking almost like frog spawn, in cemeteries of several hundreds (St Joseph 1978b), but they can also occur in ones and twos. Circular ditches are occasionally associated with them.

Square ditched enclosures of similar size, but with no visible grave, and often with a narrow ditch and sharp corners, have been noted in other parts of the country, especially in south-east Britain. These have been compared with enclosures found in excavated cremation cemeteries of La Tène date, but the only crop-mark examples to be excavated contained no surviving trace of burial (St Joseph 1966a, May 1972).

Inhumation cemeteries

Single inhumation graves are too small and inconspicuous to be identified from crop-marks with any confidence unless sited in a significant position, such as the centre of a square or circular ditch. When several graves occur together, their size and shape are confirmed by repetition and are often emphasized by a common orientation (50). Even so, it is only crop-marks of better than average fineness and clarity that will render an oblong pit 2m long and less than 1m wide with sufficient precision to be securely recognized.

With one exception, there is little indication of the date of a cemetery to be obtained from crop-marks. An east-west orientation is obligatory for Christian burials but is far from uncommon in non-Christian burials also. The siting of a cemetery in relation to a nearby settlement, church or temple of known date is often suggestive, but any chronological conclusion involves assumptions that all too often prove to be unjustified. A positive indication of date is exceptionally provided by pagan Anglo-Saxon cemeteries in which some graves were covered by diminutive round barrows, up to 9m in diameter and 0·6m high (Grinsell 1953, pl 5b). When the cemetery is

50 *Crop-marks south of Radley, Oxfordshire, 9 June 1959*

Five large ring ditches (about 30m in diameter) mark the sites of some of the Barrow Hills, a Bronze Age round-barrow cemetery beside the river Thames; the nearest one contains a narrow inner ring and a large central grave-pit. Below this are a smaller ring and an incomplete ring broken into three or four separate arcs. To the right of these is a pit circle surrounding a seemingly random arrangement of further pits of similar size (p 76); and to the left is a group of about three dozen inhumation graves, mostly oriented NW–SE (p 86). The dark squarish marks probably belong to Anglo-Saxon huts with sunken floors (p 110), but have to be distinguished from the less regular marks caused by pits of other kinds. The enclosure shaped like a pie dish (bottom left) is of unknown significance.

The archaeological marks are superimposed on a network of fossil ice-wedges (p 148).

ploughed, crop-marks may show its full extent for the first time, by revealing flat graves in addition to those beneath barrows, whose position is now marked by a narrow ring ditch, often broken for an entrance (St Joseph 1974). The presence of narrow ditches encircling certain graves in an inhumation cemetery appears to be a reliable indication of Anglo-Saxon date.

RING DITCHES AND RELATED FEATURES

Although ring ditches are the commonest of archaeological crop-marks in Britain, they remain some of the least well understood. It is frequently assumed that all but a negligible proportion are the remains of round barrows, even by those aware of their considerable variation of form and of the wealth of alternative explanations (RCHME 1960, 16–23 and fig 2). Their very familiarity has tended to inhibit detailed study, by prompting quick identification without close scrutiny; but any attempt to identify the original function must analyze differences of shape as much as size and any associated features.

A substantial number of ring ditches are so perfectly shaped as to be evidently compass-drawn. The means for achieving this are very simple—a length of rope attached at one end to a stake in the ground and at the other to a pointed stick with which to trace the line: it does nevertheless imply a desire for geometrical regularity, willingness to take the trouble to obtain it, and a cleared area free from natural or man-made obstacles. When two or more such circles are centred on the same point, it is reasonably certain that they were drawn out at the same time.

The majority of ring ditches, even if neatly made, do not attain the same geometrical perfection. Some indeed are quite irregular and only approximate to a circular form. Carefully executed or not, there are examples which are not so much circles as ovals or ellipses; the exact shape may be difficult to determine in an oblique view. Some well-formed rings will appear to be flattened on two opposite sides for reasons that are merely 'reprographic'. Crop-marks, like the images on our television screens, are made up of variations in tone along a series of parallel lines (in this case the rows of plants), imposing on them a rectilinear pattern or texture that is not ideal for rendering curvilinear forms. The slight distortion of shape that is sometimes seen is an accidental effect that is visibly related to the agricultural 'grain' of the field. This is quite different from the regular faceted outline of examples where the entire circumference is actually made up of straight lengths of ditch meeting in a series of distinct angles. These rare polygonal variants most often have eight sides and are surprisingly difficult to distinguish from proper circles (53). None of them appears to have been dug.

Many apparently complete circles turn out to be actually penannular when the marks are seen at their best; that is, the circle is broken for an entrance. The broad entrance causeways of henges or in the ditches surrounding Roman watchtowers and medieval windmills are virtually unmistakable, though they may be simulated by modern interference, when, for example, a ring ditch is cut through by a sewer-trench or obscured by a vehicle track (121). Narrower causeways, however, are not uncommon, though not easily recognized, since they can only be detected in crop-marks of good definition and even tone. If the marks are ragged or mottled, genuine causeways are lost in the more general variations, while spurious gaps may seem to be created by a random change of tone.

More rarely several causeways are present, dividing the circle into a series of separate arcs (St Joseph 1965a). Many of these interrupted ring ditches are also incomplete, comprising little more than half a circle (50, 51). It is not clear if this constitutes a distinct class of monument, or if it represents an intermediate stage in the construction of an orthodox type of ring ditch, the work remaining for some reason unfinished.

In addition to detailed variations of shape, account should also be taken of dimensions.

51 *Crop-marks south-west of North Stoke, Oxfordshire, 23 June 1970*
A variety of ring ditches cluster round a possible cursus beside the river Thames. The 'cursus' is exceptionally narrow and has open ends, the nearer of which appears to overlap some kind of circular feature (p 80). The ring ditches include multiple, interrupted, incomplete, and oval forms in several combinations, as well as simple pen-annular ones; most undoubtedly belong to round barrows, but those in the field on the right, with others of the same size, could possibly derive from circular houses.

The width of the ditch and the diameter of the circle are significant both in absolute terms and in proportion to each other. Although seldom decisive in themselves for positive identification, these data are useful in limiting the range of possible interpretations which need to be considered.

In areas where crop-marks occur ring ditches are virtually ubiquitous. This may be partly a question of terminology, considering the variety of more or less circular enclosures which tend to be collected under this one label. But essentially it is because the circular form is so simple in concept and easily executed, while at the same time meeting a deeply felt and widespread need, to enclose a feature of importance within a mark or barrier. The ditch may in fact serve as a quarry for material to build a bank or a circular mound; it may be intended for drainage or defence or as a boundary; or it may serve several of these purposes. Occasionally crop-marks of internal features provide a strong clue to the identity of what is enclosed and so to the nature of the site as a whole. These are described more fully at the appropriate places below: they include a central pit or group of pits, cross-shaped foundation-trenches, a circle of pits, and a continuous circular trench.

When we come to review the possible identifications, it is convenient to refer first to a number of circular marks of non-archaeological origin that will be discussed in greater detail in Chapter 4. Several are caused by normal agricultural activities, such as tractors turning (p 158), irrigation by rotary sprinklers (p 161), or grazing by tethered animals (p 164). Other circles are produced by recreational pursuits; these may mark the site of a football pitch, of a fête or fair (p 177) or of a riding school (p 180). Even fairy rings are visible from the air and sometimes masquerade as ring ditches (p 167). When confronted by a possible ring ditch on a photograph, the interpreter will do well to begin by eliminating these spurious circles before trying to find an archaeological explanation. Hints for correct identification are given at the places specified.

None of the marks so far mentioned is caused by an actual ditch, despite appearances. Amongst those that do represent a genuine ditch or trench there will still be some that are of no very great antiquity. Ring and penannular ditches can be successfully classified, up to a point, in terms of size and shape; nevertheless it *is* only up to a point that this can be made to work. The ditches of round barrows, for example, are so varied in size and proportion and in minor features that they will not fit comfortably inside any very systematic classification. Other categories are more easily dealt with, however, and these can be disposed of first.

Penannular ditches

Narrow penannular ditches of modest size (less than 1m wide and no more than 15m in diameter) are likely to represent the foundation-trenches or eavesdrip gullies of circular houses. These are discussed separately below (p 96).

A larger size of ditch (not less than 2m broad but still no more than 30m in diameter), with an unmistakable entrance not less than 3m wide, is likely to have enclosed something specific to which access was going to be required over a period. When traces of this inner feature can be seen, the nature of the site is not much in doubt; otherwise identification must depend on a correct assessment of other factors such as siting, surface finds, or the character of neighbouring sites, all of which can be tiresomely misleading.

a *Roman military watchtowers* either have a stone foundation about 6m square or are carried on four massive timber corner posts sunk in pits each nearly 1m across, which form a square with sides of about 3m (45b). The ditch is over 2m broad, with a diameter of 14–20m; sometimes instead of forming a true circle it has short straight sides parallel to the sides of the tower. A second ditch may be present a few metres outside the first one. If the site is unploughed, the remains of a turf rampart 2·7–3·6m broad may be visible within the ditch and a low mound of upcast outside it. On crop-mark sites the four post-pits of a timber tower can be discerned only with difficulty, but unless they are seen the identification is uncertain. Although such towers occur at intervals along strategic military roads in north Britain, the fact of being sited beside a Roman road is not in itself sufficient identification since prehistoric homesteads (45a) and burial sites of circular plan have also been recorded in such positions.

b *Medieval post-mills* stood on crosstrees whose foundation-trenches formed a cross about 10m wide overall. The crosstrees were usually embedded in, or set in the top of, a low mound surrounded by a ditch. The higher the mound, the broader its ditch, but the less likely that the timbers will have penetrated the subsoil. Crop-marks of windmill-mounds thus fall into two groups: those with proportionately broad ditches, which usually display no central cross and are liable to confusion with 'hengiform' earthworks (p 75), and those with modest ditches (2–3m wide) and a cross within (45e, 58). The ditch is ordinarily about 25m in diameter; it may have two, or even occasionally three, entrances. The central cross is such a distinctive feature that the reader should be warned of the rare possibility of seeing crop-marks of a ground marker for a disused bombing range in the form of a circle with a central cross (p 173); such a circle would be unbroken but might not appear with sufficient clarity for this to be evident.

c *Prehistoric homesteads.* While circular houses may be found within ditched enclosures of various shapes and sizes, some are clasped closely by a penannular ditch of up to 20m in diameter (45a). It requires crop-marks of exceptional clarity and fineness to show the remains of the house itself, however, and few have been recognized; others must surely remain undetected inside some of the penannular ditches that do appear on photographs. The smallest size of Irish raths would fall into this category, though not always provided with an entrance causeway.

d *Hengiform earthworks* have been described above (p 75). An example with a single entrance and no special features would yield crop-marks little different from those in (*a*), (*b*) and (*c*) above.

Not all penannular ditches of about this size have entrances that are so obvious.

e *Searchlight batteries* of the 1939–45 War had penannular earthworks in two or three sizes, whose ditches have diameters in the range 15–35m (p 170) Traces of an internal rampart are sometimes visible even in crop-marks. Entrances were as narrow as operational efficiency would allow, as protection against blast, and their presence is often not readily discerned in crop-marks.

Circular ditched enclosures with diameters greater than 30m and with a definite entrance belong to categories which are dealt with more fully in other sections of this chapter.

f *Henges* are marked by a broad ditch and smooth well-cut outline, but those of Class I (with a single entrance) yield crop-marks much like those of other circular enclosures (p 75).

g *Moats* are sometimes circular, and some are interrupted by a causeway at the entrance. Crop-marks will usually show that the ditch is not only very wide but deep and steep-sided. Circular moats are most likely to surround a circular structure such as a castle mound (p 101) or to form part of a formal garden layout.

h *Enclosed settlements and hillforts* (p 97) may also be circular, often for topographical reasons, as when a hillfort crowns the summit of a rounded hill. Small circular or oval settlements are frequently, though not invariably, found sited on top of hillocks or on the end of a spur overlooking lower ground.

Ring ditches

Narrow ring ditches of modest size, like their penannular equivalents from which they are not easily distinguished, will usually mark the sites of circular houses (p 96); but not in every case.

i *Stack stands.* This identification is tentatively assigned to the groups of very narrow ring ditches about 0·3m wide and 9–16·5m in diameter which have long been recognized from the air in the East Anglian fens (Riley, 1946), but have yet to be examined by excavation. Marks so slight can be discerned only when there is maximum tonal contrast; they are most often noticed in bare soil or as germination-marks in the silt-fen (101). The circles often overlap and are sometimes accompanied by more elongated figures with straight parallel sides and rounded ends. A few examples of double concentric circles are also known. Detailed analysis of their position in relation to the medieval strip fields indicates that these circular ditches are of broadly medieval date (Wilson 1979a); their function was presumably to provide temporary local drainage round small stacks of hay or corn. Such slight ditches might at first sight seem inadequate even for this purpose, but it should be remembered that their original width at the contemporary ground surface would have been substantially greater.

Ring ditches with diameters in the range 15–45m (as well as many that are smaller) will most often belong to round barrows, separately described below. Other possibilities do nevertheless exist. Moats and ornamental waters (*g*, above), for example, may be crossed by boat or bridge instead of on a causeway and thereby qualify for reconsideration here. Irish raths, unlike most British enclosed settlements (*h*, above), are often surrounded by a continuous ditch.

j *Circular buildings with stone foundations* would ordinarily yield negative crop-marks; but if all the surviving stonework had been systematically robbed, the same plan could then reappear as positive marks responding to the robber-trenches. Such complete robbing even of foundations would probably imply a substantial building with masonry of a high standard, such as a Roman temple or mausoleum, though other possibilities (eg a medieval dovecote) are numerous. Simple rings, without external buttresses or internal subdivisions, are unlikely to exceed 15m in diameter, but the addition of an outer ring, as in a Romano-Celtic temple (p 131), could increase the diameter to nearly twice as much.

k *Plantation boundaries* of circular form are not infrequent, especially in former parkland (p 166). There is no specific size for them, but those most liable to misinterpretation are probably those with diameters of 30–40m. Since there are no grounds for excluding genuine barrows from land that was emparked, such crop-marks are ambiguous unless identifiable as groves from documentary sources. Even quite recent maps may suffice for this purpose.

Round barrows and circular houses

Despite the variety of alternative explanations which the interpreter needs to keep in mind, there can be little doubt that the majority of ring and penannular ditches are derived from round barrows or from circular houses, though it may often not be simple to determine which.

1 *Round barrows* (p 82) have ditches with diameters ranging from 4m to more than 45m. The lower figure takes account of two varieties of exceptionally small ring ditches believed to belong to barrows. The first of these has already been described as a feature of Anglo-Saxon inhumation cemeteries, where very small ring and penannular ditches surround certain of the graves (p 86). Small ring ditches, 5–10m in diameter, also occur in clusters round rings of more ordinary size, 25m or so in diameter (St Joseph 1965a, Wilson 1975, fig 1). These ring-ditch clusters are not at all common, though several examples have been photographed in East Anglia. No grave-pits have been observed, and their identification as barrows rests solely on their close and seemingly deliberate association with other round barrows, of which they appear to be in some sense satellites.

At the other end of the scale the largest surviving barrow ditch has a diameter of 60m. This size is quite exceptional, yet it is exceeded by a small number of crop-mark circles with narrow ditches whose diameters reach as far as 100m. These can scarcely be regarded as belonging to normal barrows, but are otherwise unexplained. The examples are few and somewhat various. One near Ailsworth (Cambridgeshire) has a narrow ditch 1–2m wide describing a perfect circle 75m in diameter (RCHME 1969, pl 4). Another, not far away at Chesterton (Cambridgeshire), has a diameter of about 100m with a double ring ditch at the centre, but has a narrow entrance and is actually twelve-sided. There are other largish circles nearby (Mackreth 1979), one of which overlaps this one, but it is not clear if there is any connexion. Similar outsize circles no doubt exist elsewhere and may prove to be more informative; care must be taken, however, to distinguish genuine examples from the residual marks of boundary lines on cricket fields, which are usually of more or less circular form (p 177).

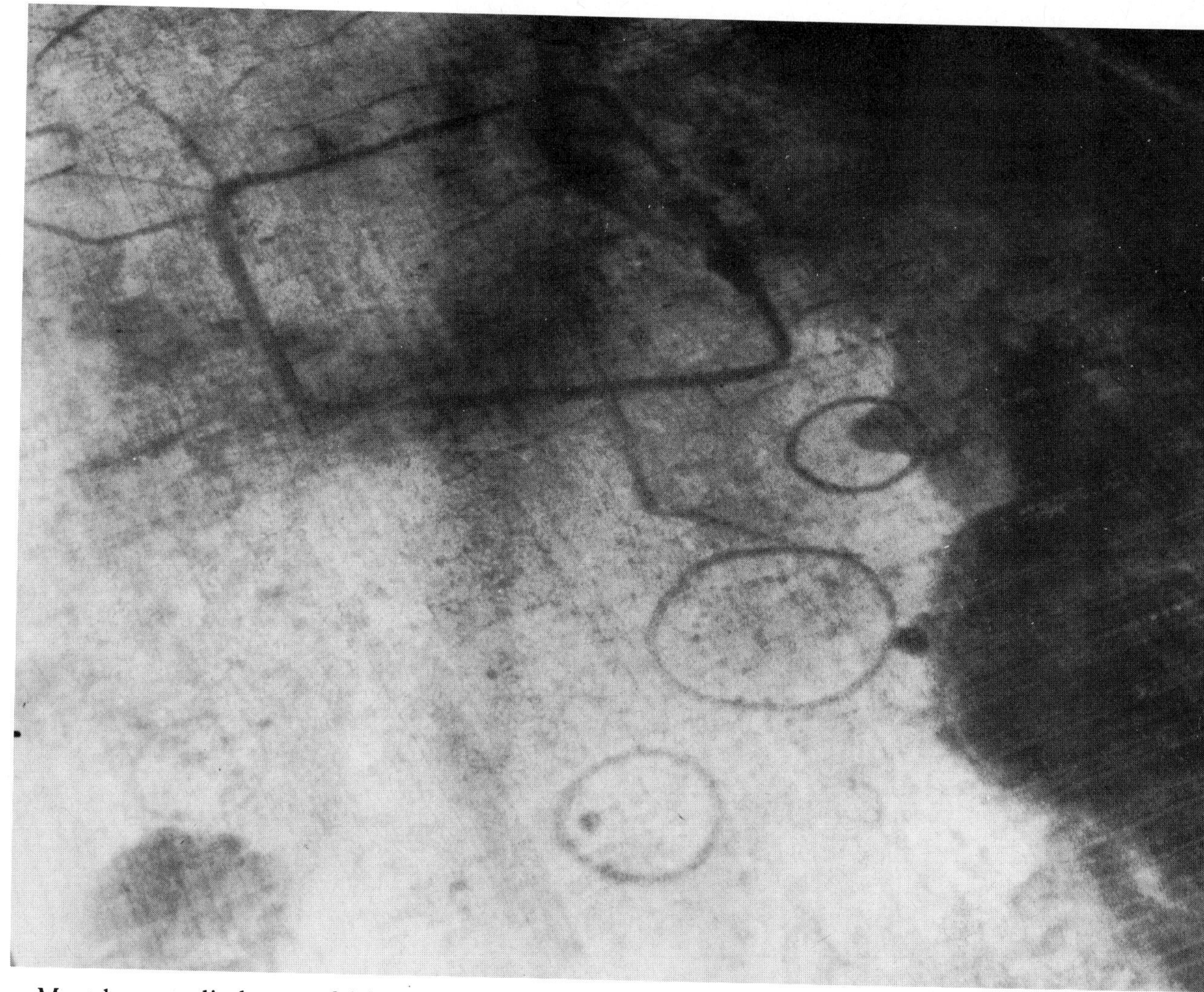

Most barrow ditches are fairly well shaped in plan, and many are geometrically perfect. There is nevertheless a minority that is distinctly irregular. The width of excavated barrow ditches has a range from 0·75m to 7·25m. There is no simple relationship between ditch width and diameter, since this depends also on the type of barrow. The ditches are normally continuous, but not invariably so, a small causeway being sometimes left for access to the central area for the performance of ceremonies or for construction of the mound itself. Some barrow ditches have several of these causeways, and similarly interrupted ring ditches can be attributed to barrows with fair confidence. Incomplete examples, showing scarcely more than half the full circuit (50,

52 *Crop-marks east of Wansford, Cambridgeshire, 26 June 1959*
In the foreground, the largest of six ring or penannular ditches contains a semicircle of large pits; these lie round the edge of a disc of darker tone which can be seen more distinctly on photographs taken in another season. Beyond, a four-sided enclosure overlaps an irregular pattern of frost-cracks. This enclosure is also crossed by a vertical band of darker tone due to variation in sensitivity of the photographic emulsion on the negative (p 182).

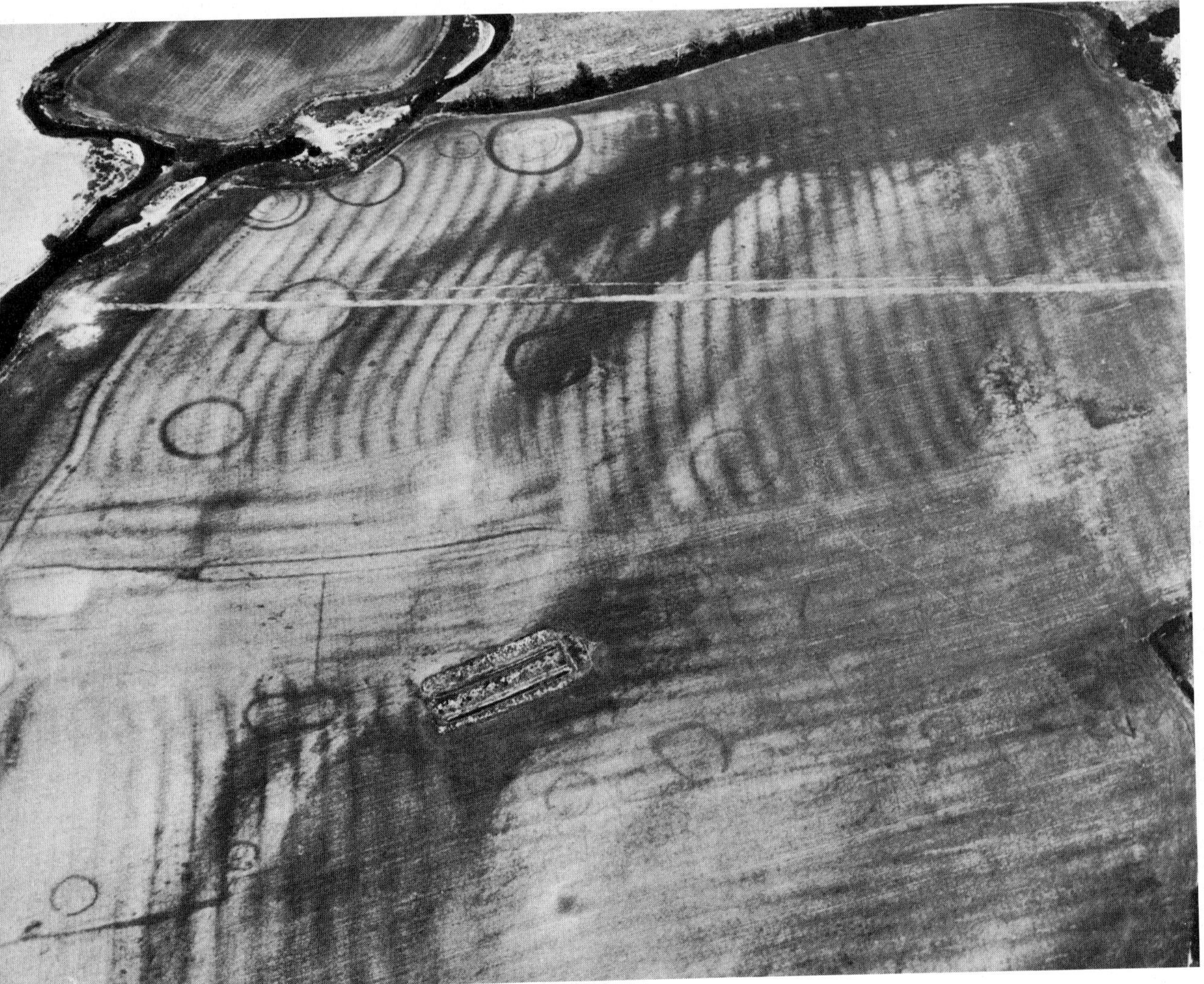

53 *Crop-marks north of Tyringham, Buckinghamshire, 30 June 1976*
Severe parching in a ley crop has revealed a group of ring ditches beside the river Ouse beneath the characteristic patterns of medieval ridge-and-furrow. One is crossed by the straight lines of two modern trenches of different width, possibly a sewer outfall (p 174). Near the centre of the picture a narrow octagonal ditch is only just discernible. The small enclosures of irregular oval plan seen rather indistinctly in the foreground are typical of prehistoric settlements in the Ouse and other Midland river valleys (p 113).

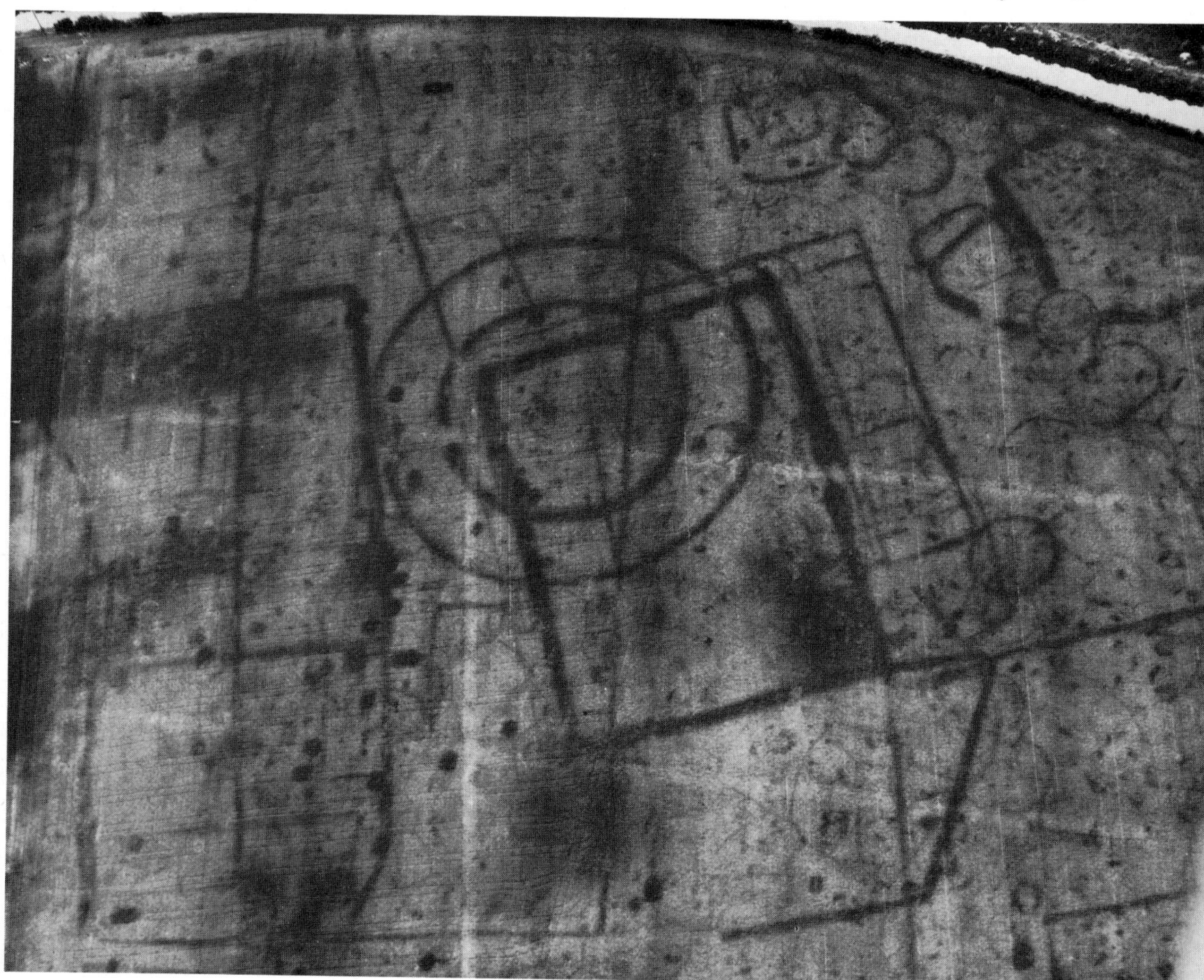

54 *Crop-marks near Mucking, Essex, 14 June 1962*

The photograph shows one part of the largest excavated crop-mark site in Britain. At the centre, two widely spaced penannular ditches (the South Rings) enclose a domestic site of the Later Bronze Age (pp 113, 193). A regular oblong enclosure overlapping this is embedded in the field system of a Roman villa. On the right, penannular gullies mark the sites of Iron Age circular houses, a few of which have substantial enclosures attached. The enclosure in the top right corner was later used for a Roman inhumation cemetery (p 86). A scatter of dark blobs with straightish sides is caused by some of the sunken huts in a large Anglo-Saxon village (p 110).

Also visible are alternately dark and light parallel lines running across the picture, caused by ploughing in 'lands' (p 156), and the broad, dark, blurred marks of natural drainage hollows at the left margin (p 155).

51), are presumably to be interpreted in the same way.

The clearest evidence for identification as a barrow is the presence of a central grave-pit. Such pits are not, however, particularly common. Other internal features that may be visible are rings of pits (52) and additional circular ditches (50, 51, 53).

Post-circles under barrows are set either in individual pits or in a continuous trench. The posts may be closely or more widely spaced. They may form either a single circle or several in concentric series. Individual circles may be truly internal or else form a peripheral revetment for the mound; the internal circles are not always concentric with the subsequent barrow. Amidst so much variation it will be seen that there is ample room for confusion with the remains of circular houses, on which more will be said below.

Multiple ring ditches (47d, 50, 51) can originate in either of two ways. The extra ditches may have been present from the first as part of the original design, intended to be covered by the mound when it was constructed; or they may result from enlarging the mound for secondary interments. There is no sure way of distinguishing between the alternatives except by excavation, though a very slight inner ring would seem more likely to be a primary feature, whether it was an actual ditch or a trench to hold a ring of posts. Whatever the actual mode of origin, multiple ring ditches can generally be attributed to barrows unless the dimensions of the inner ring are small enough for a circular house. It is necessary, of course, to distinguish them from double-ditched settlements of more or less circular form. Such settlements in Britain are more often oval or elliptical than truly circular, and they have entrance causeways; but this is less true of Ireland, where a double or triple circle with substantial ditches would be most likely to denote a rath (Norman & St Joseph 1969, fig 21).

m *Circular houses* made of wood, wattle, and wicker leave relatively little trace in the ground, even for discovery by excavation. Only the principal features of the most substantial houses are likely to yield visible crop-marks, and often all that is seen is the penannular eavesdrip gully surrounding the outer wall (54). This may be replaced by a more substantial ditch, as already observed (*c*, above). When the house itself produces crop-marks, these normally reveal either a ring or penannular foundation-trench or else a circle of post-pits. A broader interval between two of the pits in such a circle will sometimes indicate which way the entrance faces, but massive porches of Little Woodbury type are rarely seen on air-photographs. On a few sites in eastern Scotland all the pits appear to be elongated radially, as if holding pairs of posts set side by side; whether the second post was for reinforcement, repair, or replacement, or if it served some other purpose, is as yet unknown.

It will be observed that there is considerable overlap of form not only between crop-marks of circular houses and those of probably ritual pit-circles (as already noted, p 76), but between crop-marks of circular houses and those of round barrows. There is no handy rule of thumb for distinguishing them, provided that the diameter of the ditch is not excessive. Barrow ditches are normally continuous but may be broken by a narrow causeway; foundation-trenches and gullies belonging to houses are normally penannular but may also be continuous. Circles of pits may equally well belong to a post-circle under a barrow or to a dwelling (45h), and neither need be truly concentric with a surrounding ditch. In neither category are the circles consistently well shaped or consistently irregular. Moreover it is perfectly possible for the remains of round barrows and circular houses to be mingled on the same archaeological site.

The clue to a correct identification will often be given by siting and association.

Groups of houses in a single settlement will commonly be of identical construction and fairly similar size, whereas round barrows less often repeat themselves exactly. In particular, it is unlikely for several adjacent barrows to isplay the same peculiar features, such as a ost-circle, inner ditch, or entrance causeway. 'he repetition of any special feature in ring itches of similar size is thus a strong argu-nent for identification as a group of dwellings, ven though individually each could in theory elong to a round barrow (St Joseph 1970a, l 44a).

When houses occur singly, they are often nside larger enclosures. A narrow penannular litch of moderate size seen near the centre or he back or one corner of a rectangular en-losure, or in a similar position in an oval one, an thus be interpreted as a house with easonable confidence (114). It is true that uch an association could be the result of mere oincidence in any particular case, but this iting recurs with sufficient frequency to stablish it as a genuine type of settlement—nly to be simulated by chance on rare ccasions.

An unusual instance of houses distributed n individual compounds in this way is seen n fig 45g, where one of a group of similar iouses is represented by a ring of pits, mea-uring some 8m across its diameter, and by an utlying pair of pits in front of the entrance. These outlying pits are set too far out, at a listance of 5m, to form part of a porch of any lausible kind; their true explanation is sug-gested by another site elsewhere in the region. There, two houses resembled those in fig 15g, but a third was surrounded by a circular palisade whose narrow trench ended in two arge pits. These pits, which were evidently ntended for the gate-posts of a substantial entrance, occupied the same position in re-ation to the house as the outlying pair of pits illustrated here. In other words, all the houses had once been enclosed by palisades, but only at one had the palisade-trench es-caped destruction by ploughing, whereas the pits for the gate-posts, being deeper, had all sur-vived in truncated form to furnish crop-marks.

FORTS AND CASTLES

Hillforts

Hillforts were among the earliest and most spectacular subjects for air-photography in Britain. Only an aerial view could capture the full sweep of the defences of a major hillfort, and photography in oblique light could also show up the slight earthworks of earlier de-fensive circuits or the traces of modern use as a place of assembly (Crawford & Keiller 1928, pl 11). It was this same comprehensive view that first made sense of the jumbled heaps of earth at unfinished hillforts like Ladle Hill (4). The role of air-photography in hillfort studies has been reviewed by St Joseph (1965b).

Many hillforts were settlements and, when the interior remains unploughed, the remains of stone foundations for circular or subrectan-gular houses may still be visible. Alterna-tively, on sloping sites it may be possible to see the terraced platforms on which vanished houses originally stood (CBA 1981, 17). When the interior has been brought into cultivation, crop-marks of houses or enclosures appear only seldom. It is not possible to make a clear distinction between the smallest size of hill-fort and a defended homestead. In practice those with surviving earthworks have tended to be called hillforts if sited on hilltops (18), whereas those on lower ground or known only from crop-marks have been described simply as settlements or homesteads. They are dis-cussed further below (p 113).

It is most often the smaller hillforts whose defences have been levelled by agriculture. Crop-marks may then reveal not only the lines of the ditch-system, sometimes displaying several structural periods, but also the narrow mark of a palisade or a timber revetment for the rampart (55).

Hillforts may be confused with other hill-top enclosures, such as Neolithic causewayed enclosures (p 72) or plantation banks (p 166). They should also be distinguished from sev-eral features of natural origin. It is not uncom-mon for a steep-sided isolated hill to be capped with a layer of hard rock particularly resistant to weathering; this will outcrop round the brow of the hill like the base of a defensive wall, and a modern field-wall may even stand upon it, while the upper courses of

55 *Hillfort at Burncastle, north of Lauder, Berwickshire, 27 July 1967*
Two periods of defences are partly preserved as earthworks, partly revealed by crop-marks. Just inside the outermost ditch can be seen the narrow trench of a palisade.

the supposed fortification will seem to have tumbled down the slope below. In areas of arable land soil-marks and crop-marks like those of a hillfort's ditch-system may be created by the presence of horizontally bedded rock (p 143).

Roman military posts

Knowledge of the Roman conquest and occupation of Britain has been transformed by aerial discoveries of Roman camps and forts since 1930. Discoveries made from 1945 onwards have been reported in a series of articles by St Joseph (1951b, 1953, 1955 1958, 1961, 1965c, 1969b, 1973c, 1977b).

Roman camps are, in principle, shaped lik a conventional playing card: rectangular, wit straight sides and rounded corners. In prac tice the angles can be distinctly greater or les than 90° and the sides, although made up o straight lengths, may show several changes o direction. These occur most often, though no necessarily, at the camp entrances. Mos camps have an entrance in each of the fou sides, those in the shorter sides being central Small camps may have only one or two entrances; large camps, six or more. The planning of these entrances is very characteristic the principal variants are illustrated in fig 56 where the ditch is represented in solid black (as if portrayed by crop-marks) and the rampart shown by stipple. The *titulum* (16, 96

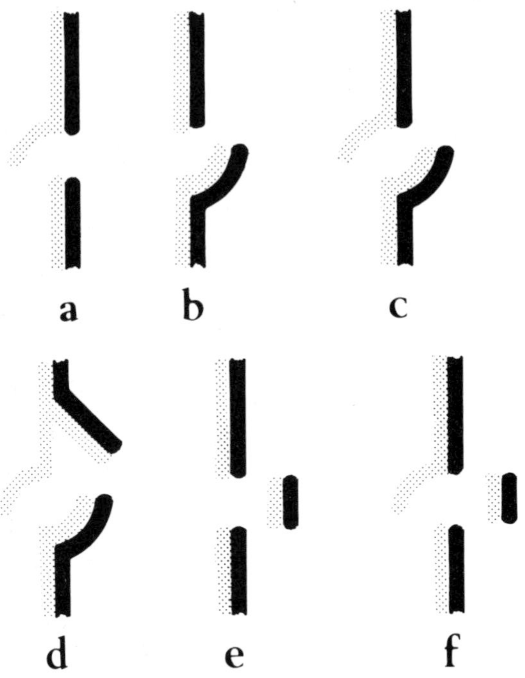

56 *Roman camp entrances*
The interior of the camp is to the left. The ditch is shown in solid black, the rampart by stipple.
a Internal *clavicula*
b External *clavicula*
c Double *clavicula*
d Double *clavicula* with external spur
e *Titulum* (or traverse)
f Internal *clavicula* with *titulum*

and the internal *clavicula* (19) are the forms most commonly found. When the defences survive in relief, the presence of any of these types of entrance is sufficient to identify a defended enclosure as a Roman camp (19, 57a). On sites where the rampart has been levelled, however, some distinctive details are lost: it is the rampart that distinguishes an internal *clavicula*, for instance, the ditch showing only a simple causeway (56a).

Roman camps vary enormously in size, from tiny enclosures as little as 12m square, built solely as training exercises (16), to vast marching-camps for whole armies covering more than 65ha. The largest camps extend over many modern fields and may have a rampart and ditch each as much as 4·6m wide, whereas the ditch of a 10ha camp may survive to a width of one metre at best. In a few camps, occupied by a military construction-party over a longer than normal period, lines of rubbish pits have been detected in the interior, presumably fronting the contemporary lines of tents (St Joseph 1951b, pl 6(2); 1965c, pl 10(2)).

Identification as a Roman camp, if not signalled by the type of entrance, depends on the general layout. Rounded corners are essential but are not limited to Roman military work. They may be found in modern fields, plantation boundaries, and enclosures of all kinds (Wilson 1975b, fig 7). The provision of entrances in all four sides, except in the smallest camps, and their orderly arrangement in facing pairs, are reliable indicators which are not repeated in other kinds of enclosure. It may nevertheless require photography over many seasons to establish the full circuit of a Roman camp from crop-marks, as different lengths of ditch come into view in different fields in different years, and identification will be only provisional until the greater part has been confirmed. Care should be taken to ensure that apparent entrances are in fact genuine, not caused by modern interfence (p 189), and conversely that genuine entrances are not missed because the causeway has been dug through in near-modern times (p 162).

Roman forts normally have the same playing-card shape as the camps up to the late third century AD, but are distinguished by their more substantial defences, internal streets and buildings. Unlike camps, which have only one ditch, most forts have two or more. The earthen rampart can be up to 15·5m wide, with towers at intervals and often with a front revetment either in timber or in stonework. A narrower rampart 3m wide with revetments at both back and front, although rare in Britain, is indicated by crop-marks at Stanway (Essex) (Wilson 1977). An entrance in each side was controlled by a gatehouse of timber or masonry matching the interval-towers; crop-marks sometimes show their post-pits, foundations, or robber trenches. The special devices for protecting camp

a

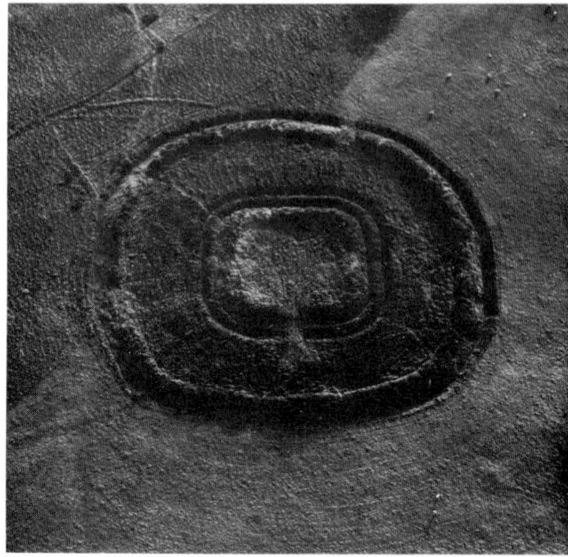

b

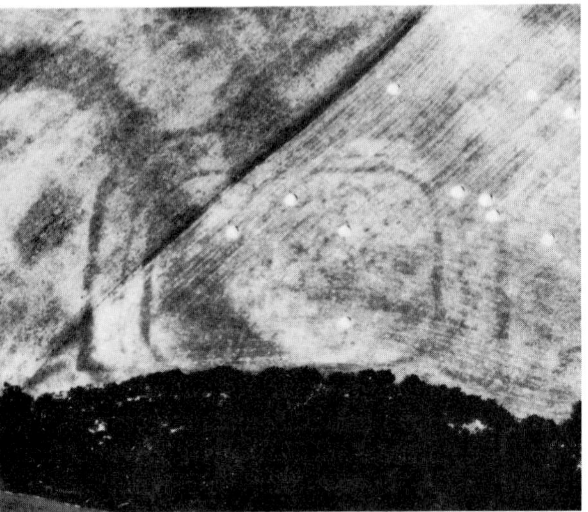

c

d

57 *Roman fortlets and other small squarish enclosures*

a Roman labour camp, Troutbeck, Cumbria, 14 July 1952; this has only two entrances, both with double *clavicula* (p 98)

b Roman fortlet, Old Burrow, Countisbury, Devon, 26 November 1969; the outer rampart, enclosing a stores compound, is less regular than that of the fortlet proper (p 101)

c Roman fortlet north of Gatehouse of Fleet, Kirkcudbrightshire, 12 July 1949; the ditches are revealed by parching in grass (the pale blobs are haycocks) (p 101)

d Iron Age homestead north-west of Kenton, Devon, 3 July 1970; the ditches on the far side of the enclosure are bowed, and the front corners of the inner ditch are rather sharp for Roman military work (pp 101, 113) ntrances—*titulum* and *clavicula*—occur occa-ionally also in fort defences, at the outer edge f a multiple ditch-system; a number of first-entury forts with two closely spaced ditches lso have *titula* at the entrances (St Joseph 973c, pl 16(1)).

From the late third century AD onwards nost forts had a free-standing wall with no ank behind it, square instead of rounded cor-ers, and projecting towers.

Not all Roman forts are rectangular and traight-sided, though the great majority are; nd not all rectangular enclosures with ounded corners are necessarily Roman. In arthwork construction it is more convenient) turn the corner in a curve, and enclosures f other periods or of other functions are quite apable of showing the same feature. The egular arrangement of gateways linked by nternal streets on a standard plan is, however, ndicative of Roman military work, and many f the internal buildings, if revealed by crop-narks, are equally distinctive (St Joseph 951b, pl 4(2)). Irregular street-systems have evertheless been observed at a number of nown Roman forts; these are attributed not o the original garrison, but to subsequent ivilian settlement spreading over the site fter its abandonment by the army.

The largest Roman military posts are nown as fortresses; besides being larger than rdinary forts they are more elaborate in their nternal planning (38). Legionary fortresses over about 20ha, and vexillation fortresses -11ha. Some vexillation fortresses have *tit-la* in front of the gateways.

The smallest posts, apart from watchtowers p 90), were fortlets, only about 35m square r little larger. They usually had a single gate-vay and accommodation for no more than 80 nen (57b, c). There is some risk of confusion vith native homesteads of four-sided plan: nany of these are of Roman date, but their litch-systems do not achieve the regularity of Roman military work, with good straight ides, true curves on the corners, and exact orrespondence between inner and outer litches (Wilson 1982). At the same time it should be understood that even at a genuine Roman fort or fortlet the outer elements in a complex ditch-system, which may themselves be secondary, are often less regularly planned (57b). Four-sided enclosures are particularly common in Northumberland, in the lower Severn valley, and in Devon (57d), where not a few have been wrongly, or at least only dubiously, identified as Roman forts or fort-lets (p 193).

Castles

Castles, whether of earthwork or masonry, are particularly photogenic. The surviving ma-sonry castles need no further comment, but their ruins, if quarried by stone-robbers, are soon reduced to insignificance, leaving little but a substantial moat as evidence. Earthwork castles are less often destroyed and, if not overgrown with trees, present an impressive appearance from the air. Castles of motte-and-bailey type are very distinctive and un-mistakable, but isolated mottes or motes are less easily identified without documentary confirmation, as noted above (p 85). St Joseph (1966b) illustrates a rare example of a motte and bailey visible chiefly in terms of crop-marks. This may be compared with fig 58, where a large enclosure appears to be at-tached to a circular moat; but close scrutiny shows that here the two enclosures overlap and should thus be regarded as independent features presumably of different date.

A large number of Norman castles made use of earlier fortifications in their defences. A motte or keep is often to be seen in one corner or at one end of a Roman fort or at the centre of a hillfort. The obvious presence of castle remains on a particular site, therefore, does not necessarily imply that all the visible defensive earthworks are of medieval date.

Civil War forts

The period of the Civil War was the last in which major new fortifications were carried out in earthwork alone. Later artillery forts invariably incorporate structures of stone or concrete. When Civil War forts survive in

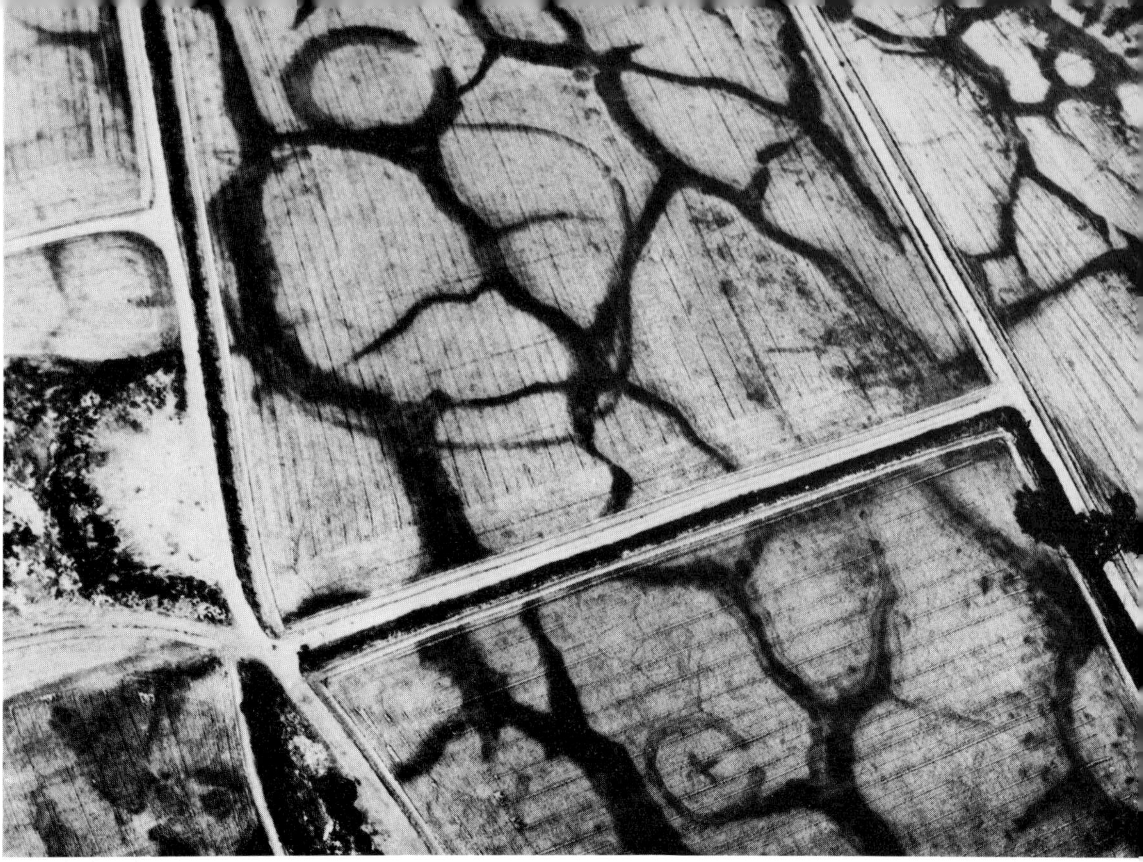

58 *Crop-marks near Romford, Havering, London, 18 June 1976*
In the foreground is the site of a medieval windmill (p 90). The large penannular ditch beyond may possibly belong to a second windmill mound of unusual size. It overlaps a large enclosure with two entrances, at each of which the ditch-ends overlap one another. The archaeological features are superimposed on a strongly developed geological pattern of ice-wedge polygons (p 149).

59 *The Bulwark, Earith, Cambridgeshire, 11 February 1978*
This fort of the Civil War period has a 'spearhead' bastion on each corner; from tip to tip of adjacent bastions is approximately 100m. The inner and outer ramparts are outlined in white where snow lies unmelted on the ice-covered ditches (p 36).

good condition, they display the characteristically angular forms introduced into military architecture in the seventeenth century (59); but their ditches tend to follow a smoother line than the ramparts, and the crop-marks of a ploughed-out fort may do no more than hint at the 'spearhead' bastions that originally controlled its corners.

LINEAR EARTHWORKS AND FRONTIERS

Linear earthworks serving as boundaries, obstacles or frontiers have been in use at least since the Bronze Age. They run across country, dividing one tract of land from another; although often preserved or traceable only in fragments, their definition would demand a minimum length of several hundred metres. Offa's Dyke is over 160km long.

Boundaries

Linear earthworks are distinguished from mere field boundaries by the multiplication of lines of bank and ditch, or by size, if single, and by their extended course. Multiple earthworks are particularly common on the Yorkshire Wolds and the southern slopes of the North Yorkshire Moors, where one example has as many as seven parallel banks. Many of these Yorkshire dykes incorporate pit-alignments in place of one or more of the ditches; dykes with a single bank are also present (119). Multiple linear ditches are known from crop-marks in many parts of East Anglia and the Midlands (60). Some form part of the prehistoric landscape, while others are known to be post-Roman. Whatever their period of origin, such distinctive features were always effective boundary markers and it is not unusual to find a county or parish boundary following the same line.

Triple and quadruple linear ditches have no common alternative explanation, but double ditches are ambiguous. Care must be taken to distinguish the crop-marks of double-ditched boundaries from those of double-ditched lanes and tracks, either of which may be found separating blocks of

60 *Crop-marks west of Long Bennington, Lincolnshire, 29 June 1976*
A triple-ditched boundary is joined by another composed of two ditches and a pit-alignment. In the foreground, a group of small enclosures appears indistinctly in pasture.

fields in an agricultural landscape. The necessary distinction can be made on the basis of spacing or on that of connexion. A pair of ditches only a metre or two apart is too close together to allow the free passage of vehicles or livestock to and from the fields; so they are more likely to border a bank than a lane, though such a bank might prove to belong to a modern hedgerow (p 167). If the ditches can be traced to a terminus of some kind, this wil usually imply a specific interpretation. Thus a lane should lead in to a field or enclosur (20, 25), whereas a boundary is most likely to be joined to another boundary. Sometimes a variation in the number of ditches strongly favours one interpretation: if at some poin the number increases from two to three, the associated feature is more likely to be a boundary; and if two ditches converge into one, the feature can hardly be regarded as a lane.

A linear feature attested by crop-marks of a single line of ditch is even less immediately recognizable. If the ditch is obviously broader than other ditches nearby, this may arouse

interest, but identification will depend on a close analysis of its course over a considerable distance. This will not only establish its 'linear' character, but distinguish it from other linear features such as abandoned canals, railways and hollow ways, sewer-trenches, pipelines and anti-tank ditches (pp 138, 172, 174).

The dykes surrounding Belgic oppida may be regarded as being linear earthworks of a kind: although closely related to a specific local context, they differ from the defences of hillforts in being physically independent of each other and in not combining to form a continuous enclosure. New elements of such dyke-systems can still be expected occasionally to make an appearance on air-photographs taken in suitable conditions (61).

61 *Crop-marks south-east of Stanway, Essex, 23 June 1976*
The camera looks along the line of two broad ditches forming part of the dyke system of Belgic Camulodunum. The ditches run along the rim of a narrow valley; the sequence of parallel hollows along one side of the valley is a common feature of fluvioglacial deposits in this part of Essex (p 155).

Two Roman boundary earthworks also call for mention. The so-called Vallum, defining the rearward limit of a military control zone along Hadrian's Wall, consisted of a ditch 6m broad midway between parallel banks which were also each 6m broad. The whole work occupied a strip 36m, or 120 Roman feet, in width overall. The Cleaven Dyke, which may have bounded land assigned for the use of legionaries in the unfinished fortress at Inchtuthil (Perthshire), was organized in contrary fashion, with a central bank 14m wide between parallel ditches 5m wide spaced 49m apart. The similarity of layout is only apparent where the two works survive intact; crop-marks depict merely a single or a pair of ditches.

Frontier-works

Linear earthworks intended as frontiers or as major obstacles to movement are normally constructed on a much larger scale than the lesser boundary earthworks so far described. Nevertheless, because they are indeed obstacles, they are just as liable to obliteration once their purpose has been served. Thus the Antonine Wall, which was the Roman frontier in Scotland, comprised a turf rampart 4·5m wide with a ditch usually about 11m wide; but in comparatively few places along its 59km length do these both survive intact. The course of the levelled frontier can in many places, however, be traced by the crop-marks of its ditch.

Major earthworks on this scale usually have a long recorded history. This assists recognition since a dyke is thereby known to have existed, and crop-marks of a broad linear ditch can be readily identified even when they are not virtually continuous with a length of surviving earthworks. Frontier-works comprising palisade and ditch leave less conspicuous remains and are thus less likely to be remembered in tradition. Identification therefore rests on a consideration of their course and will probably need to be confirmed by excavation. Two lines of ditch varying between 30m and 46m apart were revealed by crop-marks on the Cumbrian coast between Bowness-on-Solway and the inlet of Moricambe (Jones, 1976). That they formed part of Hadrian's frontier for Roman Britain is shown by the way that these ditches run up to the front and rear defences of several of the 'milefortlets' belonging to the frontier system; but the palisade running behind the forward ditch was only discovered during subsequent excavation.

MAJOR SETTLEMENTS

Some major prehistoric settlements have already been discussed. Traces of settlement inside hillforts were considered on p 97, where the rarity of crop-marks was noted, even on apparently favourable sites. Crop-marks are also rare inside Belgic oppida, except when these are sited on glacial or fluvial gravels. In the Gosbecks area at Colchester (Essex), in addition to the great ditch of the pre-Roman sanctuary, air-photography has revealed a large homestead surrounded by fields, possibly belonging to a royal farm (Crummy 1980, fig 34), whereas crop-marks within the Dyke Hills at Dorchester (Oxfordshire) show a pattern of numerous circular houses and small enclosures that suggests much denser settlement (Hampton & Palmer 1978, fig 3).

Roman towns and road-stations

The detailed contribution of air-photography to the study of Roman towns and roadside settlements has been reviewed by St Joseph (1966c) and by Wilson (1975d).

Settlements formally recognized as towns by the Roman authorities can be identified archaeologically by their orderly street-patterns and by their central municipal buildings (62). The forum and basilica housed the offices of the town or tribal council, while the grid of streets crossing each other at right angles demonstrated the council's power as a local authority. The regularity of the street-grid should not be exaggerated; even in the planned layout at the centre of the town streets were seldom equally spaced and in less central parts the development of the street-system tended to be quite informal. Towns of this status invariably had defences, which sometimes cut across already existing streets.

Growth of the town, or of the ambition of the council, could result in several successive defensive circuits, so that the crop-marks of earlier earthwork defences may be visible either inside or outside the line of the eventual town-wall (62). Internal buildings with stone foundations may be revealed by negative crop-marks in considerable numbers, but allowance should be made for other buildings constructed wholly of timber, which mostly yield no trace when observed from the air. Extra-mural buildings, being more often timber-built, are seldom detected, but the more important towns erected amphitheatres, in which an elliptical arena perhaps 65m long

62 *Roman town, Silchester, Hampshire, 23 June 1970*
Vertical photograph (scale 1:5700), with north to the left. The streets and many of the buildings are picked out by negative crop-marks, even in an area given over to pigs near the bottom of the picture where the lines of shelters make a regular pattern. The forum courtyard can be seen near the centre; in the next block to the south is a 16-sided Romano-Celtic temple (p 131). North-east of the forum crop-marks show the broad rampart and ditch of a first-century defensive earthwork running beneath the later street-system; another part of this ditch is seen outside the south gate.

63 *Crop-marks near Harston, Cambridgeshire, 25 June 1962*
On the right a ditched enclosure contains not less than three timber buildings, at least one of which has opposed entrances at the centres of the long sides. The enclosure encroaches on a periglacial geological pattern composed of spots and squiggles (p 151). On the left are a number of more or less rectangular dark marks, some of which are certainly caused by small gravel-pits, while others seem more likely to belong to houses with sunken floors.

was surrounded by a massive earthen seating-bank 20m or more wide. Unlike prehistoric henges (p 75), this bank was not accompanied by an internal ditch.

Settlements of lesser status occurred at intervals along the Roman roads. Many of these also had defences, but are distinguished by their unplanned layout (36). The defended area was naturally smaller, most examples covering less than 12ha (compared with 14–96ha for tribal capitals), but there was normally a large area of extra-mural settlement not readily appreciated from the air unless also provided with metalled streets. At a few sites an original earth rampart was succeeded by a defensive wall on a different line, both circuits being capable of appearing in terms of crop-marks. It should be remembered that many roadside settlements of considerable size were never in fact provided with defences. The streets typically run off the main road at a variety of angles; they are usually metalled and are shown by negative crop-marks, but sometimes unmetalled lanes are outlined by positive marks on the line of their side ditches. Buildings with stone foundations tend to be few, though sometimes individually imposing.

It is the metalled streets which mark these settlements as Roman, though individual house-plans may also be recognizably Roman in character. A position on a known or on a suspected Roman road constitutes useful supporting evidence, though not in itself conclusive, while the date may also be confirmed by finds made in field-walking.

64 *Crop-marks near Atcham, Shropshire, 2 July 1975*

Just below the centre of the picture can be seen the outlines of two large timber halls, each over 20m long including the projecting annexes. The nearer of the two, part of which has been destroyed by an isolated gravel-pit, is of a type familiar from Old Yeavering and other 7th-century royal seats in Bernicia. There is nothing to show if the adjacent enclosures are in any way connected. The fields on both sides of the road exhibit traces of medieval ridge-and-furrow, now completely levelled at the surface, while a belt of narrow parallel lines running horizontally across the photograph near the bottom are the shadows from electricity cables in a power line. One of the pylons is visible in the bottom right corner, next to the curving line of a filled-in disused canal.

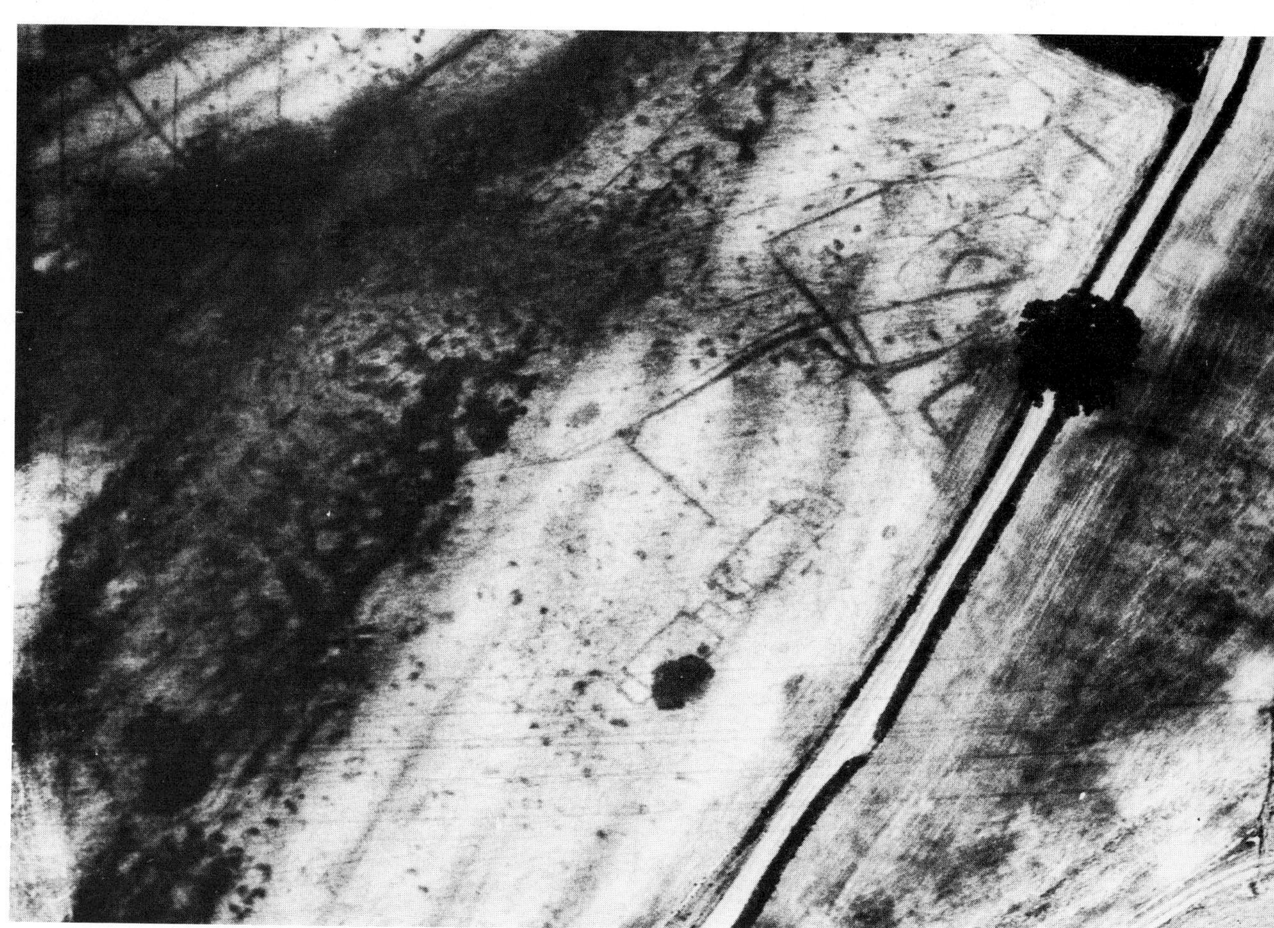

Early medieval settlements

Among the variety of buildings occurring in Anglo-Saxon settlements two call for special mention by virtue of being datable from their plan alone, while at the same time detectable on air-photographs.

The first is the sunk hut (*Grubenhaus*), whose basement consists of a steep-sided pit, somewhat longer than it is broad, with parallel sides and roughly square or sometimes rounded ends. The length is mostly between 2m and 6m. These huts often occur in some numbers, making a bold pattern of dark squarish blobs when seen as crop-marks (50, 54); but considerable care is needed in distinguishing these from a natural pattern of rounded blobs, similar in size but subtly different in shape, which are a feature of certain sands and gravels (p 152). Larger houses with sunk floors are also known (63), but are not confined to an Anglo-Saxon context, being found, for example, in Roman villas (30). These larger buildings are themselves liable to confusion with a particular kind of gravel-pit whose regular rectangular shape is governed by its position within a single strip in a larger field (p 175).

The second distinctively Saxon type of building is the rectangular timber hall with opposed entrances at the centres of the two long sides (63). This is most likely to be recognizable when the wall-posts are set in a continuous foundation-trench. The walls sometimes bow outwards slightly to the entrances, and these may be emphasized by the presence of large post-pits at either side of the opening. The normal length, except in royal halls, is between 8m and 12m. Many Anglo-Saxon halls had their doors in other positions, but the arrangement described is the only one attributable to this period from the plan alone.

It is worth noting that aisled halls like those of Roman and medieval Britain appear to be wholly absent from the early and middle Saxon periods.

Royal halls are distinguished by greater size, with lengths ranging from 14m to 25m. Two types are specially distinctive and characteristic of the period. One has rows of pits outside the main wall lines for timber buttress-posts, as seen in crop-marks at Milfield and Old Yeavering (Northumberland) (Knowles & St Joseph 1952, 271). The other has extensions or annexes projecting from each end of the hall, narrower than the body on the hall itself, as seen at three royal seats in Bernicia, at Malmesbury (Wiltshire) and at Atcham (Shropshire) (64). Besides a great hall, or more often a succession of several such halls, not always of identical plan, a Saxon royal residence can be expected to display subsidiary buildings, which may include lesser halls and bowers or even a church or moot, as well as other features such as graveyards.

Deserted medieval towns and villages

The study of deserted medieval villages from the air was initiated by O G S Crawford (1925), but was not effectively continued until after the 1939–45 War. A full treatment of medieval villages in their contemporary landscape as discernible on air-photographs has been provided by Beresford and St Joseph (1979). A selection of good air-photographs also appears in Beresford and Hurst (1971).

Unlike deserted villages, whose sites have been recorded by air-photography in their hundreds, deserted towns usually show little surviving surface trace. The remains of a village can be allowed to remain in the home pasture surrounding the farm which has inherited its name, or in the grounds of a country house, or in some remote part of a reorganized parish, without particular inconvenience; but a town occupies too much ground to be left without interference. The land will be needed for agricultural or industrial development and is sufficiently extensive to be worth the effort and expense of clearing it.

The surviving remains of deserted medieval villages display a characteristic pattern in which three main elements appear with varying degrees of emphasis. In areas where building stone is readily available, the outlines of ruined cottages form the major element in the plan, the stumps of their walls making a series of rectangles beneath the grass plainly visible in relief. Attached to these are the backyards (tofts) and garden plots (crofts) bounded by low banks composed of the tumbled debris of their drystone walls. The village streets are seen principally as ribbons of unenclosed ground between the cottages and closes. Contrasting with these are the many lowland villages where cottages were built largely of clay and timber, in which there is little trace to see at the surface of actual buildings, though buried stone foundations beneath the turf may be capable of causing lines of parching in a time of drought (15). The main element in the pattern is now provided by the village streets, whose hollow ways constitute the frame for a patchwork of individual building-plots defined by drainage-ditches or by lynchets (10, 13). The pattern made by earthworks of this type is distinctive enough to be recognized in soil-marks or crop-marks after ploughing, or even in isolated fragments surviving undestroyed within a modern village. The latter situation is not uncommon in villages at a little distance from the modern commercial and industrial centres: after centuries of decline as villagers moved away to the towns, they now find themselves conveniently placed for commuters and have re-expanded to become dormitory villages, their new housing estates often encroaching on the remains of their medieval predecessors.

The abandonment of villages has nevertheless continued to the present day, especially in the Scottish Highlands (74) and in worked-out mining districts. Although modern desertions can usually be distinguished from their medieval counterparts by the more precise shapes and fresher appearance of the earthworks, as well as sometimes by their situation (in relation to a disused mine, for example), they resemble them in being datable principally through historical documents including dated surveys. A special type of modern settlement, for which such documentation is often not available, is the army camp (p 169). Hard core underlying the concrete bases of its huts may be difficult to distinguish from other kinds of building debris after ploughing, but the regular layout is usually suggestive of a military, or at any rate non-domestic, context.

FARMS AND COUNTRY HOUSES

Prehistoric and Romano-British homesteads and minor settlements

The earthworks of prehistoric and Romano-British rural settlement survive in considerable, though decreasing, numbers on downland, moor and fell in areas where upland pasture has not yet been converted to arable use. The better preserved examples are well known, if not always fully studied, but the slight grass-covered remains of many others are not easily recognized or interpreted without the aid of air-photographs (Wilson 1975e, fig 5). Air-photography has revealed settlements on arable land in similar abundance. On chalk downland the evidence of crop-marks and soil-marks closely echoes that of recorded earthworks, as we should expect, but some of the types of settlement most often seen on the gravel terraces of the great river valleys show no close resemblance to those familiar from surviving remains.

Prehistoric sites, whether seen as earthworks or as crop-marks, may be identified as settlements on three main criteria.

a *Visible traces of houses.* Stone-walled houses, when free-standing, are usually circular. A truly circular form may be maintained when a house is incorporated in a larger structure, but more often the shape is adapted to the context so as to become more or less irregular. Rectangular houses are rare even in the Roman period, except as part of villas. Timber houses yield recognizable crop-marks or soil-marks comparatively seldom. Those that do so are almost invariably circular (p 96), but two exceptional sites have produced crop-marks of large timber halls up to 36m long (43), for both of which there is reason to suggest a Neolithic date. The method of construction in both buildings, with lines of wall-posts set in large pits, is identical to that of some early medieval royal halls (cf p 110).

Rectangular aisled houses have also been seen at some romanized homesteads, but these are more conveniently discussed in the context of Roman villas (p 116).

b *Complex internal organization.* Although many homesteads are marked by no more than a simple enclosure, many other settlements display a more complex plan. Geometrically, this is usually organized in one of two ways: either a main enclosure is subdivided internally into compartments, or several small enclosures cluster together into a group. Either way the resulting complexity indicates varied activities or social groupings within a settlement. In detail the planning of such settlements is enormously varied, but by contrast with that of adjacent field-systems the pattern is distinctively dense and concentrated. Quite often successive enclosures overlap one another, increasing the overall complexity as well as attesting continued or renewed use of the site over an extended period.

c *Identity of plan with known settlements.* This criterion, which might seem of paramount importance, is placed in third position because it applies principally to types of settlement already identifiable on criteria (*a*) and (*b*). Settlements with less explicit plans, even though identical to known examples, are also usually too similar to sites of other kinds to permit a valid inference.

In practice, secure identification will depend on a combination of criteria: thus, a group of crop-marks may form a complex pattern of a kind already familiar in the local archaeological repertoire and inferred to be a form of settlement from the partial excavation of one or two examples.

It is not possible to present here a comprehensive guide to all the different types of prehistoric rural settlement that are now known from crop-marks, since no overall survey of this material has yet been undertaken. The distribution of most of the types has still to be defined, and their great variety still awaits analysis in terms of geographical, social and chronological differences. Some of the commonest types can nevertheless be described, with special emphasis on features that are ambiguous or misleading. Some comparisons will be made with earthwork sites, but it is mostly taken for granted that these are already familiar and need no further description. It should be recognized, therefore, that what follows is selective and requires to be supplemented by detailed study of known and suspected settlements in the area with which interpretation is actively concerned.

Unenclosed settlements, comprising a group of circular houses with no surrounding ditch, are seldom seen on air-photographs because of the difficulty of detecting such houses in terms of crop-marks. Much of the photographic evidence relates, for some reason, to Scotland north of the Forth (Maxwell, forthcoming), but the distribution was probably very widespread. In addition to traces of the houses themselves (p 96), crop-marks may pick out the levelled platforms on which the houses stood. Sometimes the platform is indicated by a complete disc of darker tone (St Joseph 1967a), but more often there is only a crescent where the rear of the platform was terraced into a gentle slope. Such crescents, if seen on their own, could hardly be interpreted, but in the company of narrow-ditched circles they can be understood as marking houses in the same settlement.

It should always be remembered when studying groups of houses that they were probably not all in use at the same time; this becomes quite evident when their crop-marks overlap, but is always fairly probable.

The absence of an enclosing ditch around the settlement does not mean that individual houses necessarily have no enclosures of their own. In some settlements a surrounding ditch or palisade echoes the outline of the house so closely and is so consistently present that it effectively forms part of the definition of a standard type of house (cf 45g). Elsewhere, small enclosures are less intimately and consistently associated with houses; they are more irregular in plan and may either surround or simply adjoin a house. Such enclosures may be limited to only a few houses in the settlement (54) or may extend to most of them. Only excavation can show if the enclosures belong to a distinct chronological phase.

One type of settlement commonly seen in crop-marks from the Thames to the Trent displays a moderately dense pattern of such enclosures, roughly oval or trapezoidal and mostly about 15–20m in diameter. Many of the settlements display a linear axis, but the layout is seldom orderly, and overlaps frequently show that the crop-marks record a composite pattern built up over a period. Extension, modification or replacement of individual enclosures can create agglomerations of a kind well known from earthworks (cf Standlake in Wilson 1979b, with Woodcuts in Hawkes 1948). Further complications are sometimes to be seen where a sequence of connected rectangular enclosures is superimposed on all or part of the original settlement pattern (St Joseph 1968a).

The settlement at Butterwick (Humberside) illustrated in fig 34 is more unusual. A number of much larger enclosures, 45–55m across, are packed closely together. Each is defined by a ditch many times re-cut and each seems to contain a circular house and a number of internal compartments. The planning appears superficially similar to that of courtyard-houses in Cornwall or enclosed hut-groups in central and northern Wales; but amongst crop-marks this site is virtually unique.

Smallish enclosures containing just one or only a few houses occur widely both in lowland and in highland areas (114). Although such enclosures may be grouped in a larger settlement, as already noted, it is commoner for them to be found in isolation or loosely associated with only one or two other examples. If there is no visible trace of an internal house, it is not easy to correlate a simple isolated oval, rectangular or trapezoidal enclosure with any specific function or archaeological period. In hilly country there is a tendency for homesteads to perch on a local summit or on the end of a spur, but this siting is neither invariable nor unique to prehistoric settlement; it would be appropriate to a vanished clump of trees, for example.

There are, however, features which make identification as a settlement more probable. The presence of pits within the enclosure, if not those in which trees have been planted or from which they have been pulled out (p 166), is strongly suggestive of settlement (65). The pits must be limited by the enclosure: if more widely distributed or part of a more general pattern, they will need to be interpreted in relation to that wider context.

Another indication is given by the presence of one or more outer ditches (94, 117). These ditches are usually closely spaced, but an exception is provided by a few circular settlements of the Later Bronze Age in which the outer ditch has a diameter that can be as much as 1·6 times that of the inner one (54). Multiple ditches are not a feature of medieval and later wood-banks, nor of the more or less informal enclosures which may be created for a variety of purposes in almost any age; but care must still be taken to distinguish prehistoric settlements from those of other periods. When the plan is rectangular, it may resemble that of a Roman fort or fortlet; criteria for telling the alternatives apart have already been presented (p 101). Many of the rectangular settlements with two or more ditches did indeed have a Roman phase, so the mere presence of Roman pottery in a trial-trench across the ditch-system proves nothing about the character of the occupation, which can only be determined from examination of the internal buildings. Medieval moats can also assume quite elaborate forms with several ditches but these multi-ditched examples, besides being uncommon, usually mark places of importance about which something is already known. On all types of site it should be remembered that the two ditches of a double-ditched enclosure are often shown by excavation not to have been in contemporary use but to have been successive.

65 *Iron Age settlement east of Lower Bullington, Hampshire, 6 September 1976*
The settlement is of Little Woodbury type, with 'antennae' at the entrance and numerous pits in the interior. The marks are seen in grass pasture and their reversed tones, paler over the ditches, are typical of chalkland after prolonged drought (p 55).

Other special features occur in a number of settlement-types known principally from Wessex (Perry 1970). More or less circular enclosures 125–175m in diameter often exhibit traces of pits and working-hollows within, less often those of circular houses. Little Woodbury (Wiltshire) is the type-site (Palmer 1978). Occasionally, flaring ditches are attached to the outside of the single entrance like a pair of antennae (65). In another type one elliptical enclosure lies concentrically within another, the intervening space being divided into a number of compartments by cross ditches. The type-site is at South Wonston Farm (Hampshire), with overall dimensions 150m by 190m (St Joseph 1972a, St Joseph & Wilson 1976). A smaller size of enclosure, 50–90m in diameter, is approached down a funnel-like passage; the ditches bounding the funnel run parallel for 50–150m from the entrance, but then turn outwards, sometimes continuing to form a very large enclosure of several hectares, to which other small enclosures may be similarly attached. The type has been colloquially termed 'banjo enclosure' from its shape, but in addition to the examples where the inner part is truly circular there are many more where it is irregular (St Joseph 1972a) or more or less rectangular, while a triangular example in Humberside would presumably qualify to be known as a 'balalaika enclosure'.

Just as smallish enclosures may occur on their own as well as in larger groups, so too may the agglomerations previously described, where a number of enclosures have effectively fused together into a larger whole. Cohesively planned settlements of this kind are no less common than simple enclosures, both in upland areas where they tend to survive in relief (St Joseph 1969b, pl 6 (2); Wilson 1975e, figs 3–5) and in lowland areas where they are seen as soil-marks or crop-marks (St Joseph 1972b). While the distributions of simple enclosures and of these agglomerations are certainly not co-extensive, there is a very considerable degree of overlap.

Many of the prehistoric rural settlements known from air-photographs, both as earth-works and as crop-marks, now appear to be totally isolated. By contrast, others are seen embedded in their contemporary landscapes, the settlement differentiated in plan from the surrounding fields and often approached by a lane which leads up to or through or past it

66 *Crop-marks north-east of Barholm, Lincolnshire, 22 June 1960*
A five-sided enclosure is subdivided by probably secondary ditches; in the nearest compartment can be seen the double row of post-pits for an aisled house of 7 or 8 bays. Elsewhere in the enclosure are less certain traces of both rectangular and circular buildings. A number of more-or-less rectangular paddocks are attached to the outside of the enclosure, and the whole complex was originally skirted by a winding double-ditched lane, apparently suppressed at a later stage.

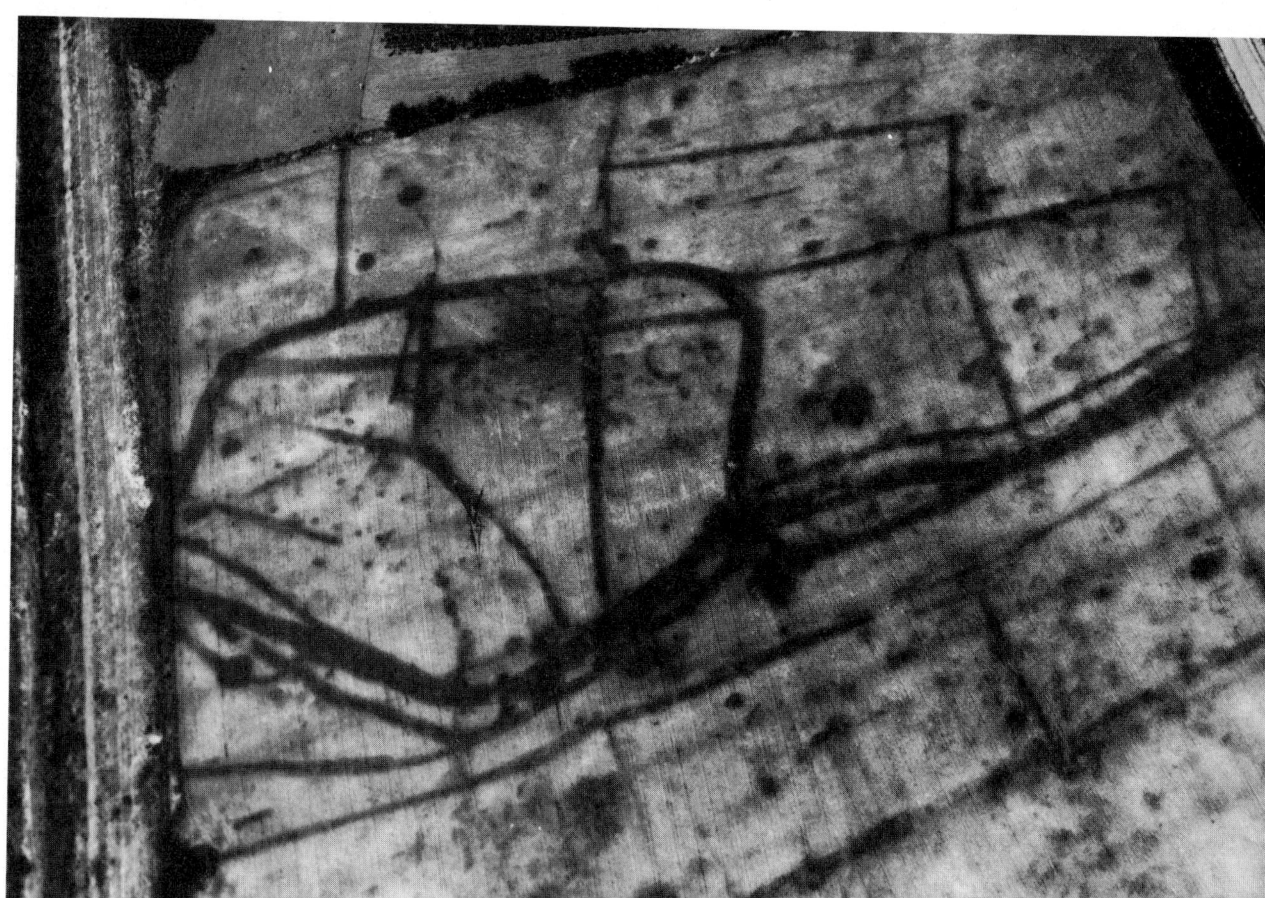

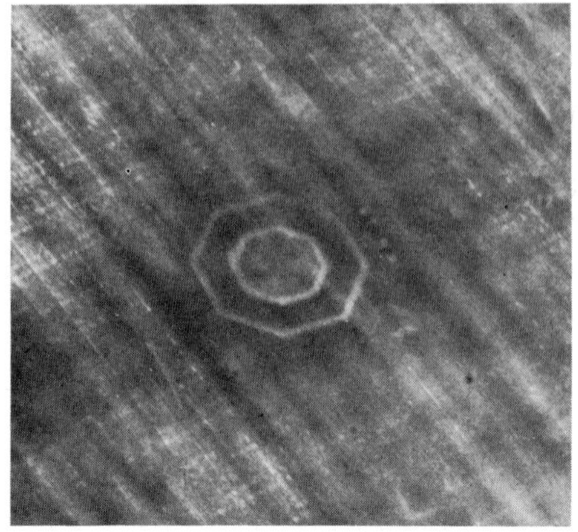

67 *Roman buildings*

a Dwelling-house of Roman villa explored by wall-tracing, Car Colston, Nottinghamshire, 29 November 1974 (pp 116, 176)

b Crop-marks of octagonal Romano-Celtic temple with four-columned porch, Weycock Hill, Berkshire, 19 June 1959 (p 131)

(20, 89). Indeed, when a lane does run between the fields to end at the entrance to an enclosure, this may be taken as evidence that the enclosure had some special function, whether this was agricultural, domestic or industrial (25). It may be possible to distinguish those that are homesteads from those that are industrial by the results of fieldwalking.

Roman villas

The appearance of Roman villas from the air has been reviewed by Wilson (1974b). Their remains principally comprise a dwelling-house, outbuildings, farmyard and paddocks. The farmyard may be bounded by a wall or simply constitute as open space between the farmhouse and the outbuildings. Many of the latter may be too insubstantial to be seen in terms of crop-marks, so that the main house appears on the photograph in misleading isolation. At a number of villas the buildings are sited within a ditched oblong enclosure, typically about 90–160m long; the size, shape and regular outline of such enclosures is sufficiently characteristic to suggest the presence of a Roman villa even when no internal buildings are visible. Very occasionally the enclosed area is bounded by a wall instead of by a bank and ditch. At other villas the buildings are surrounded by irregular paddocks (30) or else stand within a larger field-system presumably more or less contemporary in date.

Apart from the humbler farmhouses and mere sheds the majority of villa buildings fall into one of three categories.

a *Circular houses.* In a Roman context these usually have stone foundations, and there may also be a concrete floor. It is hardly possible from air-photographs to distinguish between actual houses, more mundane farm-buildings, and religious shrines. All of these may occur within a villa.

b *Aisled houses.* With varying degrees of elaboration these may serve as barns, halls or dwellings. The simplest form is an all-timber building, principally attested by the double row of post-pits for the roof supports. Crop-marks of such a building can be seen inside certain enclosures whose plans otherwise recall a prehistoric homestead more than a Roman villa (66): this combination suggests the partial romanization of a native type of homestead. Pits for the posts of the side walls are only rarely seen.

c *Corridor-houses.* In these a rectangular block of rooms is served by one or more corridors. The front of the house is very often marked by projecting wing-rooms on the corners, one at each end of the front corridor

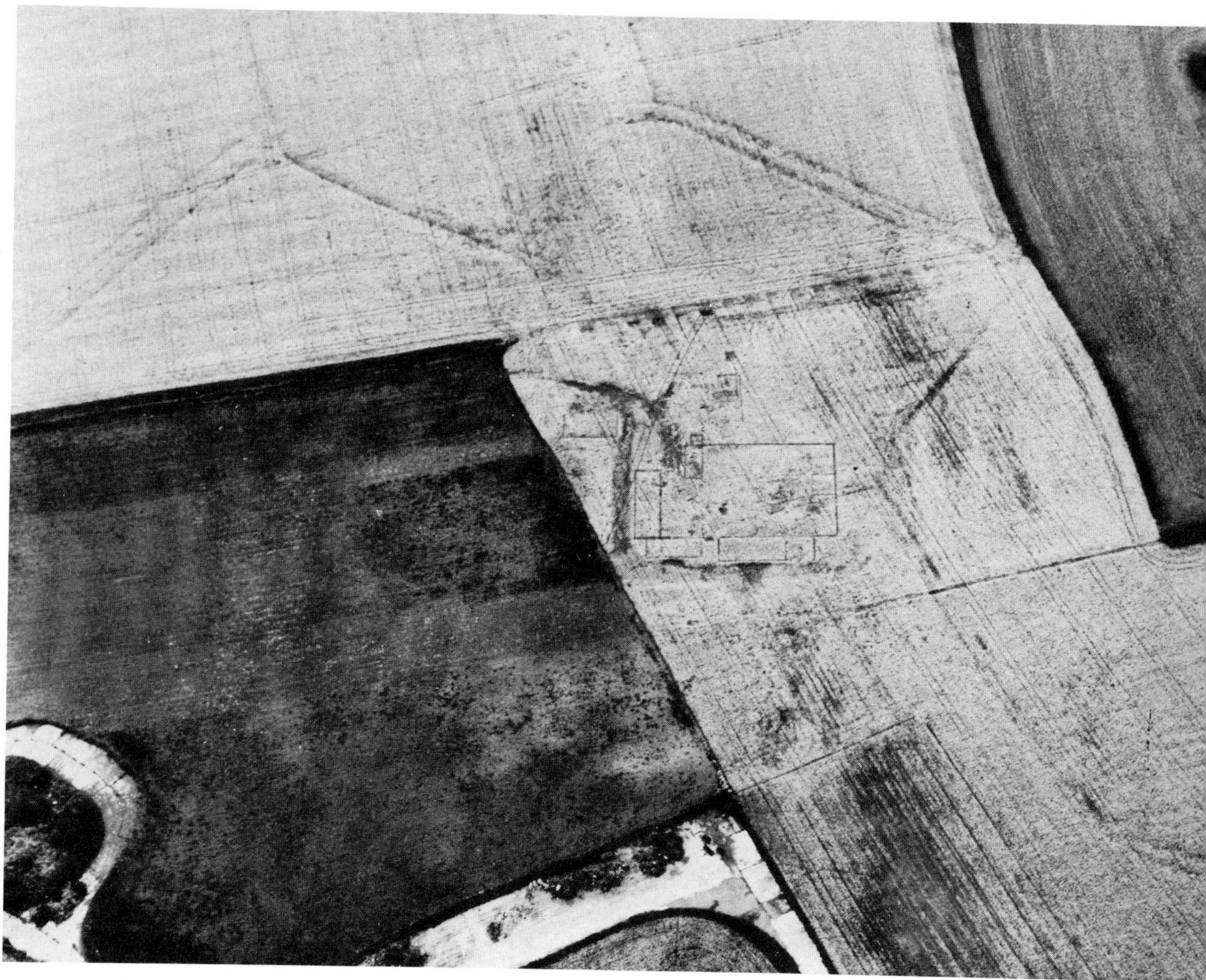

(67a). This arrangement might also be repeated at the rear of the house, to give a sort of H-shaped plan; and wing-rooms were also sometimes fitted even onto an aisled house of category *(b)*.

The combination of wing-rooms with a front corridor may be taken as a reliable indicator of Roman date. Also distinctively Roman is the provision of a suite of baths, either in a separate building or else included in the main house, usually at side or rear. The baths can normally be recognized by the presence of small semicircular or rectangular apses projecting from one or more adjacent rooms to contain hot or cold immersion baths and by

68 *Crop-marks north of Kimbolton, Northamptonshire, 12 August 1975*
Negative crop-marks in a ripe cereal crop reveal the plan of a group of buildings with stone foundations ranged round a rectangular walled yard and served by a metalled road. This is the site of Old Mill Farm, cleared away to make room for a wartime airfield, part of whose concrete tracks are still to be seen in the foreground. The irregular shapes of the modern fields on the site have produced a complex elaboration of the familiar 'envelope' cultivation-pattern (p 158).

the detailed planning of the flues leading to the hot rooms. Heated rooms may be indicated either by areas of negative crop-marks, where the upper floor of the hypocaust has survived, or by areas of positive crop-marks, where the upper floor has been destroyed and a depth of soil has accumulated within the hypocaust itself.

In the absence of recognizable baths or of a 'winged corridor' façade, the plan of a Roman villa does not differ markedly from those of farms of later ages (68). Identification may thus depend on the evidence obtained from fieldwalking.

Medieval manors, granges and farms

The manor house would normally be the most substantial building in the village after the church; its ruins, if any, should thus be more massive and more extensive than those of any cottage. Often too the site of the manor is marked by one or more moats. But when the house was originally timber-built, there is little visible difference between the remains of the manor with its closes and earthworks in other parts of the village. And moats and manors are not necessarily connected: many manors were unmoated, while the moats themselves can have a variety of functions.

Similar arguments apply when traces of medieval settlement are detected at a distance from the body of the village. If they do not belong to a castle or abbey, substantial ruins or negative crop-marks of stone foundations could well indicate a manor house, or perhaps a monastic grange. Between these last two there is no systematic difference of plan, and documentary evidence will be needed to distinguish them. A moat, if present, might reasonably have enclosed any isolated farm, regardless of its status. Often all that in fact survives is a small isolated group of earthworks, whose medieval date can be inferred by comparison with those of deserted medieval villages; but whether they indicate a farm or hamlet can hardly be determined from air-photography alone.

Country houses

The classic English country house is associated with a stable block and a walled kitchen-garden and stands within a park. If the house itself has been demolished, its former presence may be implied by the survival of some of the other features. The park, even if now converted to arable farming, can usually be recognized by surviving groves and plantations, especially those around the former perimeter (p 166). Tree-lined avenues were most often designed to converge on the house, though other focal points are possible, and the approximate site of a vanished house may also be suggested by that of the stable block, which was seldom far removed (69).

Around the house, whether standing or demolished, may be the terraced remains of ornamental parterres or tennis courts (12) and the less obvious traces of paths, flower beds and pools of formal gardens. In places where a formal geometrical arrangement has been abandoned in favour of simple lawns, the former layout may re-emerge as a pattern of differential parching in the turf at a time of drought (Binney & Hills 1979, 10, 13). Beyond the garden earthworks around the house there can usually be discerned some traces of early fields predating the creation of the park. These traces will sometimes be of ridge-and-furrow, sometimes of small enclosed fields, according to the local agricultural tradition. In addition, the act of making the park may well have required the total removal of an existing village, whose abandoned remains may still be preserved within it. This is to be strongly suspected at sites where the parish church stands inside the park apart from the modern village, which is sited outside the park boundary. Earthworks of the original village should then be carefully sought in the vicinity of the church.

FIELDS AND CULTIVATION

Field-systems

The boundaries of ancient fields tend to have inconspicuous remains and individually they

furnish few clues for detailed interpretation. They take on more definite meaning only when viewed in a broader context and perceived as elements in a composite system of fields. Air-photography is of particular value in the location and study of such field-systems, which are often difficult to trace on the ground but more readily identified from the air. The recognition of general pattern in the landscape is one of the classic roles of air-photography, and it is appropriate that the first exercise in archaeological photo-interpretation published in Britain should have dealt mainly with prehistoric field-systems (Crawford 1923).

In upland areas, where fields are normally bounded by dry-stone walls, the remains of prehistoric field-systems are generally marked by broad low banks two metres or more across. These contain the spread rem-

69 *The site of Hoxne Hall, Suffolk, 24 June 1975* The stable-block still stands, but the hall itself disappeared more than 60 years ago. Lines of parching over its foundations trace out much of the plan, testifying to its spacious proportions.

nants of former field walls, tumbled and overgrown after falling into disrepair (70). Sometimes, however, the early walls have continued in use and have survived, embedded like fossils in a later field-system, where they tend to cause local disruptions in its pattern (71). It is worth studying anomalies in the layout of modern fields in case they should be explained by survivals of this kind.

On the chalk downland of southern England prehistoric fields are divided either by banks or by scarps where the field has been partly terraced into the slope (72). When these have been ploughed over in modern times, the

70 *Settlement and fields, Crosby Garrett, Cumbria, 6 February 1970*
A settlement of late prehistoric or Roman date surrounded by fields is approached by two lanes. Some of the fields radiate from the settlement and must be directly related to it. Traces of ridged cultivation on the left override the ancient field boundaries, whereas similar traces in the foreground conform to them, indicating their continued existence as field boundaries (or at least significant obstacles) even into post-medieval times.

71 *Outgang Hill, Conistone, North Yorkshire, 15 February 1973*
A vertical photograph (scale 1: 5900) of part of upper Wharfedale under snow discloses remains of the prehistoric and medieval landscapes picked out by winter sunlight amidst the modern fields. Over much of the picture low banks form an irregular pattern outlining prehistoric and later settlements and fields whose walls have tumbled into ruins. Elsewhere, near the edges of the photograph, this pattern has been replaced by the strip lynchets of medieval cultivation. The modern walls incorporate fragments of both the prehistoric and medieval patterns.

72 *Celtic fields, Pertwood Down, Wiltshire, 8 May 1967*
The fields partly survive in relief unploughed and partly appear as soil-marks on the slopes of a piece of chalk downland. A line of dots in the ploughed field, dropping towards the bottom right corner, is part of the 'envelope' produced by square ploughing (p 158). The pale spots at the top of the pasture field are bare places worn in the turf by animals crowding round feeding-troughs.

pattern reappears most clearly in terms of soil-marks: dark bands show where the old ploughsoil accumulated at the foot of scarps or along both sides of field-banks, sandwiching a central core of paler chalky material (cf 100).

On arable land elsewhere, including the chalk wolds of Lincolnshire and Humberside, early fields can usually be detected only when bounded by ditches. An occasional variant is provided by pit-alignments, described more fully in the next section of this chapter (p 127). Both field-ditches and pit-alignments are capable of yielding clear positive crop-marks, but an unditched boundary consisting solely of a fence or hedge will furnish little or no trace even when first removed, let alone after centuries of ploughing. In attempting to reconstruct prehistoric and Roman field-systems from crop-marks allowance has to be made for possible fields with boundaries of this sort.

Those groups of fields which can be studied, either as surviving earthworks or through the appearance of crop-marks, fall into two main categories as regards their organization in plan. Those in the first category cluster round one or more dwellings and seem closely related to them, as garths or paddocks. Examples range from the irregular plots attached to Bronze Age settlements to the rectilinear closes which surround many Roman villas (30, 66). In the second category are blocks of fields laid out on a common orientation within a common boundary. Settlements may be incorporated within the field-system or be closely linked to it, yet they do not really control its layout. Such blocks of fields may cover several kilometres, but their internal organization is often relatively unplanned and does not exclude piecemeal enclosure. Particular interest attaches therefore to the late-prehistoric or early-Roman field-systems discovered from the air between East Retford (Nottinghamshire) and Doncaster (South Yorkshire), in which long strips of land, mostly 50–100m wide, are divided by cross-ditches into fields forming a kind of brick-work pattern (Riley 1980b). This arrangement seems to be more closely regulated; it is seen also in surviving Neolithic fields in Ireland and in Bronze Age fields on Dartmoor, but is apparently unmatched by crop-marks elsewhere in Britain. There are strong hints in the crop-mark evidence that the main fields were subdivided. Many of the cross-ditches show offsets or changes of direction, and these are sometimes articulated with narrow ditches dividing the fields lengthways. It seems probable that more of these sub-divisions originally existed, either marked by ditches too slight to survive later ploughing or formed by movable barriers leaving no trace at all.

When field-ditches are revealed by crop-marks, they are not necessarily of any great age. Field-boundaries removed in modern times can usually be recognized from their relationship to the surviving field-pattern or by reference to maps. Two or even three phases of superimposed fields may sometimes be detectable in a complex pattern of crop-marks (117). Care must be taken, however, to distinguish genuine field-systems from crop-patterns resulting from other causes. These include geological patterns produced by jointing in bedrock or by fossil ice-wedges in once frozen ground (pp 143, 150), modern cultivation patterns (p 158), and systems of war-time anti-glider trenches (p 173). Any of these may overlap with genuine fields to cause a pattern of notable complexity (85, 89, 100, 103).

In an area of surviving Celtic fields the parallel firing-positions on a disused rifle range might also be possibly taken for an isolated fragment of a former field-system (p 173).

Ridge-and-furrow

In many parts of Britain the field pattern has developed continuously from prehistoric times to the present day. There is, however, a broad band of country extending from Wessex through the Midlands to the east coast from Norfolk to Northumberland in which

'3 *Ridge-and-furrow, Frisby, Leicestershire, 13 Лay 1966*

\ series of three parallel green lanes divides the idge-and-furrow into short lengths. Two of hese old lanes are followed by modern roads or netalled tracks; the third one, in between them, uns towards the site of two windmills (top left), out no longer reaches them. Both windmills have eft cross-shaped depressions from which their rosstrees have been withdrawn (pp 85, 136). To ight of these a line of bumps shows where a ormer headland has been cut through.

A modern pipeline has been laid in a trench hrough the ridge-and-furrow from near the top eft corner to the bottom right. An attempt to estore the original appearance of the ridges has ailed to understand the layout: instead of running straight through, the ridges near the bottom right corner now make a series of doglegs along the course of the pipeline (p 174).

this development was interrupted by the creation of the medieval open fields. These fields, although undefined by boundary walls and ditches, can still be traced through the remains of their ridge-and-furrow. The layout of the ridges corresponds exactly to that of the strip holdings in the fields, as may be readily seen from a comparison of air-photographs showing ridge-and-furrow with the corresponding village maps (Beresford & St Joseph 1979).

These medieval ridges have to be distinguished from other forms of ridge-and-furrow which will be described later in this section, but in general they are sufficiently distinctive in size, shape and overall planning to be identifiable with confidence. The individual ridges typically have a width of 5–6m (or one rod) from the centre of one furrow to the next. Along their length they may be completely straight, but more often curve gently to the left as each end is reached, so making the shape of a shallow reversed-S (10, 53). This curve assisted the plough-team to manœuvre onto the unploughed headland running across the ends of the ridges. Each main field was subdivided into furlongs, identifiable as groups of parallel ridges with a common orientation, sometimes interlocking with each other in an intricate pattern (23). Access to most parts of the field could be obtained along the headlands, but when there was no other way through, a balk was left unploughed between the furlongs.

The patterns of ridge-and-furrow seen today are the result of a long process of development eventually terminated by enclosure. In many places there are clear signs of alteration in the layout. Ridges may have been enlarged by running adjacent pairs together, or else subdivided to produce ridges of half the normal width (23). Such subdivided ridges have a close resemblance to the post-medieval 'narrow rig' described below, but are distinguished by their position within a block of conventional ridge-and-furrow.

Ridges could be also shortened or extended, a new headland being constructed across their abandoned ends, or an old headland being ploughed right through. It is not unusual for two furlongs meeting end to end to be run together by ploughing through the intervening headlands. This gives rise to a tell-tale kink if the two sets of ridges were imperfectly aligned, and the junction is also marked by a line of spoilheaps forming humps on all the ridges, caused by cutting through the former headlands to join up the sets of furrows (73).

The open fields were enclosed at various times from the fourteenth to the nineteenth centuries. Where the land has since remained in pasture, the pattern of ridges, balks and lanes appears very plainly in oblique lighting and may also be discernible at other times through growth of rushes in the furrows. Some visible relief will survive moderate or intermittent ploughing; and even when all other surface traces have been levelled off, there may still remain a rise or swelling of the ground along the line of former headlands. These swellings are low and unobtrusive but quite definite; their interpretation is not obvious to the uninitiated, but careful study of their disposition will show their relevance to the vanished medieval layout (Taylor 1975b).

In bare soil there are usually lines of darker tone along the furrows, caused by the greater depth and greater humic content of the soil (23). It was noted in Chapter 2 that on some soils a reversed pattern could also be produced as a temporary effect of differential drying after rain; the surface dries off more quickly on the line of the furrows and thus appears paler than damp soil to either side (pp 47–48). When former ridge-and-furrow has been totally levelled, the chance of seeing conventional soil-marks is much reduced, but crop-marks may still be produced if the bottoms of the furrows have penetrated below modern plough-level into the subsoil. These marks often have a soft blurred appearance and do not jump to the eye, but their meaning is shown by the overall pattern (53, 104, 112, 114).

In some places, especially when the open fields were enclosed by voluntary agreement,

he later field-boundaries closely follow the ›utlines of former strips or furlongs and there-›y reproduce the characteristic reversed-S :urve (Beresford & St Joseph 1979, fig 53). If urface traces of ridge-and-furrow have all lisappeared, the occurrence together of a ıumber of field-walls or hedges of this charac-er may be the only visible clue to the layout ›f the medieval fields.

The creation of ridge-and-furrow on heavy and, especially when other forms of drainage ıave been found ineffective, is a practice that ıas continued to the present day and was par-icularly prevalent in the eighteenth and nine-eenth centuries. The post-medieval ridges

74 *Deserted crofts and lazy-beds near Uig, Lewis, Ross and Cromarty, 22 June 1977*
The ruins of an abandoned settlement on the sea shore can be seen around the right and bottom edges of the picture. The remaining area, unless too rocky or too boggy for cultivation, is covered with the ridges of lazy-beds. These are crossed by modern field-walls in a rigid rectangular pattern, which contrasts with the more irregular walls of the earlier phase.

differ, however, in their size and in their planning, being no longer related to strip-holdings in the open fields or designed to accommodate a long plough-team. The individual ridges were low and narrow, less than 5m wide and

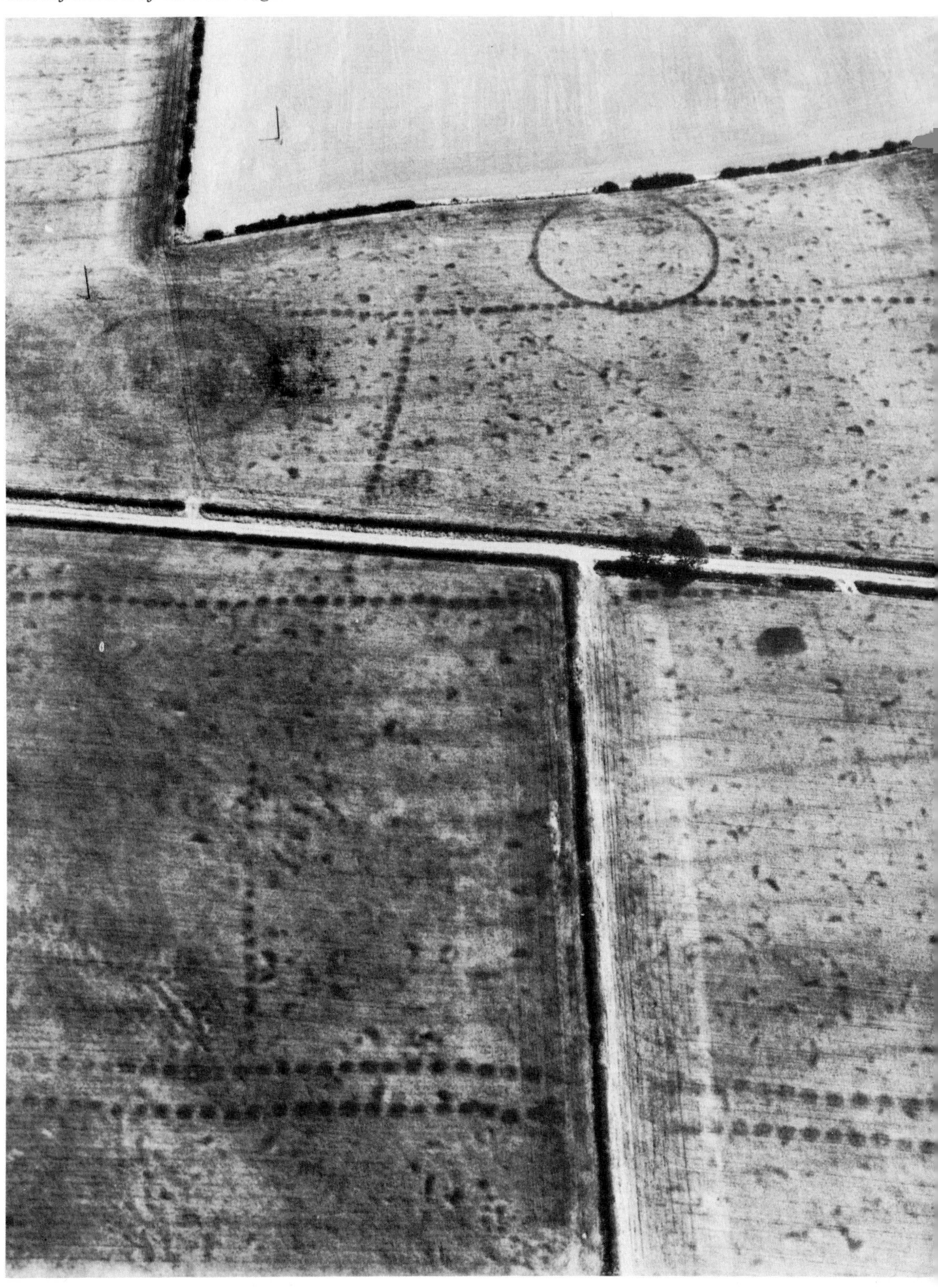

sometimes as little as half the width of their medieval equivalents, giving rise to the term 'narrow rig' to describe them (111). The lines were straight, and the ridges normally fit the fields in which they are found. Narrow ridges may, however, be found overriding earlier earthworks, including those of earlier field-systems (70) and of deserted medieval villages (Beresford & St Joseph 1979, fig 10).

Cultivation-ridges in the form of 'lazy-beds' are also a feature of spade agriculture as practised in the Western Isles, on the coasts of Ireland, and in other parts where the rocky terrain makes the use of a plough impracticable. The individual plots are naturally smaller than those intended to be ploughed and the layout more flexible; although straight parallel ridges are not uncommon, there is nothing to stop the creation of patterns that are remarkably contorted (74).

The various types of ridge-and-furrow need not only to be distinguished from each other, but also from an assortment of geological and agricultural patterns. As so often, there is no great problem if the pattern can be studied over a large enough area, but identification is more difficult if it can be seen only in part. On marginal land it may require close scrutiny to tell the difference between abandoned narrow rig and a relatively recent system of closely spaced surface drains (16). In bare soil certain types of patterned ground could be mistaken for ploughed up ridge-and-furrow (p 152). The most misleading pattern in growing crops is caused by the application of nitrogenous fertilizer in overlapping bands; darker growth along the overlaps produces a series of parallel stripes with blurred edges at much the same spacing as medieval furrows (p 158).

75 *Crop-marks near King's Bromley, Staffordshire, 2 July 1975*

Pit-alignments form a system of fields on the south bank of the Trent. The shorter alignments making the cross-divisions do not come right up to the main alignments at the T-junctions, as if leaving space for an accompanying bank. The two ring-ditches form part of a group of four, each about 35m in diameter, presumably marking the sites of round barrows (p 92). If so, the far pit-alignment has neatly skirted both the mounds but has ignored their ditches, perhaps already filled up and forgotten. Over all can be seen the repetitive pattern of medieval furrows (p 124).

PIT-ALIGNMENTS AND FENCED ENCLOSURES

This section is concerned with crop-mark sites in which closely spaced lines of pits occur in positions where continuous ditches might have been expected. It is far from clear if these are to be thought of as forming distinct classes of sites in their own right or merely as variants on the normal forms; but the feature is so distinctive as to call for separate description. The sites can be divided into linear boundaries (pit-alignments) and enclosures.

Pit-alignments

The distribution and general appearance of pit-alignments have been described by Wilson (1978). The individual pits are about 1·5m in diameter, usually circular or elliptical, and spaced at intervals of about 1·8m (75). Crop-marks of particular fineness show that sometimes the pits are exceptionally well shaped, with a perfect circle or rectangle exactly repeated. More often the pits are somewhat irregular and the close spacing makes it difficult to be certain if a particular line in the crop is actually continuous or really broken into dots (60). A continuous ditch running across the agricultural 'grain' of the field may appear to be broken merely because of the spacing or treatment of the crop plants; so it is important to consider the spacing of a supposed pit-alignment in relation to any agricultural pattern that may be visible in the field. If the two coincide consistently throughout, extreme caution should be used in inferring a genuine pit-alignment. In addition it is not unknown for a line of ditch to be continued by a pit-alignment, so that it is not always safe to extrapolate from one part of the line to another. In cases of doubt it is useful to have photographs taken in more than one season, especially if the direction of cultivation has varied from one season to the other.

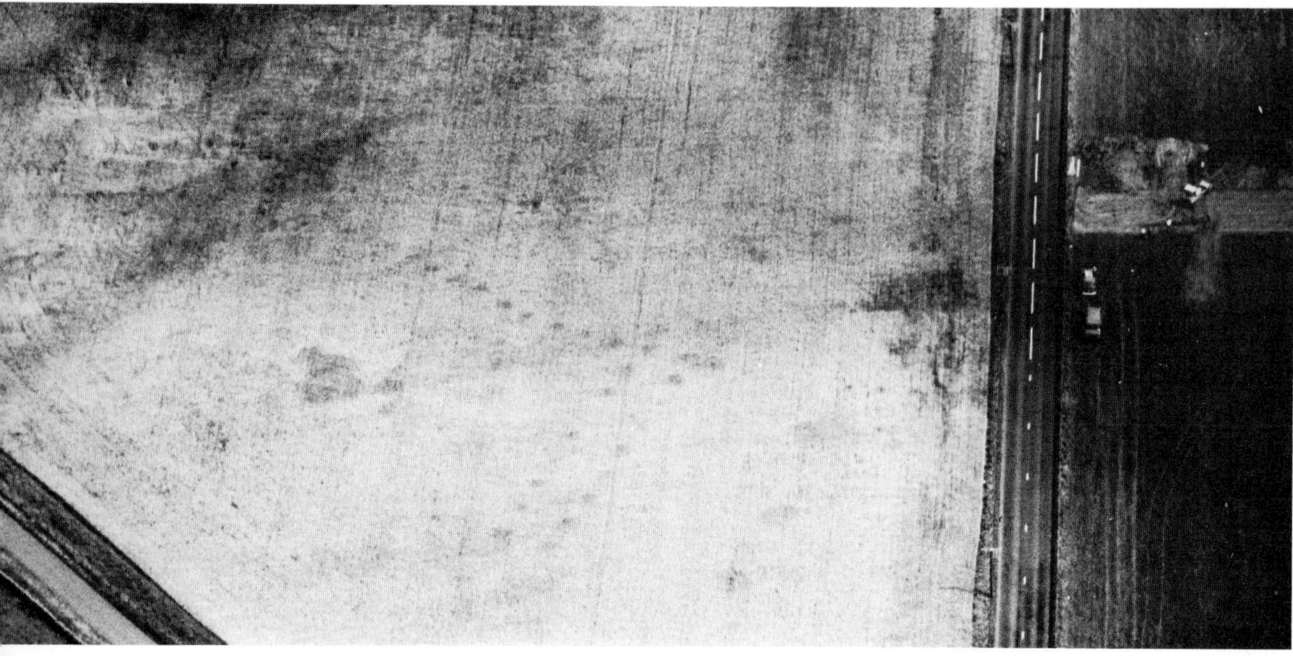

76 *Neolithic settlement, Meldon Bridge, Peeblesshire, 31 July 1975*
Eight pairs of post-pits forming two lines about 3.8m apart lead to a probable entrance through the perimeter fence of the settlement. The main posts of this fence are spaced at 3–4m intervals; smaller intervening posts discovered during excavation do not seem to be detectable on the photograph.

Excavation and historical documents show that pit-alignments may be of any age from the Neolithic to the Middle Ages, so they are unlikely to have always served an identical function. Nevertheless the majority of known examples appear to form an integral part of the late-prehistoric landscape. On the Yorkshire Wolds, the Vale of Pickering and the Corallian outcrop to the north, pit-alignments form part of the system of dykes for which the area is well known, with one to four lines of pits occurring either on their own or in combination with linear ditches (cf 60). In the English Midlands and in Lowland Scotland pit-alignments bound fields or larger blocks of land. It can be argued that in the Welland valley pit-alignments seem to define pre-Roman estate boundaries (Simpson 1966), but elsewhere their incidence is much less regular. At King's Bromley (Staffordshire) an orderly system of rectangular fields is defined entirely by pit-alignments (75), but such a concentrated and consistent use of pit-alignments is most unusual.

When excavated, the pits show no sign of ever having held posts, and it is generally supposed that they served as quarry-pits for a continuous bank. The junctions between ditches or pit-alignments and other pit-alignments should be carefully examined for any clue to the siting of such a bank. Gaps may be left in an alignment to provide a way through, as in a continuous ditch; very occasionally a pit is placed in front of this gap, offset from the main alignment, rather in the manner of a *titulum* in front of the entrance to a Roman military camp (p 98). Double pit-alignments, like double ditches, may be either boundaries or lanes; the same criteria must be employed to discriminate between them (p 103). Triple and quadruple pit-alignments are rare, but occur in similar contexts to triple and quadruple ditches; thus, on the Yorkshire Wolds they are directly comparable with multiple dykes like the Scamridge Dykes, and in the

Midlands they may be related to the multiple ditches which are becoming increasingly known from crop-marks. None of these multiple pit-alignments has yet been excavated, however, and the possibility cannot be excluded that they formed ceremonial monuments composed of rows of posts, like a timber Carnac. But their close spacing does not suggest this interpretation, which seems better suited to lines of pits like those illustrated in fig 46.

Reference has already been made to the difficulty sometimes experienced in distinguishing pit-alignments from continuous ditches. Considerable care must also be taken to identify and exclude agricultural patterns. Some of these are caused by defective machinery, as when lines of dots are produced in a crop by dribbling tanks or spray-bars during fertilizer application. A line of dots is also one of the forms in which the 'envelope pattern' of cultivations on the square (p 158) may make its appearance (72). Again, there is a geological pattern caused by periglacial action on sands and gravels which is composed of spots or blobs (p 151), but these do not occur in simple lines except occasionally when bordering an obvious frost-crack.

Fenced enclosures

We turn now to lines of pits which describe a closed figure. The description 'fenced enclosures' is convenient and vivid but begs a fundamental question, whether these enclosures were indeed fenced or not. Such examples as have been excavated have been found to have traces of actual posts; but the sites are very various and there is no reason why many or most of them should not have been bounded by earthwork banks like those attributed to pit-alignments. This is a question that must await the results of further excavation.

Such enclosures are not very commonly seen. Some have closely spaced pits only 1m in diameter, not capable of being discerned except in crop-marks of particular fineness and clarity. In others the pits are larger and more widely spaced, but are still less readily detected than a continuous ditch of similar width.

There is much variation in size and shape, and in general these enclosures have little in common but their method of construction (Maxwell, 1979). Some of the more distinctive shapes do nevertheless recur, and these may be regarded as forming individual types. The most clearly defined are the Neolithic settlements typified by Meldon Bridge (Peeblesshire), at which a more or less oval space of 6–8ha is enclosed by a fence whose main timbers are spaced at intervals of 3·3–6·8m (Burgess 1976, St Joseph 1978a, 1980). At each of the three examples so far recognized (all located through air-photography) there is an entrance approached down a similarly fenced passage 6–12m wide and 35–75m long (76). The straight parallel lines of pits defining the entrance passage are more readily noticed than the single curving line of the main fence and, if interpreted in isolation, might seem to belong to a great hall (p 111).

Another distinctive form of enclosure has the elongated proportions of a cursus, 18–30m wide and over 200m long, with the pits 3–6m apart (St Joseph 1973a, 1976a). Two examples at Stracathro (Angus) are flanked by other lines of pits, not yet fully traced or understood, while that at Bainton (Lincolnshire) ends in a separate smaller enclosure measuring about 14m by 20m, defined by close-set pits perhaps half the diameter of those in the long enclosure. The significance of such special features is as little known as that of main enclosures themselves.

A third recurring shape is the circle, already discussed at an earlier stage in this chapter because of its common ritual associations (p 76).

Specific warnings against misinterpretation already given in relation to pit-alignments and pit circles need not be repeated here, though they should still be borne in mind. In general terms it can be said that the interpreter should be equally wary of the regular patterns produced by modern agricultural activities and of random patterning caused by natural

77 *Crop-marks, Ormesby St Margaret, Norfolk, 29 June 1976*
Beside the curving line of a vanished road can be seen negative crop-marks of the former church of St Peter. This was a relatively simple building without side aisles, the chancel once extended, with prominent buttresses along the side walls and a round tower at the west end. The church appears to have stood in a double-ditched enclosure. Positive marks show a number of former field boundaries, most of which are contemporary with the curving road and church, though two which override them are evidently later. In the upper part of the picture part of the later field-system has been subdivided into allotments.

processes, in both of which it is possible to see apparently meaningful combinations of pits—or, alternatively, fail to see such groupings as really do exist.

RELIGIOUS BUILDINGS

Prehistoric ritual monuments of various kinds have already been discussed at the beginning of this chapter. Here we deal with roofed buildings of known religious use.

Pagan temples

Although Iron Age temples have been tentatively recognized in excavation, it is not until the Roman period that such structures become sufficiently substantial and their plans sufficiently explicit for detection from the air. Stone foundations are normal for all but the smallest Roman temples, which are thus capable of showing their presence by means of negative crop-marks.

Temples of traditional Classical form are usually rectangular but, unless they are very modest, usually stand on a vaulted podium. This feature makes it easier to recognize their remains as belonging to a public building of some kind than it is to identify them specifically as a temple.

The Romano-Celtic form of temple is more explicit, with two concentric foundations of rectangular, circular or polygonal plan, the outer approximately twice the diameter of the inner (67b); known examples in Britain range from 10m to 22·5m overall. Here too the floors were often raised but without any modification of the plan, extra earth and gravel being dumped in the compartments between the walls. In Britain it was not unusual for subsidiary rooms to be attached to the outside of the temple, usually placed symmetrically each side of the entrance or at the sides.

In a simpler form of temple the outer foundation is omitted. This leaves the plan ambiguous, though circular or polygonal buildings seen in an urban context would be more likely to be temples than anything else. A similar plan would seem to be seen if the outer foundation of a Romano-Celtic temple were made of materials too slight to appear in terms of crop-marks. Large rectangular rooms or halls are similarly ambiguous, though sometimes dedicated to religious cults; the addition of an external or internal apse on either the long or the short axis would, however, normally indicate some public or official use, most often as a temple.

In identifying temples from crop-marks it should be remembered that the forms of Roman temples of Classical type were deliberately copied in post-medieval times for garden buildings, monuments and mausolea; and there is also some overlap of plan between Roman mausolea and Roman temples. The Romano-Celtic plan was virtually unknown to eighteenth-century improvers, yet it might be inadvertently reproduced in a garden pavilion, or indeed in any functional building like a kiln or windmill in which a tall central structure happened to have acquired a covered gallery around its base.

Churches

The fully developed plan of the medieval parish church is easily recognized when reproduced through the medium of negative crop-marks (77), but earlier or lesser churches had simpler plans indistinguishable from those of other plain rectangular buildings with no internal subdivisions. Identification as a church must then depend on historical records or tradition, or on associated features. Especially in Scotland and in Ireland the traditional sanctity of an early church is often manifested in the continued use of the graveyard as a burial ground long after the church itself is ruined and the neighbourhood apparently deserted. At such sites search should be made for any sign of a surrounding circular enclosure, whether field-wall, bank or ditch, which might indicate the presence of an early Celtic monastic site. Such enclosures might be from 60m to 140m in diameter (Norman & St Joseph 1969).

Religious houses

The abbeys, priories and other religious houses of Britain, as seen from the air, have been described by Knowles and St Joseph (1952). Even when their remains have been extensively robbed, the stumps of the walls and the associated spoilheaps leave surface traces which reveal the essential outlines of the plan, if viewed and photographed in appropriate lighting (9). The easiest feature to recognize is the great cloister, normally the only area of smooth ground free from disturbance within the main building complex. Often the church is the least recognizable of all the buildings, apart from its position, because most thoroughly robbed of its stonework. In addition to the remains of actual buildings, there are often monastic fishponds, which may well turn out to be the clearest features on the whole site.

78 *West Dereham Abbey, Norfolk, looking west, 8 July 1976*
Negative crop-marks reveal much of the layout of a vanished Premonstratensian abbey. In a field of sugar-beet on the right can be seen the gate-house and entrance drive, with a great barn sited conveniently nearby. In a field of corn on the left are the main abbey buildings. The robbed-out abbey church is scarcely visible, but it is possible to recognise the cloister, the octagonal chapter-house, and numerous subsidiary buildings.

79 *Site of Coggeshall Abbey, Essex, 12 July 1976*
The buildings on the left include some survivors of the original Cistercian abbey and a sixteenth-century house built from parts of its remains. In the lawn and adjacent pasture bands of parched grass trace out much of the plan of the abbey church, whose foundations still lie beneath the turf.

80 *Spoil-heaps from coal-mining near Tankersley, West Yorkshire, 6 April 1972*
Half-a-dozen rows of spoil-heaps survive where they have been incorporated into a golf course beside the M1. The considerable diameter of the heaps may be judged by comparison with the width of the motorway.

81 *Former lead-mining area west of Elton, Derbyshire, 9 April 1968*
The area has been worked and reworked over several centuries. Most of the shafts are too shallow and closely spaced to have produced more than a narrow raised rim of spoil, but a few are surrounded by more substantial mounds. There are also small areas of opencast working as well as tip-heaps.

When a site of this character is ploughed up but not systematically cleared of all remaining stonework, the general extent of the buildings can be perceived from spreads of rubble in the ploughsoil, at least for a good many years. Little detail is, however, to be expected. On a long-ploughed site any surviving foundations will tend to produce negative crop-marks (78), while robber-trenches from which all stonework has been removed may themselves be the cause of positive marks.

After the Dissolution many demolished priories and abbeys became the sites of mansions and other secular buildings constructed from their masonry. The undressed stonework of the foundations was commonly left in place with the result that, in times of drought, the plan of the principal buildings reappears as lines of parching in the turf of lawns or parkland beside the later house (79).

INDUSTRIAL SITES

Mines

Abandoned mines, unless revealed by subsidence into the disused galleries (p 143), are most readily identified by their spoilheaps. The actual shafts are less conspicuous, but not invisible; aerial survey has in fact been used for plotting old mine-shafts which might otherwise be a serious danger to walkers.

An exception is provided by Neolithic flint-mines, in which it seems to have been normal practice, instead of tipping spoil on the surface, to dump it down a disused shaft. There is thus little visible surface debris, but the shafts themselves are marked by hollows where the filling has sunk as it has consolidated. The diameter of the shaft is typically 5–7m where it passes through the chalk, but greater at the surface, individual hollows measuring over 10m across. The shafts are closely grouped together, being spaced at not much more than 15m intervals (Curwen 1930, pls 1, 13). This close spacing serves to distinguish flint-mines from dene-holes, a specialized form of marl-pits which were needed only one or two to a field, and from natural solution-holes (p 143), which, although occurring in chalk, do not do so in such clusters.

The spoil from much medieval and early post-medieval mining was heaped around the mouth of the shaft in a bun-shaped mound. The size of the spoilheap depended on the thickness of the seam being worked and the length of the radiating galleries as well as the depth of the shaft. The larger the spoilheaps, the more widely they are spaced (Beresford & St Joseph 1979, fig 34), a development likely to reflect improving technology. The largest heaps are associated with iron- and coal-mining and can reach a diameter of over 30m (80). Spoilheaps associated with lead-mining never reach such dimensions and are in general smaller than those for coal and iron. In the Yorkshire Dales, where lead-mining and coal-mining went on in much the same area, it is possible to distinguish between them on air-photographs simply from the size of their spoilheaps. In Yorkshire the heaps of both sizes tend to be evenly spaced, yielding a pattern on the ground that is generally tidy and sometimes extremely regular. Lead-mining in Derbyshire and on the Mendip Hills, by contrast, shows a less orderly pattern in which numerous small shafts are used to follow what are often quite narrow lodes (81). There is a disorganized look to these mining areas that invites comparison with the irregular groupings of solution-holes that also occur in the Carboniferous Limestone (p 143). There need be no confusion, however, as long as the area remains unploughed, since virtually all mine-shafts have some kind of a raised rim, which solution-holes are bound to lack.

Other kinds of mining, eg for tin, tend to leave less distinctive patterns on the surface of the ground, though signs of disturbance of a more general character are plentiful enough.

Spoilheaps most often remain intact on moorland or common land, but may occasionally be preserved in less expected settings such as golf courses (80). Identification rests upon the number, size and spacing of the mounds, and upon the characteristic hollow in the mouth of the shaft, in addition to occurrence in a known mining area. Where spoilheaps have been levelled, both soil-marks and crop-marks have occasionally been observed. Although identically spaced to the original mounds, these marks tend to be irregular in outline and, if derived from coal-pits, make obvious coal-black patches in the soil.

The spoil from mines of the industrial age, being too abundant to store at the actual pithead, was transported to a distance, where the tips formed patterns of a different and more familiar kind: mostly they either radiate from a series of focal points to form fans of ever increasing radius, or they are piled up into single cones of enormous height and girth. These present no great problem of interpretation. Mention should, however, be made of the nineteenth-century practice of mining for chalk and limestone beneath agricultural land. These mines have usually been long forgotten until they make an unexpected reappearance when their galleries eventually fall in (p 143).

Pits and quarries

The most striking difference between medieval and early post-medieval pits and quarries and their modern equivalents lies in the small scale and piecemeal nature of their working. Even when large areas have been worked over, as at Barnack (Cambridgeshire), the individual hollows and piles of quarry waste are very modest by modern standards and suggest a limited scale of operations (Beresford & St Joseph 1979, fig 106). Once again, as at the contemporary mines, the waste was dumped as near to the working area as was feasible, with no attempt at subsequent making good, creating an untidy scene of disturbed ground readily identifiable from the air. Gravel-pits in particular were often worked in small compartments separated by solid baulks of undug gravel and backfilled at the end of each season (p 175), though on land no longer in cultivation they would be left permanently open. Peat-diggings too were left open. Those of Roman date in the Fens became choked with silt like nearby river channels (p 154) and now display a remarkable pattern of pale silt-filled basins surrounded by black peaty soil, while those of medieval date in the neighbourhood of Norwich once flooded have remained filled with water to become the Norfolk Broads (Beresford & St Joseph 1979, figs 114–15).

The crop-marks of filled-in pits and quarries are described in greater detail in Chapter 4 (p 175).

Kilns and furnaces

There are two ways in which the industrial processes carried on in kilns and furnaces can cause soil-marks, allowing their former use to be inferred.

One is the reddening of the soil caused by the action of high temperatures on it in oxidizing conditions. Where this has occurred to any depth, as, for example, when the firing-chamber of a pottery kiln is sunk into the ground, reddened soil brought up by the plough will make an obvious mark or pattern. The colour of the 'Red Hills' of the Essex coast is due to the same cause, these Iron-Age and Roman saltern mounds being composed largely of fire-reddened earth and clay remaining from the salt-making process. The red colour is, nevertheless, more apparent in excavation than to aerial observation, unless the area has been reclaimed from the marsh and is now subject to ploughing. On the whole, the identification of salterns, whether prehistoric, Roman or medieval, depends chiefly on recognition of the artificial origin of the mounds (Beresford & St Joseph 1979, fig 111).

The second kind of soil-mark is black rather than red and is caused by concentrations of cinders from iron-smelting. Some Roman iron-making sites had a considerable output, and large parts of one or more modern fields may be blackened by the accumulation of cinders on ground now given over to cultivation.

Windmills

The medieval post-mill commonly had its crosstrees embedded in a windmill-mound, to give it greater height. The possibility of confusion with a round barrow has already been noted (p 85). Windmill-mounds were not always purpose-made, however, and some were adapted from existing mounds, such as prehistoric barrows, whose siting happened to be favourable. Identification of a mound as having supported a windmill, therefore, does not in itself exclude identification as a barrow.

The crop-marks of windmill-mounds have been discussed above, in the context of ring-ditches (p 90).

In its more developed form the post-mill did not stand on an earthen mound, but the crosstrees were raised on substantial piers enclosed within a round-house. The structure of the piers at least was normally of brick or masonry, but parch-marks of two of Great Yarmouth's vanished windmills suggested they had been entirely of timber. Measurements kindly provided by Mr D A Edwards showed that a central post had been encircled by others in 4 concentric rings,, with successive diameters of 12m, 24m, 38m, and 56m. Although at first sight these concentric circles of post-holes recall the circular structures associated with henges (p 76), their disposi-

tion does differ significantly, the circles being closer together towards the middle of the windmill, where the prehistoric structures always seem to leave an open space.

LINES OF COMMUNICATION

Roads

The line of a forgotten road may be shown by the remains of the road itself or by traces of the roadside ditches. On unploughed ground the road will often appear as a low causeway, its ditches (if any) picked out by lines of darker vegetation. Such a causeway may still be discernible after ploughing, and even under crop, if favourably lit. In bare soil the road is more likely to be marked by a band of stonier soil between the dark lines of the ditches (82). In growing crops the rammed gravel composing roads, streets or metalled yards produces negative marks where it has not been destroyed by ploughing or by deliberate removal

82 *Roman roads near Badbury Rings, Dorset, 8 April 1949*
The main Roman road from London to the South-West (Ackling Dyke) crosses from left to right; only a length on the right survives unploughed. In the ploughed field soil-marks show the ditches of Ackling Dyke crossing and completely cutting off a superseded line of road, while a third road can be seen crossing the field obliquely near its apex. Other marks are of natural drainage, post-Roman tracks, and a modern plantation-boundary, while a short horizontal black line above Ackling Dyke (darker and sharper than the other marks) is caused by damage to the negative.

(37), whereas the ditches cause positive marks. It is not unusual to see crop-marks of a road without any ditches, or of roadside ditches with no visible road (25); these may reflect either the original construction (the road being unditched or only lightly metalled), differences of preservation, or limited sensitivity in the crop-marks at the time of photography.

The course of a Roman road may also be marked by lines of irregular quarry-pits on one or both sides, from which the road material was originally derived. After ploughing these may be seen in terms of crop-marks as lines of irregular blotches.

The approximate period of use of an abandoned road can be inferred from that of the places it served, though correlations will not be exact, since a road constructed for one purpose may well be adapted to another. This kind of inference is of most use when the places served are isolated and known to have been only briefly occupied. Thus, a road leading to London might be of nearly any date, but one linking two Roman forts, neither of which became a centre of medieval settlement, would most likely itself be Roman, while a road aiming directly through the park towards the site of a demolished mansion might well have been a carriage-road in use during some part of the mansion's existence (Wilson & Wilson 1982). In fig 77 it is reasonable to assume that the former road once served the former church and that the disuse of both reflects the changing pattern of local settlement; but it would be rash to conclude that both were either constructed or abandoned at the same time, since neither was actually necessary to the other.

The crop-marks of roads may be distinguished from other linear marks by reference to their course, if a sufficient length is visible. Negative marks of the causeway are most likely to be confused with pipelines and sewers, which often have lengths of notable straightness and will sometimes produce negative marks, especially when newly cut; but these will also include sharply angled changes of direction unlikely in a road (p 174). Pairs of parallel ditches, besides marking out a road, might have belonged to a linear earthwork (pp 103–4), to a vanished plantation-belt or windbreak, or even to a narrow cursus (p 78).

In addition to the occurrence of actual roads and their remains, former lines of communication may sometimes be shown by the presence of multiple trackways worn into the surface of commons and wasteland and in other places where the passage of men and animals was not closely confined by fields and hedges into following a precise line, whether metalled or not. These trackways occur, or are preserved, especially on hill-slopes, where travellers or animals prefer to follow their own line; but they are by no means restricted to them (Beresford & St Joseph 1979, fig 116). In places where former moorland has been ploughed up, the complex braided pattern of trackways will sometimes reappear in terms of soil- or crop-marks.

Canals and railways

Although obviously different in their actual construction, canals and railways are similar in cutting across the landscape with a fine disregard for previously existing boundaries and lines of communication. Their remains, whether overgrown, filled or levelled, catch the eye because of the bold sweeping curves or straight alignments that divide so many former fields and woods into two complementary parts.

Canals take a more sinuous course than railways, being more closely controlled by the contours. Disused canals are more difficult than railways to document in detail, some having already been abandoned at the time that the Ordnance Survey began its work. The remains are often fragmentary and inconspicuous, their meaning only becoming apparent when two or more of the fragments are connected by fieldwork or documentary research. The presence of former locks, inclined planes and reservoirs should be sought; where they can be found in recognizable form, singly or in conjunction, then identification as a canal is no longer in any doubt.

The main railway lines are very well documented on the various editions of Ordnance Survey maps, and there should be no difficulty in identifying even isolated fragments of an abandoned track. The various spurs and links may give more trouble if their relation-

ship to the main line is not immediately perceived. For example, the link between a high-level and low-level track might have been carried for much of its length on an arched structure, whose foundations now produce a curving line of rectangular negative marks across one corner of a field in crop. The marks do not in themselves speak strongly of railways, but their layout in relation to the adjacent tracks (even if disused) should prompt the true explanation.

Light railways serving industrial concerns are numerous and differ little in appearance on the photograph from the public lines. They are sometimes short-lived and not readily traced from available maps. Those serving military ordnance depots (pp 170–1), whether in current use or not, are unlikely to appear on a map of any kind.

Canals and railways have another point of resemblance in their use of major engineering works, such as bridges, viaducts or aqueducts, and tunnels. Unexpectedly, tunnels have features of interest from the air. In long tunnels there are ventilation shafts at intervals, each opening screened for safety by a lofty wall. Other shafts were used in the actual construction work for extracting some of the spoil, which forms a series of bun-shaped heaps identical in appearance to those produced in coal- and iron-mining (83). The correct interpretation is implied by their position in a single line continuing that of the visible length of canal or railway.

83 *Canal tunnel near Crick, Northamptonshire, 29 October 1969*
The Crick Tunnel on the Grand Union Canal is nearly 1400m long. Its line is marked by a row of large spoilheaps, like those associated with iron or coal pits, overriding the ridge-and-furrow.

MISCELLANEOUS

There is a sense in which this chapter, useful though it may be, is grossly misleading. In the thirteen previous sections it has sought to describe a good sample of the most distinctive archaeological sites at present recognizable on air-photographs. These sites are not truly representative of what the photo-interpreter can expect to see for at least four reasons:

1 The majority of archaeological sites, even if visible from the air, are not so distinctive or readily classified as those picked out here.
2 A large part of those that are visible are too poorly preserved, or at least too imperfectly rendered on the photographs, to be classified at all.
3 Amongst those that can be clearly seen, most are too simple in form and associations to be given a description more informative than 'bank', 'ditch' or 'enclosure'. Some indeed are so mysterious as virtually to defy description, as happens, for example, with several of the features visible at Minchinhampton Common (Gloucestershire) (St Joseph 1968c, RCHME 1976, 81–4).
4 Even among crop-marks, the majority are not of archaeological origin, but have natural geological or modern agricultural causes. (These are discussed further in Chapter 4.)

Most archaeological sites on air-photographs, therefore, come into the miscellaneous category; but for that very reason there is little more to be said about them. Two groups call for some further comment: these are enclosures, which offer encouraging scope for future morphological analysis, and pillow-mounds, which are described last only because they do not fit into the conventional categories used in the remainder of the chapter.

Enclosures in considerable variety have already been described in earlier sections of this chapter, but it is those that remain undescribed that are in fact the ones most commonly seen. Some, like the double rectangular enclosures noted by St Joseph (1967b), are of distinctive plan but as yet unknown archaeological character. Most are very simple in form, yet still show much variation. It is hoped that taxonomic studies at present in progress can isolate a number of distinct varieties which subsequent investigation may prove to have archaeological significance. If this work turns out successfully, it will transform our understanding of a major sector of British field archaeology.

Pillow-mounds are normally rectangular, 12–50m long and 5–9m wide, in fact almost always longer in proportion than a modern pillow. They are no more than half a metre in height and are surrounded by a narrow ditch on all four sides. The name was coined by Crawford (in Crawford & Keiller 1928) for a type of site whose nature was at the time mysterious but soon recognized as providing artificial warrens for managed colonies of rabbits. Some flat circular mounds appear to have served the same purpose. Pillow-mounds are usually found in groups of half-a-dozen or more and this serves to distinguish them from other elongated mounds such as long barrows. Where similar mounds occur in ones or twos, it is much less easy to be certain of their attribution.

4

Identification of Non-Archaeological Features

Air-photographs show the landscape in its full complexity, and archaeological information has to be sought amongst a mass of non-archaeological detail. The interpreter cannot afford to dismiss any part of this complex pattern as irrelevant, for unless he has some understanding of everything on the photograph, how is he to discriminate between what is archaeological and what is not? There are many natural features and many effects of modern activity that simulate archaeological sites with sufficient exactness to cause considerable difficulty in interpretation. Only a detailed familiarity with the kinds of mark involved will prevent frequent misidentifications. Moreover someone who disregards geological data is depriving himself of environmental evidence relevant to the sites he does identify, and if he cannot recognize at least the commoner agricultural processes, he has little basis for the detailed evaluation of soil- and crop-marks.

Many of the features to be described in this chapter may be seen in any of several transformations. What is plain and obvious in its original state may become ambiguous or misleading in a secondary form, especially if this is incomplete. Thus, a football field in use poses no problem of interpretation. In summer, when the white lines have been washed away, lines of darker grass may remain in their place, and, if only one part of the pitch can be seen, it may appear as though a rectangular enclosure or a large ring-ditch is present (84). The darker growth is caused by the continued application of chalk throughout the season; this produces such a build-up of calcium in the soil that it can still promote crop-marks in growing corn if the field is brought back into cultivation. The unwary observer seeing part of a football field reproduced in a cereal crop could easily be misled into thinking he had seen an archaeological site. Similarly, farm animals at feeding-troughs or confined in pens wear the turf into bare patches of characteristic shape (72). When the trough or pen is removed, the grass recovers and the same shape is reproduced in the vivid green of new growth enriched by droppings. Even after ploughing the same patterns may re-emerge, but their meaning will only be clear to someone familiar with all features of the agricultural scene.

Non-archaeological patterns should become so familiar that they can be recognized, or at least suspected, from mere fragments. For the aerial archaeologist every flight is an opportunity for self-tuition in the varied aspects of the countryside. The earthbound interpreter does not have the same opportunities, but he can learn much from the systematic study of blocks of vertical photography takes at various times of year. Being non-selective the vertical photographs will show much that does not come into specialist photographs of archaeological sites, and he will soon learn to recognize such things as crop-trials, abandoned airfields, and the sites of grass-track racing with comparative ease.

GEOLOGICAL FEATURES

Crops respond to differences in the depth of soil caused by geological processes in just the same way and in just the same conditions as they do on archaeological sites. The natural features revealed by crop-marks have a wide

84 *Parch-marks in grass near Woodham Walter, Essex, 17 May 1976*

In May 1976 permanent grassland had still had little chance to recover from the drought of 1975 and was already showing the effects of parching as another dry summer followed. Air-reconnaissance of parks and playing-fields was beginning to reveal many archaeological marks: here an oblong enclosure appears to have parched out in the turf of a two-hole golf course. But the pattern is suspiciously familiar, as comparison with the fading lines of a football field beyond quickly shows; the 'enclosure' proves to be the penalty box of the 1974–5 football pitch, which was laid out in the other direction. Similarly, traces of superseded bunkers are visible beside the right-hand fairway of the golf course.

The field on the left, behind the pavilion, shows the characteristic regular layout of an orchard (p 166).

range; they include jointing in the underlying rock, ancient frost-cracks and 'patterned ground', former creeks in reclaimed marsh, lines of subsurface drainage, and simple accumulation of soil in natural hollows and at the foot of slopes. Most of these features are also visible in bare soil, especially when the subsoil is brightly coloured. Geological and archaeological patterns are often superimposed, and especially when composed of elements of similar dimensions they may be difficult to disentangle (85, 86). Geological features seen in relief, by contrast, cause little difficulty. Often, indeed, mounds and scarps that seem ambiguous on the ground take on a clearer meaning when viewed in suitable conditions from the air.

The comments and illustrations that follow are mostly limited to patterns in soil and crops. These patterns occur widely in conjunction with archaeological marks, but are seldom described or illustrated in geological textbooks and are therefore unfamiliar. The novice interpreter finds himself in the same position as O G S Crawford in 1936, seeing crop-marks of ice-wedge polygons for the first time: 'Nothing quite like these markings has been encountered before elsewhere.... They are probably medieval' (Crawford, 1936). No further justification is needed for including a substantial geological section in a book on archaeological interpretation.

Solid geology

On arable land sedimentary rocks are responsible for two main patterns liable to mislead the archaeologist. These reflect respectively the stratification and the jointing of the underlying rock.

The first pattern is produced by the alternation of hard and soft layers in the rock. Where this occurs, differential weathering at the surface causes a corresponding variation in the depth of soil, making a distinctive pattern both in soil and crop. Where the bedding plane is horizontal, the pattern follows the contours, and on a hilltop or isolated knoll it may easily resemble the defensive circuit of a ploughed-out hillfort (87). Clues may be given by the presence of faulting across the strata (Wilson 1975b, fig 4) or by similar patterns appearing at the same height nearby. Failing any definite indication of a geological or archaeological origin, marks seen enclosing a hilltop should be identified only with some caution.

The second pattern is caused by jointing in the bedrock. Natural joints in marl and limestone are enlarged by weathering to form troughs of deeper soil detectable by crop-marks. There is normally no pattern visible in bare soil. When sets of joints meet at right angles, they form a system resembling a regular layout of ditched fields (88). Although master-joints may continue over a considerable distance, the joint-system is seldom as regular as its overall organization would imply if interpreted in archaeological terms. There are usually offsets, discontinuities and other illogical details difficult to accommodate to an archaeological explanation, but these may not be apparent if seen only in fragments or indistinctly. Crop-marks of particular fineness and clarity will, however, reveal minor joints and fissures within the main pattern, leaving no doubt as to the geological origin of the system as a whole (89).

On limestone moors and chalk downland a further source of confusion is the presence of solution-holes. These are formed by chemical weathering at points of weakness in the rock such as joint intersections. The basic form is a cylindrical shaft, but the top may be weathered back into the shape of a wide-mouthed funnel. When solution-holes occur in some numbers, as in parts of the Carboniferous Limestone (90), or conspicuously follow a single line along a particular joint or stratum, they could easily be mistaken for old mine shafts. The natural shafts, however, are of varied size and irregular spacing and never have a raised rim, whereas mine shafts are more uniform, more closely spaced, and normally surrounded by a bank of spoil (81) except where the ground has been brought into cultivation. Less easily distinguished from solution-holes are the voids formed by subsidence into the collapsing galleries of old chalk and limestone mines (91). These, however, are found in agricultural land and occur within well-defined areas, being limited by the extent of the original mine rather than by the broader geological context.

Glacial and periglacial features

During a period of glaciation the effects of intense cold are felt over a periglacial zone extending far beyond the margins of the ice-sheet. Most of the ground in this zone is perennially frozen ('permafrost'), but an active layer at the surface is subject to regular seasonal thaw followed by re-freezing. The alternation of freeze and thaw causes movements within the active layer, coarse- and fine-grained sediments having different rates of expansion on being frozen. Considerable

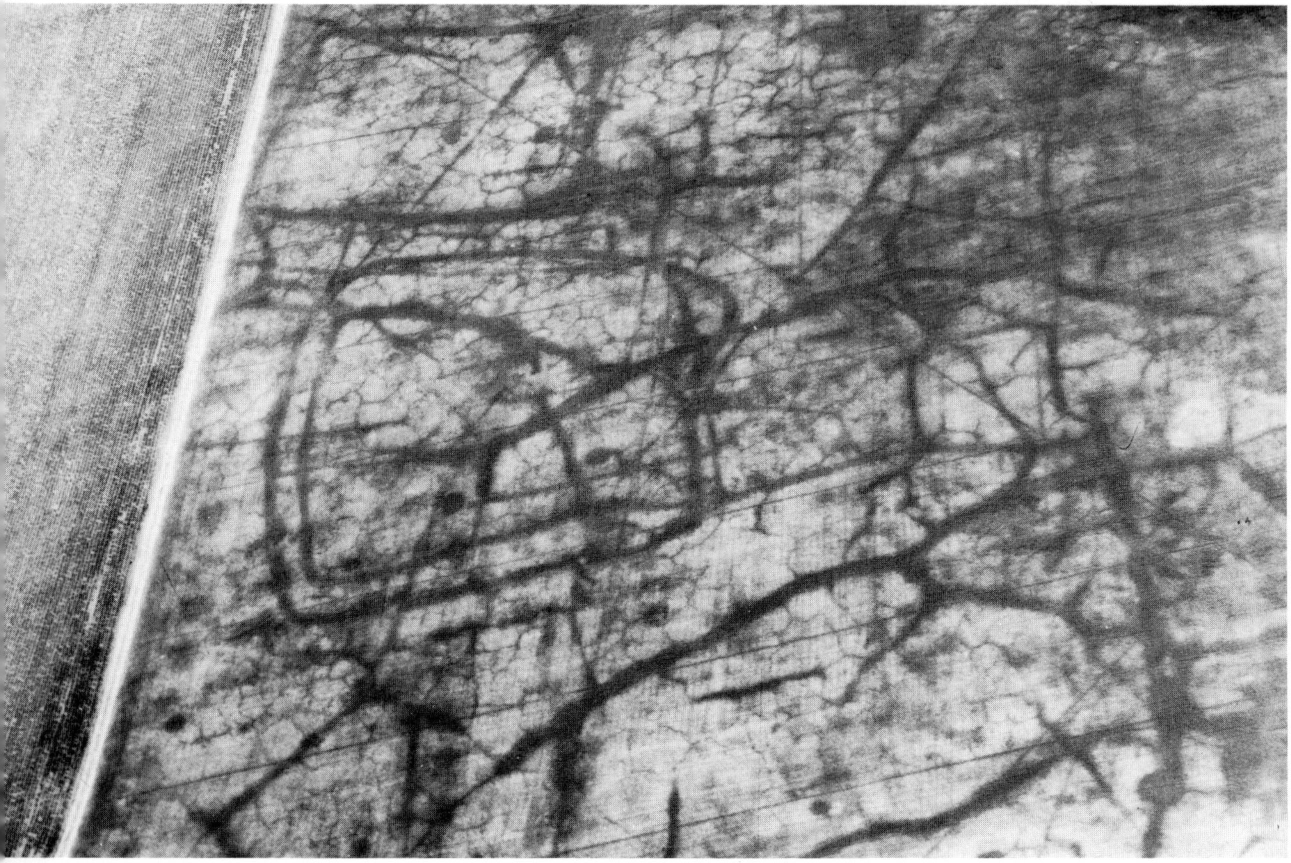

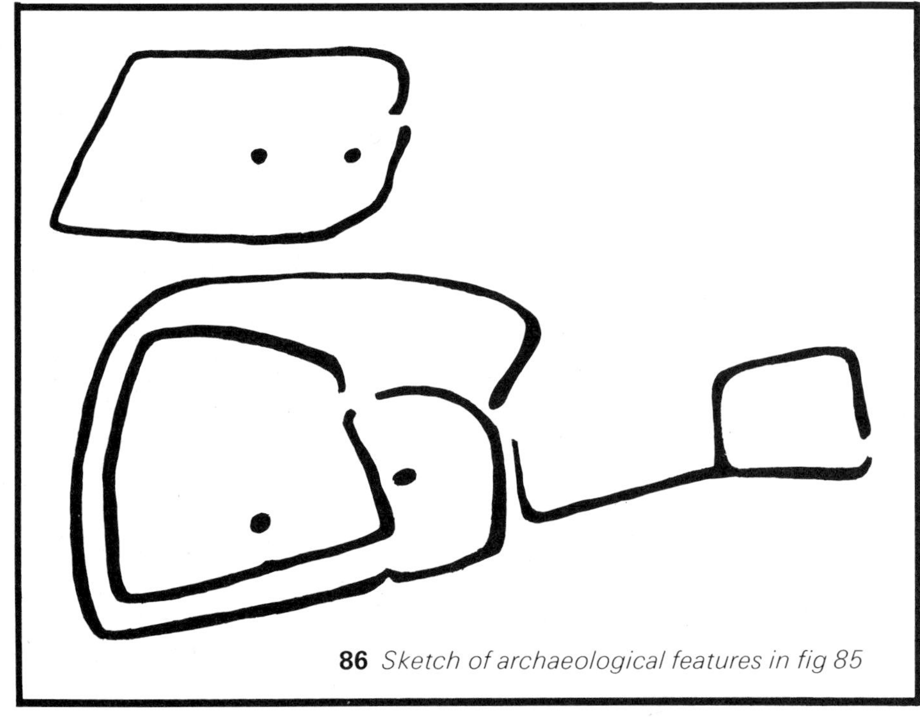

86 *Sketch of archaeological features in fig 85*

85 *Crop-marks south-west of Orton Longueville, Cambridgeshire, 26 June 1959*
Three kinds of pattern are superimposed here on a gravel terrace south of the R. Nene. (*a*) There are two networks of periglacial polygons: the larger is irregular and incomplete, with ice-wedge casts 8–10m wide; the smaller is very fine, with many polygons no more than 25m in diameter (p. 149). (*b*) The broad ditches of three subrectangular enclosures, probably belonging to a Roman farmstead, can be distinguished by their relatively coherent outlines (see diagram, fig 86). Dark spots in the two larger enclosures are presumably caused by wells. (*c*) A herring-bone pattern of straight, narrow, dark lines marks a system of modern field-drains, draining towards the lower right (p 162).

87 *Soil-marks, Upper Coscombe, Gloucestershire, 20 December 1966*
Two concentric bands of dark soil encircle a hill-top in the Cotswolds, the winter sun emphasizing the hollows in which they lie. The site looks like a ploughed-down hillfort, though there is no sign of an entrance and its defences seem too massive to have been nearly levelled by ploughing. Detailed investigation showed that the features were entirely geological in origin, caused by the presence of bands of clay within the limestone of the Great Oolite Series with which the hill is capped (Bowen, 1972). The soft clay has weathered more rapidly, forming hollows containing deep, clayey, humus-rich soil of dark appearance.

pressures build up during the freezing process, which works progressively downwards from the surface, squeezing unfrozen material against the permafrost beneath.

Periglacial features due to these and other causes can be observed in arctic regions today; they can also be detected in fossil form in temperate regions including the British Isles, from characteristic patterns of disturbance in the ground (Williams 1973, French 1976, West 1977). Some of these patterns can be recognised on air-photographs: they include collapsed frost-mounds, ice-wedge polygons, and other types of patterned ground.

Frost-mounds occur where ground water is frozen into lenses of ice beneath the surface, making the ground swell upwards. The largest examples, known as pingos, are built up over a period of many years and may be hundreds of metres wide and up to 50m high. Less spectacular hummocks only a few metres across form annually, only to decay again within the same year. As each mound grows, surface sediments tend to slide off towards the edges, exposing the ice to the sun, which eventually melts it, causing the mound to collapse. Typical remains of a collapsed frost-mound comprise a more or less circular wet hollow with a surrounding bank forming a raised rim. Composite shapes replace the simple circle when several mounds have coalesced

88 *Jointing in limestone near Colston Bassett, Nottinghamshire, 22 July 1971*
A joint-system forming squares about 60m wide merges into an irregular pattern of broader 'gulls' towards the bottom left of the picture. Fine lines within the squares hint at a subsidiary system of minor joints. To left of centre a sharply defined area of dark tone marks the site of a disused quarry (p 175). At '4 o'clock' from the quarry a rectangular enclosure overlies the geological pattern at an oblique angle to it. Note that none of the sides of the enclosure is exactly aligned on the lines of cultivation, though two of them are very close (p 186).

or have succeeded one another over a period of time.

In the British Isles most of the remains so far identified have been of medium-sized mounds 50–100m in diameter clustering together in large groups on low-lying nearly level ground that was probably supplied by artesian springs. Within such groups the remnants of individual mounds are seldom distinct but run together in complex patterns. Composite hollows may be up to 300m long; at their most irregular they develop long arms bordered by sinuously winding ridges 10–40m wide, but depressions of simple form are usually also present. A few sites in Norfolk, Dyfed and Co. Wexford have survived unploughed, but the majority are on arable land, with surface relief reduced to a metre or less. From the air the peaty soil in the hollows contrasts well with the sandy or chalky material of the ridges, and cereal crops respond strongly to the difference in soil moisture (92). Soil- and crop-marks of collapsed frost-mounds have been recorded on air-photographs in East Anglia, in the river valleys of south-east England, and in the Welsh Marches. They are most likely to deceive the archaeological interpreter when only a small

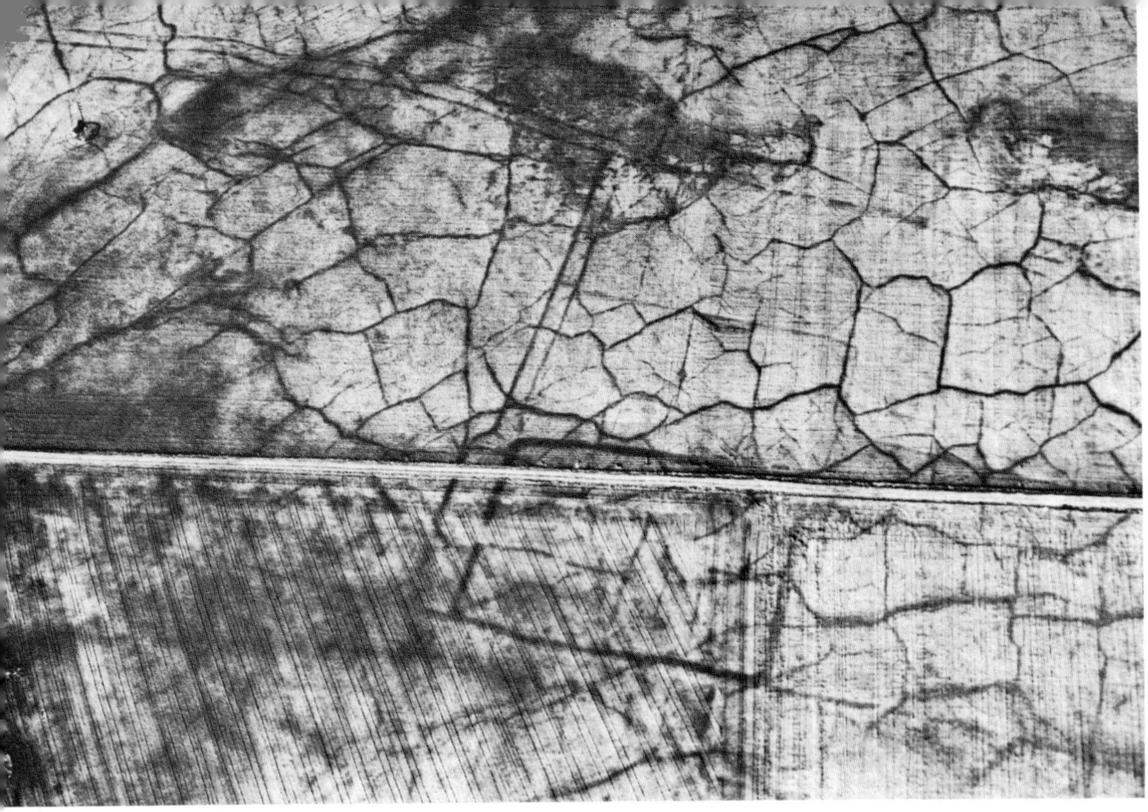

89 *Jointing in limestone near Brodsworth, South Yorkshire, 5 July 1975*
The joint-system here is more irregular than in fig 88. Minor joints are visible within the main network and explain some of its sharp angles. Across the geological pattern run the smooth continuous lines of a rectangular farmstead-enclosure with its associated fields and lanes.

90 *Solution-holes in limestone, Fforest Fawr, Powys, 4 March 1977*
This desolate landscape appears at first sight to have suffered industrial devastation, but apart from a few vehicle tracks there are in fact negligible signs of human activity. The largest holes are certainly grouped together suggestively and sometimes interconnect, but they are much too large (over 60m in diameter) to be the result of small-scale medieval mining, and nowhere is a spoilheap to be seen (cf fig 81).

91 *Subsidence near Little Addington, Northamptonshire, 29 November 1974*
The photograph shows the site of a forgotten limestone mine south-east of Kettering shortly after large parts of its galleries had collapsed. The crop growing in the left-hand part of the field has been cut, but the remainder has had to be abandoned.

part of the pattern is clearly visible, isolated in the agricultural landscape by the varied treatment of different fields. The natural rampart of a collapsed frost-mound could then be taken for the artificial bank of a henge or some other earthwork. Other parts of the pattern might nevertheless be expected to show up faintly and, if detected, would confirm the natural origin of the marks.

It is not always easy to distinguish the remnants of frost-mounds from other geological patterns on air-photographs involving ill-drained hollows, such as former marsh or end-moraine. Fortunately, this need not trouble the archaeological interpreter since it is only the more obvious and well-formed examples of frost-mound hollows that invite an archaeological explanation.

Ice-wedges are formed when moisture collects and freezes within fissures in frozen ground. It should be remembered that although water expands when it solidifies into ice at 0°C, the ice itself contracts when it is further cooled. Thus, when ice-rich soil is chilled to −15°C or less, it tends to shrink and develop cracks. In the spring, meltwater from the surface seeps down into the open cracks and, immediately freezing, prevents them from closing up as the ground temperature slowly rises. In succeeding seasons cracking recurs along the same lines, and the resulting veins of ice coalesce, building up over the years into wedges of considerable size. Modern examples are commonly 3–5m wide at the top and exceptionally can exceed 10m. When seen in plan, the wedges form a network composed of polygons 15–40m in diameter, often of four sides though the shapes tend to be irregular. The intersections are usually either at right angles or at 120°.

When an ice-wedge melts, it is replaced by sediments slumping in from the surface and from the sides of the fissure, more or less preserving its shape. Crops responding to the greater depth of soil in the ice-wedge cast reproduce the polygonal network as a pattern of positive crop-marks. Not every element in the network will be faithfully represented, however, since the material filling some of the fissures may be unconducive to crop-marks, and other fissures may not have survived at all. Shapes are therefore liable to appear illogical as well as irregular and the sides of the polygons frequently fail to close (85, 95). These fossil polygons tend to be larger than their modern arctic counterparts: in Britain they generally range from 40m to 150m in diameter, with wedges 1–5m thick (50, but cf 58). A much smaller and finer network can sometimes be seen subdividing the main polygonal cells, but it only appears with any clarity in specially favourable conditions (85).

92 *Crop-marks of collapsed frost-mounds in the Kennet valley south of Englefield, Berkshire, 23 June 1970*

The complex pattern of banks and hollows is not untypical, though there are few simple circular forms. Crop-marks of archaeological features such as ring-ditches and enclosures can be seen at several places on the banks. An obvious dark triangle to right of centre shows where a small triangular field has at some time been largely dug for gravel. Single or double lines mark the former boundaries of this and other fields thrown together in modern times.

93 *Crop-marks of frost-cracks west of Gording, Ribe* amt, *Denmark, 26 July 1966*
Such unusually orderly systems of frost-cracks are widespread on the glacial sands of west Jutland. Although when first seen from the air, they were taken for Celtic fields, their individual shapes and overall organization are actually much less regular than those of surviving prehistoric fields in Denmark. The pattern seen here (in a ripe cereal crop) includes a number of triangular and pentagonal forms; and even on the most extensive sites of this character there is never any sign of a lane giving access to the supposed 'fields'.

Remains of ice-wedges can be found in unconsolidated sediments of most kinds, but their crop-marks are virtually limited to sands and gravels and are especially typical of river terraces. They often appear in company with archaeological crop-marks, from which they may be difficult to separate in detail, particularly if only a small area happens to be visible. Individual frost-cracks may be mistaken for archaeological ditches or palisade-trenches, even in excavation (J Evans 1972). Complete polygons, if predominantly four-sided and regularly arranged, can look like small ditched fields, apparently furnishing evidence of prehistoric agriculture (93). But even these more orderly networks are irregular in detail and do not maintain their regular lines for more than three or four units at a time.

In addition to ice-wedge polygons, which are mostly large and irregular, there are various kinds of *patterned ground* in which numbers of smaller components are repeated. Patterns of this sort may be seen in bare soil or in crops, and occasionally also in natural vegetation.

The shapes involved vary according to the nature of the subsoil and the slope of the ground. The clearest patterns in bare soil are seen over chalk or chalky drift. On level ground these take the form of small polygons about 10m in diameter, each with a nearly circular nucleus of white chalky soil within a darker perimeter. On gentle slopes, of up to 5°, the darker soil makes stripes, usually 1–3m wide, at intervals of 4–10m. These two patterns grade into one another, producing inter

mediate forms with polygons elongated in the direction of slope. Below plough-level all these patterns are found to consist of alternate ridges of chalk or chalky drift and troughs containing non-chalky material, such as sand or loam. Normally, positive crop-marks develop above the troughs, but during a severe soil moisture deficit this pattern may be reversed by the release of moisture from the chalk bedrock after that in the troughs has been exhausted (94). In the Breckland of East Anglia, where the material filling the troughs is normally an acidic sand, the alternation of acidic and alkaline soils has a marked effect even on the natural heath vegetation, with calcifuge plants such as ling (*Calluna*) growing only over the sand and more tolerant species such as grasses on the chalk.

94 *Crop-marks of patterned ground south of Barnham, Suffolk, 3 July 1967*
Both stripes and polygons are visible. The arrangement of the pattern shows that positive marks are occurring over the chalky ridges rather than over the sand-filled troughs despite their greater depth of soil. By contrast, the double ditch of a four-sided enclosure is also shown by positive marks, though in places these are less intense than those of the natural pattern. We may conclude that the natural troughs are rather shallow and their water content soon exhausted, whereas the archaeological ditches reach to a greater depth and still contain a reserve of moisture, though this is coming to an end.

Similar polygons have been observed in bare soil over sandstone and limestone, but are difficult to detect because of low tonal contrast.

Over sands and gravels comparable patterns are not normally seen in bare soil, but occur quite commonly in crops. There is a considerable variety of forms: these include irregular and disintegrating polygons, short interlocking 'squiggles', and spots or blobs (63, 64). The different patterns grade into each other and may also be associated with fossil ice-wedges, either bordering the individual frost-cracks (95) or filling spaces within the network (93).

Two of the patterns described may be confused with archaeological features.

95 *Crop-marks, Baker Street, north-east of Grays, Essex, 16 June 1970*
Natural and archaeological marks are superimposed. The broad, rather irregular, linear marks of ice-wedge casts partly coincide with a neat system of lanes, fields and closes bounded by ditches of several phases. At least two penannular ditches, not necessarily contemporary with the other archaeological features, presumably mark the position of circular houses (p 96). The numerous circular blobs are of natural origin, and some of them follow the ice-wedges. They should be contrasted with the marks of Saxon sunken huts at Mucking (fig 54), less than 5km to the east.

Soil stripes may be mistaken for ploughed-up ridge-and-furrow, especially when this is likely to be 'narrow rig'. The natural stripes, however, are not organized in neat parcels with well defined limits; they follow the slope of the ground closely, diverging or forking where necessary in order to do so. On a uniform slope the stripes will be parallel, but other characteristics of ridge-and-furrow will be absent, such as headlands, the reversed-S curve, or the juxtaposition of different alignments.

Where the pattern is composed of spots or blobs, these can easily resemble crop-marks of archaeological pits. Small blobs look like storage, rubbish or latrine pits and give the impression of intensive ancient settlement; but they pay no heed to archaeological divisions such as enclosure ditches, and they tend to be very closely packed. Larger blobs are similar in size to Saxon huts with sunk floors, but crop-marks of actual huts have flattened sides (54), while those of natural origin are more nearly circular (95).

Natural drainage

Under this heading we have grouped the traces of former streams and creeks; dry valleys, in which drainage takes place beneath the modern surface; and the sites of former lakes and mires. Apart from some exceptions peculiar to the Fens, all the features concerned are revealed by positive crop-marks or by a darker tone in bare soil, caused by its greater depth and organic content.

96 *Floodplain of the Evan Water east of Beattock, Dumfriesshire, 7 July 1949*
In addition to a complex pattern of successive river channels the crop-marks show parts of two Roman camps. In the grass field on the right the firm line of a straight ditch is interrupted for an entrance protected by the characteristic Roman device known as a *titulum* (p 98). In the cereal fields on the left a similar ditch turns in a rounded corner, suggesting the presence of a second camp beside the first. The two camp ditches cut through the old river channels, which are therefore prehistoric, but they are also truncated by the modern river as it now returns again northwards.

Some of the small specks in the grass field are sheep; but most of the other spots in the photograph are caused by dust on the register-glass of the camera (p 180).

Streams may be displaced from their channels naturally, as they migrate across their flood-plain, or artifically, by deliberate diversion. The abandoned meanders of major rivers can be encountered at quite a distance from the river-channel in use today. Those that retain some water, even if overgrown, resemble a derelict moat or ornamental lake. Others, now reclaimed for agriculture, will yield strong crop- and soil-marks suggestive of an artificial enclosure bounded by a deep broad ditch. A modern field boundary usually runs across the neck of the meander, obscuring its true nature and seeming to explain why the visible traces of the 'enclosure' are not complete. A similar relationship is seen, at a smaller scale, where a minor stream has been artifically straightened in the rationalization of fields. Crop-marks of its old meanders emerge here and there from the edge of the field and, especially if these happen to be visible on one side of the field boundary only, they may seem to form a line of small ditched enclosures (Dassié 1978, ph 14).

The traces left by a river in the gravels of its flood-plain are not limited to simple, distinct channels of recent origin. More typical is a complex pattern in which countless former channels have left their mark in disconnected intersecting fragments (96). This reflects the state of many rivers at the end of the last (Devensian) glaciation, when enormous quantities of detritus were washed into

97 *Roddon of the Little Ouse east of Littleport, Cambridgeshire, 17 April 1969*
The original confluence of the Ouse and the Little Ouse, before both rivers were diverted into artificial channels, can be seen in the bottom right-hand corner. The bed of the Little Ouse finally dried out in the early seventeenth century. Note the siting of modern farms on the firm ground of its roddon. Soil-marks of the lesser roddons of tributaries and minor creeks extend over the remainder of the picture.

their valleys, and their braided streams occupied a number of channels amid shifting banks of sand and shingle.

The pattern of *former creeks* in reclaimed marshland is usually of interest only to agriculturalists and engineers, but in the Fens of East Anglia, where reclamation began in Roman times, the changing patterns of natural and artificial drainage have obvious relevance to both Roman and post-Roman settlement.

The Fenland can be divided into two areas on the basis of its soils. The southern, more inland area, or peat-fen, retains an appreciable depth of black peaty soil. The light-toned silt levees of extinct watercourses crossing this dark expanse show up from the air with notable clarity when the fields are bare (97) and also furnish negative crop-marks. Within the broad banks of accumulated silt, known locally as *roddons*, narrow ribbons of darker soil mark the final channels of the dying rivers. The roddons now stand up to 2m proud of the surrounding fields, whose level has been lowered by shrinkage and wastage of the peat. In Roman and medieval times roddons provided the only firm ground for crossing the peat-fen from island to island, and they still offer the soundest foundation for modern farms and villages. In the northern area, or silt-fen, virtually all the surface peat has disappeared, exposing a spread of silt identical with that forming the levees. In most parts of the silt-fen such levees are actually indistinguishable on air-photographs from their surroundings, and it is the dark-toned channels which record the natural drainage pattern (25, 101). It can be seen from fig 25 that on Spalding Common the natural drainage had already been superseded at the time the Roman road was laid out, in the second century AD.

Dry valleys are a feature principally of limestone, chalk and sandstone country, though also occurring in gravels and elsewhere. The upper end of each valley system nowadays usually lies in arable land, where it forms a series of hollows in the fields, marked by soil-marks and crop-marks. The pattern made by these hollows is *dendritic*, that is, it resembles the forking branches of a tree, with minor valleys coalescing to form larger ones in several successive stages. Details of this pattern can be an aid to accurate location of archaeological sites seen on air-photographs, especially where fields are large and uniform in shape, since the marks on the photograph can be correlated with contours on the map or with actual topographical detail on the ground. Minor valleys may also occur further down the system, cut in the sides of the main valley. If we return to an arboreal analogy, these are like lesser branches attached directly to the trunk of the tree. They are found both in dry valley systems (61) and also occasionally in the sides of river valleys (54).

The darker tone in soil and crops is caused by the greater depth of soil lying on the valley floor (49). This material is derived from the higher ground either by solifluxion in periglacial conditions (*head*) or by hillwash in the postglacial period (*colluvium*). Similar deposits occur at the foot of slopes of most kinds, especially when they are under the plough. Archaeological sites occurring at the foot of slopes are gradually buried beneath the accumulation, but while this protects the features from subsequent damage, it also conceals all traces from ground and air observation. Thus air-photographs can assist in locating hillwash deposits, but will furnish no clue to the presence of sites buried beneath them, unless these are sufficiently large to extend uphill beyond the limits of the deeper soil.

Although the existence of *former lakes* is often attested by documentary sources, their extent has usually to be established by fieldwork. Observation of soil-marks and crop-marks of the basin will greatly assist in this task (Wilson & Wilson 1982). The extinct shallow meres of the Fens are unusual in two respects. Their bottoms are covered with a white layer of shell-marl; and shrinkage of the surrounding peat has now left the lake beds higher than the general ground level. The sites of the meres are marked by a vivid white ploughsoil which makes the strongest possible contrast with the black soil of the surrounding peat-fen.

Bogs and marsh are usually less well documented than lakes, despite their historical importance as an influence on settlement and a barrier to movement. Former mires are indicated by the blacker colour of the soil, caused by its greater organic content, and by positive crop-marks.

MODERN AGRICULTURAL FEATURES

On arable land the commonest markings to be seen in soil and crop are those resulting from normal farming activities. Almost every agricultural process leaves its traces, and these must be understood if archaeological and geological marks are to be correctly identified and interpreted. Many marks of purely agricultural origin happen to resemble those in which the archaeologist is interested—ring ditches, square enclosures, pits, linear ditches—and great care must be taken in distinguishing them.

Cultivation patterns

The description of ploughing given in Chapter 2 must now be amplified. Ploughing and other cultivations may proceed in accordance with either of two basic schemes. The tractor may work up-and-down the field, keeping parallel with one of its sides, or it may work round-and-round (*on the square*), following each side in turn. In ploughing, it is necessary for successive furrows to be turned in the same direction. The standard mouldboard plough turns to one side only and is thus well suited to square ploughing, but when working

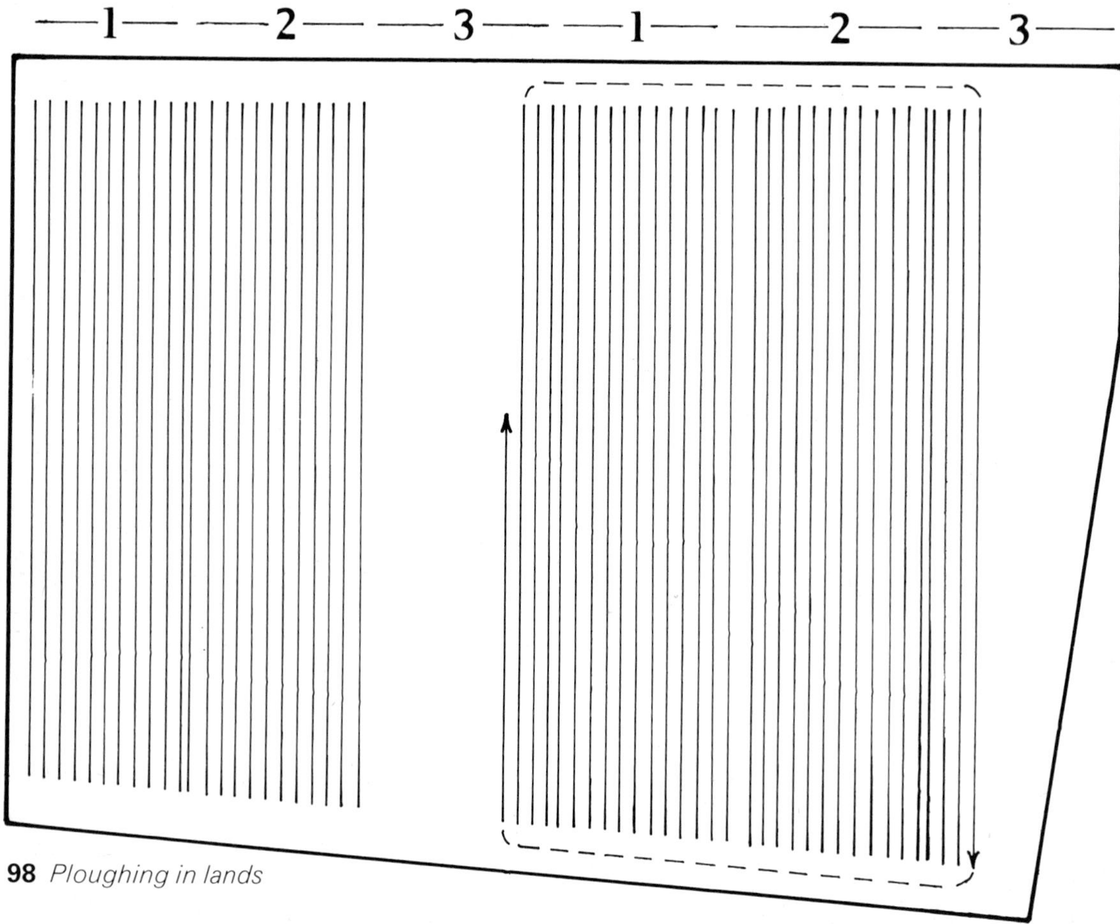

98 *Ploughing in lands*

back and forth it must do so in separate blocks, or *lands*, alternate blocks being ploughed in opposite directions (98, cf 23, 26). A reversible plough, capable of turning the soil either way, need not work in lands, but makes a simple progression from one end of the field to the other (*one-way ploughing*). Headlands are left unploughed at each side of the field for the tractor to turn on and are then ploughed out at the finish. In square ploughing, the headlands run inwards from the corners but are otherwise similar.

Modern tractor-drawn ploughs are capable of making several furrows at a time. Reversible ploughs can manage 2–4 furrows, while standard ploughs may go up to seven (Lambrick 1977, Culpin 1981). The action of ploughing gradually shifts the soil across the field, so the direction of work must be reversed at successive ploughings if the field is to remain even. In square ploughing this means working alternately from the sides to the middle and from the middle to the sides. When a field has been ploughed in lands, there is a slight extra depth of soil where the furrows of adjoining lands have been turned towards each other. This often appears as a positive mark in cereal crops, making a somewhat blurred darker line across the fields (3, 51). At the other side of the land the reverse effect is seen. Adjacent furrow-slices have been turned away from each other, leaving a deeper *open furrow*, usually marked by a clear pale line in the crop (35, 50, 112).

The parallel course of the various cultivations creates a texture or 'grain' in the field as seen from the air. Newly ploughed ground has the appearance of corduroy, but even after

99 *Cultivation pattern north-west of Nafferton, Humberside, 13 February 1970*
A light dusting of snow picks out the individual furrows, emphasizing the envelope pattern characteristic of square ploughing. In the upper field two successive cultivations have followed slightly different courses, causing displacement of the 'envelope'; but the eye tends to ignore this discrepancy and to read the headlands together as a four-sided enclosure.

100 *Longbridge Deverill Cow Down, Wiltshire, 13 April 1955*
A prehistoric field-system adjoins a D-shaped enclosure on chalk downland. Only the 'D' remains unploughed. Dark lines made by young seedlings of a cereal crop mark the envelope pattern of modern cultivation and the ditches of several ancient enclosures. One enclosure is attached to the straight side of the 'D', while a circular enclosure in the foreground only just extends into the ploughed area. The lemon-shaped figure surrounding the 'D' is not archaeological, but an elaboration of the envelope pattern to accommodate the uncultivated ground.

it has been weathered, rolled and harrowed, a directional grain is still present. This effect is repeated in the growing crop, this time through the parallel rows in which the seed is drilled. Any interruption of the even grain is noticeable, and this can make headlands unexpectedly conspicuous through a change of tone in the photograph (54, 100, 102). Crop-marks can seldom be traced across the headlands; but the headlands themselves are very liable to masquerade as crop-marks. This is especially true of fields ploughed on the square, where the diagonal headlands are responsible for a characteristic 'envelope pattern' in the crop (34). When two such fields of equal width lie end to end, a very plausible square enclosure seems to result (99). This is shown to be spurious by the fact that each of the lines of which it is composed exactly bisects the angle made by the sides of the field and runs directly into the corner—a multiple coincidence too improbable to be accepted. When several adjacent fields are square, these apparent enclosures can build up into an extensive system resembling gigantic ancient fields (Wilson 1975, fig 8). Fields with irregular shapes present a special problem to the interpreter, since the siting of the headlands becomes somewhat arbitrary (68); close study of the 'grain' of the field will nevertheless show if it changes direction consistently along a suspected line. Obstacles to ploughing such as electricity pylons, unfilled quarries or boggy ground dislocate the normal cultivation pattern; fig 100 shows how an unploughed archaeological site can distort the envelope into an unfamiliar and misleading form. On a smaller scale, a tractor turning in a tight circle round an electricity pole can create the effect of a ring-ditch; the pole itself is quite inconspicuous from the air, even in an oblique view.

Manuring, crop spraying and irrigation

Organic *manures* are ploughed into the soil before the seed is drilled. Farmyard manure is usually applied in the form of a slurry, but old-fashioned methods of muck-spreading still survive, with successive loads of manure being dumped in the field in a series of heaps, which may stand for a period before being spread. The spots on which these heaps have stood receive more of the liquid content of the manure than the remainder of the field and the crop responds with locally lusher growth. If the manure heaps were originally set out in an orderly array, the resulting crop-marks may seem to indicate the post-pits of a massive timber building (Wilson 1975b, fig 6).

Artificial fertilizers are usually applied in the form of granules from a mechanical spreader, but liquid fertilizers are now being adopted more widely. We have seen in Chapter 2 that nitrogenous fertilizers stimulate vigorous growth and visibly enhance the greenness of the crop. Any unevenness of application is shown by the plants themselves. Those that receive a double measure become greener still (101) and through over-rapid growth develop weak stems susceptible to being laid by storms. Those that are missed remain conspicuously pale. The fertilizer is applied in a broad band, from three to eight times the width of the tractor according to the method used. Fig 113 shows the effect caused by overlapping between bands using a conventional spreader, while fig 107 illustrates the curious pattern made by uneven distribution of granules with a spinner. The pattern of fertilizer application sometimes reinforces that of the previous cultivation, but often takes a different line, crossing the furrows. Large fields are subdivided for convenience into parcels capable of being treated with the contents of a single hopper. The parcels often do not run the full width of the field, but meet near the middle, where additional overlaps (or gaps) are therefore liable to occur (107).

If some fertilizer remains over when the field has been completed but is too little to be worth taking away, it is run out over the field in a second application. The track followed at this stage may be random, whimsical or methodical; it appears on the photograph as an additional line superimposed on the systematic basic pattern. If the tractor should turn in a circle, the interpreter will seem to see a ring-ditch (Wilson 1975b, fig 1); this is parti-

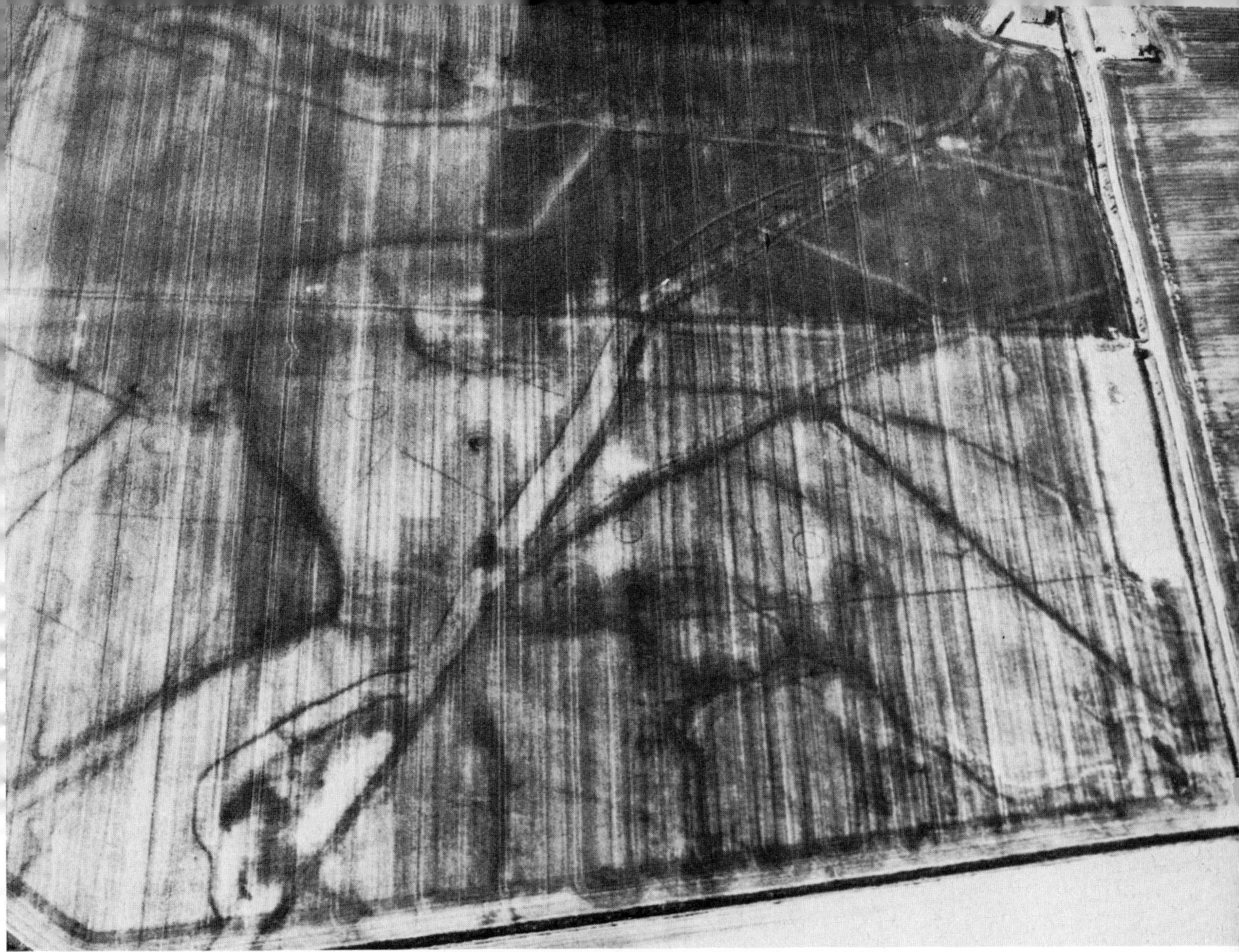

cularly misleading if it lies near the edge of the field where the rest of the track is liable to be lost in the confused pattern of the headland. The tractor will sometimes be driven in a series of concentric circuits in the middle of the field, creating the semblance of a multi-ditched enclosure (St Joseph 1975, pl 23b). Close inspection should reveal that the marks actually form a spiral, but with the fertilizer running out the pattern may not be distinct in every particular.

A top dressing of fertilizer may be applied in the spring or early summer when the crop is already up, and selective *herbicides* are used at much the same time. Timing is important: if the crop is too far advanced, it will be cut back by the herbicide (101), while plants crushed by the tractor wheels will be slow to recover. Clear vehicle tracks often remain visible as well-spaced pairs of parallel lines running through the crop long after all fertil-

101 *Crop-marks beside the Old Croft River, south of Upwell, Norfolk, 29 May 1975*
A spring-sown cereal crop in the silt-fen displays a complex pattern of geological, archaeological and agricultural marks. Differences of tone show where part of the field has received a double application of fertilizer (top right) and where part has been missed altogether (bottom left). In the lighter-toned areas bare soil is still visible between the rows, except where the dark soil filling old watercourses, drains and ditches has favoured early germination, resulting in denser growth (p 56). The field has also been sprayed with a chemical herbicide. In the area that received extra fertilizer, plants forming the crop-marks were too far advanced and were badly affected by the spray; this has caused an abrupt change of tone in the natural and archaeological marks from one part of the field to the next (*interpretation by R Evans*).

Groups of circles bounded by narrow dark lines are just discernible in the foreground. Such circles are a feature of the silt-fen and are probably post-Roman (p 91).

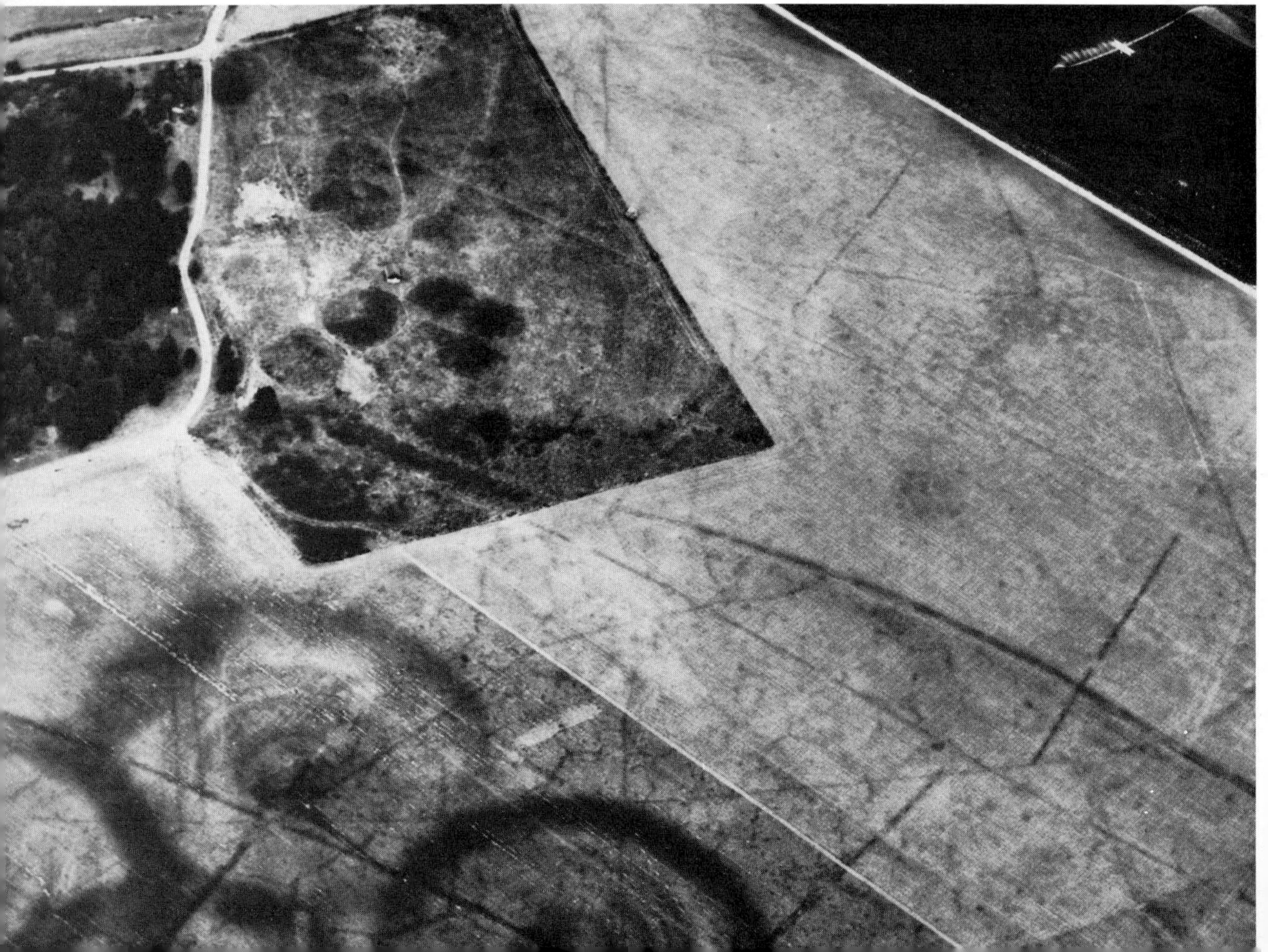

102 *Irrigation-marks south-west of Elm, Cambridgeshire, 21 May 1976*
Three fields in bare soil show residual marks of irrigation with varying degrees of freshness. In the foreground these are being virtually obliterated by harrowing. The shape of the remaining marks in this field indicates that the wind was blowing from the left during irrigation. In the field on the left a single narrow ring appears with clarity; other parts of the irrigation pattern can be identified by comparison with adjoining fields, but would they be detected if seen in isolation?

103 *Irrigation-marks, Sutton Hoo, Suffolk, 15 June 1976*
Irrigation-marks in the foreground have started to fade; they were made by the use of a large rotary sprinkler of the type seen in the top right corner. In the unploughed area to left of centre is the group of Migration-Period barrows which included the Sutton Hoo ship burial. Partly encroaching on the same area is a rectangular system of anti-glider trenches constructed in the 1939–45 War; crop-marks show regular gaps left for pedestrian access (p 173). Other marks are of former field boundaries and of ice-wedge polygons (bottom left).

izer marks have faded (45). Every manœuvre leaves its trace, and tractor turning-circles are particularly deceptive. Similarly, if two U-turns should neatly overlap, as may occur when two areas of work join in the middle of a field, a pair of concentric circles is fashioned which appears at first glance to be unconnected with the main pattern. The fact that it takes a keen eye and a careful search to detect this feature enhances the satisfaction of discovery; but an even closer inspection will show that the double ring exactly corresponds with the other tractor marks and is continuous with them.

Irrigation is carried out as the need arises, either on bare soil or on the growing crop. Mobile irrigation systems are composed of spray-lines, rotary sprinklers or 'rain-guns'. All except the spray-lines are rotating devices which water the surrounding ground in a circle. The smaller size of sprinkler is used in rows about 10–15m apart, which are moved together down the field; the larger devices are usually deployed in ones or twos. In either case irrigation produces a system of overlapping circular marks which are likely to be fresher at one end of the field than at the other. Spray-lines water the field is parallel strips with very little overlap.

On bare soil the immediate effect is to make the soil darker because it is wet, but as the surface dries the areas that received most water are left lighter-toned than normal, because of sorting of the surface particles under the downpour (102). In crops irrigation produces darker growth which lasts until the extra water is used up (103). The water is seldom distributed completely evenly, so the dampest areas show irrigation-marks the longest. This means that the originally uniform disc of darker tone begins to resolve itself into a series of concentric rings (Wilson 1975b, fig 9). An obvious broad ring usually marks the outer limit of the disc, and one or more narrow rings may enclose the centre. These rings will sometimes be distorted into an eccentric oval by the wind. All may appear to represent ring-ditches of some kind, especially if only one or two specimens are visible. The largest size of ring, produced by a large sprinkler or a 'rain-gun', is particularly misleading, since it can readily overlap the field boundary as if unconnected with modern agriculture (St Joseph 1975, pl 23c). If the irrigation has been systematic, however, there will be other rings repeating and overlapping the first, though becoming progressively fainter and thinner across the field.

Field drains and water-pipes

Field drains carry away excess surface water and help to control the height of the water table. They are typically laid in parallel trenches below the ploughsoil, with one or more sets feeding into a main drain or ditch, and are often arranged in herringbone fashion. The narrow trenches cause positive marks in crops (85) and differential drying of the surface in bare soil (p 47).

It is estimated that about 40 per cent of arable land in Britain is well enough drained by nature (Eddowes 1976, 50–1, quoting Trafford 1970), but on medium and heavy soils artificial drainage is a necessity for efficient agricultural production. Crop-marks of field drains are a normal feature of young cereal crops on heavy land, and archaeological marks are not to be expected until well after these have faded. On the lighter soils, where most archaeological marks are in fact seen, field drains are generally required only to cope with special local problems, and their rare appearances can easily deceive. They may combine with other marks to yield a complex pattern of which only certain parts are genuinely archaeological; or a pair of adjacent drains showing more clearly than the rest may be taken as the parallel ditches of a cursus or a Roman road. Parallel drains are normally spaced equally, but this is not invariable.

Field drains will sometimes be sited in relation to archaeological features no longer visible above ground, which still survived in some relief at the time the earliest drains were laid. This occurs in areas to which arable farming came very late, such as parts of Scotland. The hollow of a half-filled ditch, not yet levelled by ploughing, would collect surface water and need to be drained. In Roman camps in Scotland it is not unusual to find an early tile drain inserted in the bottom of the ditch for this purpose. From the air such a drain is concealed within the broad mark of the camp ditch except at entrance causeways, where the ditch comes to an end but the drain is liable to continue. When this happens, there is a danger of falling to recognize the entrance, if the crop-marks are not particularly well defined, since a mark can be seen to continue throughout.

Water-pipes are also laid in narrow trenches below the ploughsoil. A water-pipe may be suspected when crop-marks form a narrow straight line aiming directly for a farmhouse or its outbuildings.

Crop trials

Crop trials are carried out principally at agricultural research stations and experimental farms, where they may extend over several fields (104). When undertaken on ordinary farms they are on a much smaller scale, occupying just a small area sited on the edge or the corner of a field for ease of access. The experimental area is divided into a series of small plots planted with different varieties or managed according to different programmes. It is obviously important to ensure that there is no interference from routine operations in the remainder of the field, and cautious fertilizer application around the trial plots may leave a margin of unfertilized crop which can easily produce a rectangular mark like that of an archaeological enclosure (105). If the crop trials are effective, however, there will be traces of a chequerboard or other regular pattern within the supposed 'enclosure', which will itself be laid out in direct relation to the boundaries of the field.

Further misleading patterns are created if samples are cut from the trial plots before the field as a whole is harvested. The cut areas of crop are small but numerous and form an orderly if not wholly regular pattern; they are linked by the neat paths of the people taking the samples. The resulting pattern looks

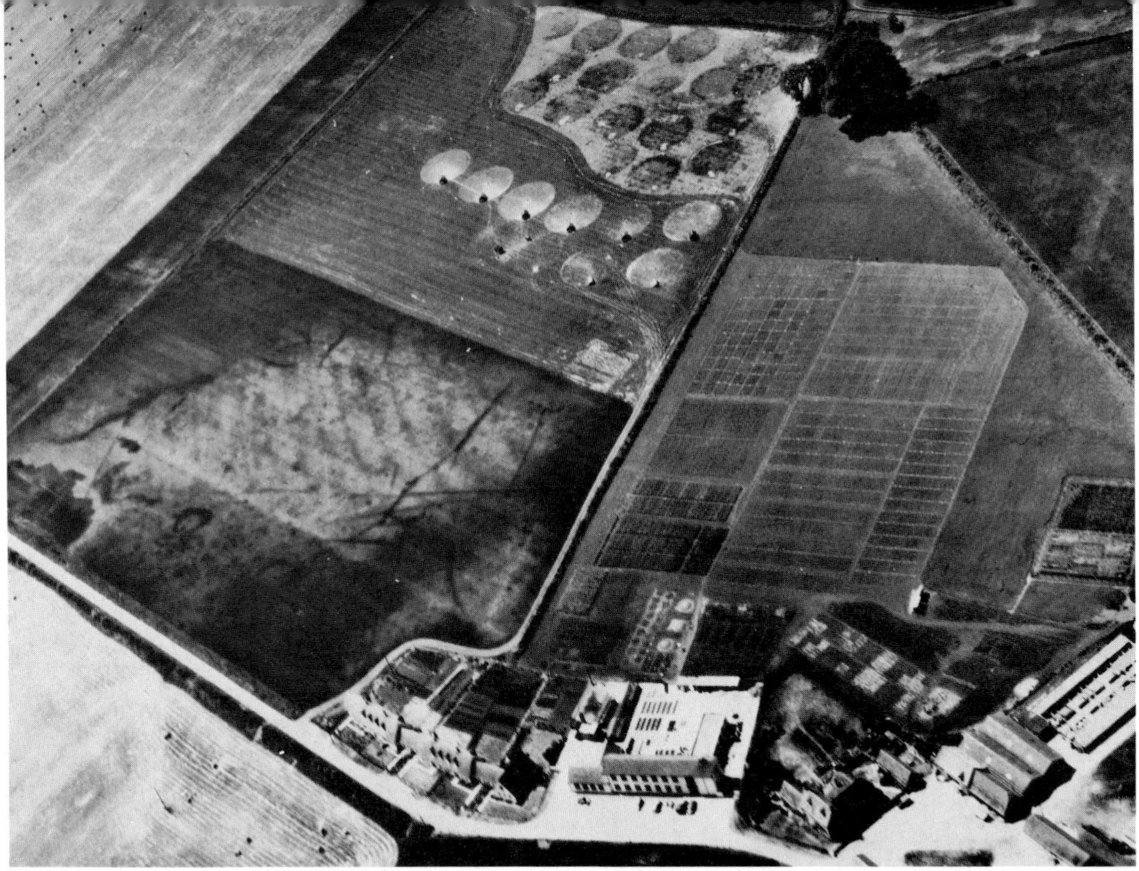

104 *University Field Station, Wytham, Oxfordshire, 19 June 1959*
A variety of agricultural activities is illustrated. Crop trials are visible on the right and controlled grazing in the centre. At the top of the photograph the same grazing pattern is shown at a later stage, when this end of the field has been newly mown, but the grazed areas are already producing new growth. Further to the left a field of cereals shows the faint curving traces of medieval furrows and the bold marks of a filled-in gravel pit. Bales of straw stand in two stubble fields in the two left-hand corners of the picture.

105 *Crop trials, Stracathro, Angus, 22 July 1960*
A square arrangement of 64 small plots is sited close to the edge of the field. A narrow strip along the margin of the experimental area received no fertilizer and therefore ripened first, appearing now as a darker line in the yellow crop. If these marks were regarded as being of archaeological origin they would suggest a square walled enclosure with triangular bastions on two sides, while the lines of plots in the interior might seem to imply its use as a graveyard. The darker triangles, however, are simply the spaces left between bands of fertilizer where the spreader had to turn to avoid the area of crop trials.

106 *Parch-marks east of Southminster, Essex, 16 June 1976*
In the foreground, immediately below a row of pig-pens, parching has revealed an oblong ditched enclosure and various periglacial features in a pasture field. To the right of the pens are clear traces of their former successive positions, while more subdued marks of the same kind to the left indicate that the same pens have crossed this ground before, earlier in the season. Further marks in the field to the right of the road show that this has been grazed in the same way. Both fields contain unpenned animals: sheep on the left, and pigs on the right. In the cereal field beyond, the clearest crop-marks are of a filled-in gravel pit opposite the farm.

something like the plan of a very large aisled structure seen in terms of the negative crop-marks of its foundations (Corbishley 1979). In fact, when examined in detail, this resembles the plan of no known or even probable building, but if the layout of the original trial plots has left no visible trace, no other explanation may seem to be available.

Grazing

The grazing of livestock can be controlled by fences, pens or tethers. As the birds or animals are moved on systematically across the pasture, they leave a distinctive grazing pattern behind them. Heavily grazed areas, only recently abandoned, appear light in tone because the short stems and reduced leaf area of the grazed crop reflect more light (104). As the crop recovers and makes new growth, this effect is reduced so that the marks grow progressively fainter as they are traced back towards the beginning of the sequence (106). If part of the field should have been left ungrazed and is subsequently cut for fodder, there will be a dramatic reversal of tonal values: by this time the grazed areas will be actively growing again and picked out in vivid green, whereas parts that are newly mown will have the same pale appearance as the grazed areas had before (104).

Each method of grazing control gives rise to its own pattern based on a particular geometrical shape. Movable fences are used chiefly for grazing in strips; pens are normally

rectangular; fixed tethers make circles, and sliding tethers produce rectangles with semicircular ends. When these shapes are repeated in close succession across the grazed area, they make an easily recognized pattern, but they may be misunderstood when occurring singly or in small groups. Circles are the most likely to mislead: in a well-known early example a group of five circular marks, obviously suggestive of round barrows, was found to have been caused by the grazing of five tethered goats (Deuel 1971, 25, quoting O G S Crawford). It is entirely to Crawford's credit that prompt field investigation allowed a provisional identification from the photograph to be revised in the light of better information. This story carries a moral for all photo-interpreters.

107 *Site of former wood, north of Petham, Kent, 11 June 1973*
The whole field is covered by a bizarre fertilizer pattern, caused by uneven distribution of granules with a spinner. A line of alternate pale and dark ovals near the centre of the picture is produced by gaps and overlaps in application along the junction between two pieces of work (p 158). Through this pattern can be seen an irregular enclosure, several times reshaped, and speckled with scattered pits, which is still shown on recent maps as being woodland. At its further end the former wood contains a small enclosure, presumably older than the wood but hitherto lost to view beneath the trees, now ploughed and rediscovered through crop-marks.

Woods, hedges and orchards

The former presence of woods, hedges and orchards can be detected on air-photographs by a variety of tell-tale signs, although it is also possible for these to disappear virtually without trace. Among the features which may be preserved, if only below the ploughsoil, are the wood-bank or its accompanying ditch and the cavities from which individual trees have been grubbed out. Details of the surviving field pattern may also furnish clues for the identification of vanished woods and hedges.

Woods more than a century old are almost invariably bounded by a substantial bank and ditch (Rackham 1976). Where a wood has been reduced in size and the ground left unploughed, the wood-bank can be easily traced as an earthwork following the old outline. After ploughing, its buried ditch produces positive crop-marks along the same track. Total clearance of a small wood may thus be marked on the air-photograph by crop-marks of a ditched enclosure perhaps of a shape and size to be mistaken for a prehistoric settlement (107). The shapes of ancient woods are, however, fairly distinctive. Most of those going back to the sixteenth century or earlier have a sinuous outline made up of numerous short curves, though some are partly bounded by straight lengths in zigzag. The groves of eighteenth-century parks take two forms. Those that made a screen of woodland round the margin of the park conform to its perimeter along their outer edge but make a series of varied sweeping curves on their inner side. Those that formed isolated clumps within the park are more liable to mislead, being frequently surrounded by a circular bank and ditch. Large ring-ditches are by no means an uncommon feature of parks that have been converted to arable use, and it is often far from clear without documentary research if these are the remains of contemporary groves or of prehistoric round barrows. Circular and oval plantations are also a feature of the agricultural landscape of the eighteenth and nineteenth centuries, as are narrow belts of woodland whose parallel sides and square ends invite comparison with those of a cursus. Many modern woods, on the other hand, are identical in shape with neighbouring fields.

Cleared woodland can be identified on air-photographs with greater confidence when the interior of an enclosure is dappled with the crop-marks of tree-holes. The marks are usually irregular and often quite vague and ill-defined, merely creating a mottled effect within the enclosure that does not continue outside it. They correspond to the ragged holes left by the dragging out of tree stumps, their outline further blurred by ploughing. There is a strong contrast with marks seen in certain parkland groves which have a distinct rounded outline. These seem likely to represent the pits in which sizeable young trees were originally planted at the time the park was landscaped. The appearance of such obvious pits inside a ditched enclosure enhances its spurious resemblance to a prehistoric settlement (Wilson 1975b, fig 5), but the pits are very large and their spacing leaves little room for actual habitations. Conversely, the plough-damaged remains of a genuine prehistoric settlement can on occasion leave soil-marks or crop-marks that could well be taken for those of former woodland. Correct identification will depend on documentary research and field-walking. Tree-pits on the site of former orchards are seldom deep enough to furnish crop-marks, but when they do occur they show the same highly organized pattern as the living trees (cf 84).

There is also a natural pattern of much smaller holes, which is not confined to specific ditched enclosures but extends like a stippled background across whole fields together (45, 75). These holes are not of a size appropriate to mature timber, but to small trees and bushes; they must derive from the wholesale clearance of scrub on the last occasion that the ground was brought into permanent agricultural use. The pattern is not widely seen because in most places such small tree-holes have not survived; and when they have not been destroyed by ploughing and natural erosion, they may instead be hidden beneath a deep layer of hillwash. These marks are archaeologically important as an index of preservation, since they imply that the subsoil has been little eroded and that even quite shallow archaeological features may therefore be encountered in excavation (45).

Recently cleared woodland may be marked by dark patches of burning in the soil, caused by the scattered bonfires in which unwanted loppings were consumed. These recent fires leave only superficial traces which are soon dispersed. They should be distinguished from the more substantial remains of charcoal-burners' hearths in ancient forest, which have apparently not as yet been recognized from the air in Britain, but are known from parts of the Continent (Agache 1964, fig 263; Léva & Hus 1975).

The removal of hedgerow bushes seldom leaves any trace on air-photographs, but may sometimes be indicated by a blurred darkish line in the crop, marking a narrow band of recently disturbed ground. The lines of vanished hedges are more usually given by the crop-marks of their ditches occurring along one, or occasionally both, of their sides (92). These may be identified as belonging to former hedgelines either by reference to old maps and plans or from their position in the surviving field pattern, which they supplement and may to some degree explain (117). Mature hedgerow trees are sometimes left standing when the rest of the hedge is grubbed out, furnishing a clue to its former presence by their curious isolation.

Other agricultural features

'*Fairy rings*' in grassland can closely resemble ring-ditches. The darker growth of these rings is caused by the outward spread of fungal attack from a central focus of infection. Usually these fungus rings are imperfectly shaped, being modified by local factors or else coalescing with neighbouring rings to form composite figures, but now and again a perfect circle is produced. This can be distinguished from an archaeological ring ditch by the fact that its diameter increases with time. To detect this growth, photographs taken in different seasons are required, but it is not easy to achieve the necessary precision of measurement unless the ring lies close to another feature. The distance between them may then be estimated in terms of the diameter of the ring itself. Best of all for this purpose is the grouping of two or more rings together, since the space between them should diminish at twice the rate and be easily observed.

A distracting feature of grassland in winter is the *distribution of fodder* to grazing livestock. This happens principally in areas of permanent pasture where the slight remains of minor earthworks are most likely to survive. The light-toned streaks across the field where hay has been strewn from a trailer seriously disrupt the subtle pattern of highlight and shadow revealing the earthworks (110) and makes any attempt at detailed interpretation somewhat unsatisfactory. It has to be accepted that this is one of the hazards of earthwork photography in winter.

Farm tracks and footpaths occasionally pass through a growing crop instead of going round the outside (34). If the route is well established, its character as a line of communication to an obvious destination should be tolerably clear, even if it does not actually appear as such on the map. Casual or isolated incursions into the crop are less easily recognised, especially after the crushed plants have had some chance to recover. The mark left by a farm vehicle on some unidentifiable piece of business may thus seem to resemble that of an archaeological site such as a ditched enclosure; it will nevertheless usually lead to a gate or the end of an unmistakable track, which should then arouse suspicion.

The irregular tracks of straying animals make a confused pattern like a tangled ball of string; this is somewhat mystifying when seen for the first time but does not look like anything of archaeological significance.

DISUSED MILITARY SITES

The disused remains of airfields, military camps and modern defensive works could well be regarded as archaeological sites in their own right, with a place in Chapter 3. They have excited little interest as yet, however, amongst archaeologists, who tend to see them as modern intrusions into the 'genuine' archaeological record. Although the line between ancient and modern is arbitrary, it must be drawn somewhere; and the photo-interpreter is usually more aware of twentieth-century military structures as a source of error and confusion than as objects

108 *Crop-marks south-east of Bramham, West Yorkshire, 5 July 1975*
Very clear negative crop-marks in the foreground reveal the foundations of four large buildings, easily identifiable by reference to the hangar still standing beyond them. Other buildings can be traced in a fodder crop beyond and in the turf of former parkland to the left. The curving layout of the buildings is typical of a position on the margin of an airfield. In the absence of surviving buildings, would remains such as these be attributed to an airfield or to an abbey?

worthy of study for their own sakes. Hence their position in the present chapter, despite their considerable intrinsic interest and the importance of air-photographs in recovering details of their former extent and character.

Airfields and military camps

Now that the Ordnance Survey has begun to include details of abandoned airfields on its maps, there is no difficulty in becoming familiar with the characteristic shapes of runways, perimeter track and dispersal points which go to make up the plan of a war-time airfield. Much of this pattern often survives in modern agricultural or industrial use (Taylor 1975b, pl 9); the concrete surfaces, even if overgrown, are easily recognized (68) and may furnish a clue to the identification of other features seen only in terms of soil-marks or crop-marks. Hangars and associated buildings may nevertheless mislead when seen in isolation (108), while bomb-stores and other dispersed buildings may not obviously belong to the airfield at all. On vertical photographs it should be possible to appreciate the significance of scattered buidlings in the area, but detailed views of individual sites could well not be self-explanatory.

The most obvious relics of abandoned military camps and depots are the concrete hut-bases and hardstandings, arranged in orderly sequence along roads or tracks. Even after the concrete has been torn up and the ground ploughed, conspicuous soil-marks are made

109 *Abandoned military camp north of Martin, Hampshire, 3 December 1975*
The water tower serving the camp still stands, but all other buildings this side of the road have been dismantled and removed, and much of the site has been ploughed. Rectangular concrete bases survive in the grass by the road; their sequence is continued by bright, if somewhat vague, marks in the bare ploughsoil and by almost imperceptible crop-marks in a fodder crop.

Soil-marks near the top corner of the photograph are of a ploughed-up round barrow.

110 *Earthworks south-east of Clotherholme, North Yorkshire, 30 January 1975*
A very orderly pattern of rectilinear earthworks covers 25ha between Ripon and Studley Roger. The remains, although mostly unploughed, are extremely slight and can only be recorded in very oblique light. They derive from a temporary hospital and barracks of the 1914–18 War.

The pale slanting streaks near the top of the picture and in the left foreground are where fodder has been distributed for grazing animals (p 167).

by remnants of the hardcore foundations (109). These marks are seldom very precise, and identification will usually depend on recognition of the overall pattern. Sometimes the marks can be related to features of known age: soil-marks of a wartime motor transport park at Naunton (Gloucestershire) clearly overlay those of medieval ridge-and-furrow. Such installations were never marked on contemporary maps, but are often still remembered in local tradition.

Military camps of the pre-concrete age leave less obvious traces, but may still be recognized from the even greater regularity of their layout (110).

Ordnance depots are distinguished by

111 *Earthworks of a searchlight site near Cradley, Hereford and Worcester, 15 December 1972*
The circular searchlight and gun emplacements and rectangular command-post all show very clearly in the midwinter sunshine. Beneath them run the denuded remains of post-medieval ridge-and-furrow.

112 *Crop-marks west of Haynes, Bedfordshire, 6 July 1959*
The photograph displays evidence of four phases of landscape history. The furrows of the medieval open fields appear as dark parallel lines curving slightly towards the top right corner. Scattered isolated trees are relics of the subsequent conversion to parkland (Hawnes Park). A group of penannular ditches in various sizes accompanied by a small rectangular enclosure shows where a searchlight battery was established in the park during the 1939–45 War. And the restoration of this land to arable use since the war, while levelling the earthworks, has also furnished the mechanism for their rediscovery through crop-marks. The pale lines running at intervals across the field are caused by the open furrows (p 156).

113 *Crop-marks north-east of St Michael at Wade, Kent, 26 June 1975*
The zigzag line of a trench-system passes between two ring-ditches, which are presumably prehistoric. To right of the lower ring the trench forks to describe a hexagon. Cultivation patterns crossing each other at right angles make a checked background through which the geological pattern caused by soil stripes is only faintly visible (pp 150–1).

structures devised to minimize the effects of possible explosion. Substantial earthwork banks commonly surround each store, and these were sometimes supplemented by water-filled moats. Stores are usually sited in small groups, with plenty of space between the groups. Movement of explosives was normally by rail, inside as well as outside the depot, each store being reached by its own branch line. When an abandoned depot is overgrown, the fan-shaped system of distributory tracks remains the most distinctive feature.

Searchlight sites

Remains of searchlight batteries are found across much of England. They typically comprise penannular earthworks in two or three sizes, enclosing the gun position, searchlights and ancillary equipment, and usually a rectangular earthwork for the command-post. When these earthworks survive unlevelled, they look very fresh and unweathered and are sometimes obviously later than other datable features, such as ridge-and-furrow (111). After being ploughed, the banks may yield soil-marks (Wilson 1975b, fig 3) and the surrounding ditches positive crop-marks (112). It is the crop-marks that are most likely to deceive, for the grouping of ring-ditches in several sizes is also a frequent feature of round barrow groups. The modern rings will always be interrupted for entrances, however, and will usually be accompanied by a small rectangular enclosure. At some of the sites three middle-sized rings are arranged back to back in a tightly knit cluster which is quite unmistakable (112, cf Wilson 1975b, fig 3).

Modern defensive earthworks

Military trench-systems in Britain, unlike most of those on the Continent, can be identified as practice-works dug during training exercises at the time of the 1914–18 War. They occur widely through much of England but are most frequent in the Isle of Thanet (Kent). The trenches have normally been filled in for safety, but on unploughed ground there is often some residual relief due to compression of the filling. Sites that have been ploughed yield clear positive crop-marks. The trenches were dug in short straight lengths meeting at obtuse or right angles so as to make a zigzag or a castellated pattern respectively (cf Agache 1964, figs 253, 258; Dassié 1978, ph 22). Occasional spurs lead off into dugouts. Fig 113 shows an elaboration in the form of a regular hexagon, offering two alternative routes along the system.

Practice trenches are unlikely to be mistaken for features of another age except perhaps in parks, where fragmentary remains might appear to belong to an abandoned formal garden or to some medieval structure older than the park itself.

In the 1939–45 War various defensive systems were devised to block or hinder possible invaders. Areas of open level ground were made inhospitable to gliders either by rows of concrete 'dragons' teeth' or by a grid of open ditches (103). Crop-marks show causeways across these ditches at regular intervals for pedestrian access, a feature that distinguishes them from ordinary field ditches.

Other areas were crossed by anti-tank ditches, linear obstacles of substantial proportions in which a ditch 6m or more across was bordered by banks of upcast. They were dug for the most part in long straight lengths with angular changes in direction (Edwards 1978b, fig 11·8) and on air-photographs their remains look not very different from Roman and later drains in the Fens and elsewhere (Bradford 1957, pl 5). The changes of direction made close to modern field boundaries are typical of other machine-cut trenches such as pipelines and sewers; but whatever damage may once have been caused to hedges by anti-tank ditches has long ago been made good, whereas the course of pipelines is normally marked by obvious damage (p 174). When crop-marks of this character are associated on the photograph with broken hedges, it is relevant to take account of the date of photography. Before about 1960 an oil or gas pipeline is not at all likely; after that date an incompletely restored anti-tank ditch is equally improbable. The ultimate criterion, in default of ground examination or documentary evidence, must be the actual course of the feature, which can be analysed in terms of its apparent destination (a sewage works—or pumping station?) and its use of the ground.

Other military features

Active artillery and bombing ranges contain many strange objects used as targets or reference markers, but in the nature of things they are photographed seldom, and since the extent of the range is well enough known, few misinterpretations are likely to result. The same cannot be said of abandoned wartime ranges, whose very existence is half forgotten. The most misleading features are ground markers originally laid out in crushed chalk to guide aircraft into the range area. Besides simple arrows, the commonest symbols used were circles, usually with a central dot or cross. Surviving soil-marks could well resemble those of a disc barrow in chalk country (Edwards 1977, pl 11), but would look out of place elsewhere. Crop-marks due to the increased calcium are not so obvious, being usually of low contrast, but tend to suggest some kind of ring-ditch.

Bomb craters, although more commonly noted on the Continent than in Britain, seem surprisingly infrequent. If occurring singly, they are unlikely to be identifiable, but a stick of bombs more or less equally spaced should make a recognizable pattern.

On rifle ranges the most distinctive features are the level platforms of the firing positions, set out at ever increasing distances from the butts. On level ground these are usually raised on low banks, but when there is a slope, the platforms are terraced into it. The resulting lynchets, widely spaced and parallel, may seem like fragments of an early field system, especially if the intervening spaces are in modern cultivation; but if the range is active, they will be linked by a track, which will also lead to the butts, behind which will rise a large, though sometimes seemingly unrelated, earth bank. Other details, such as the flagpoles for red warning flags at each end of the range, may also be visible, if sought with a magnifying glass.

EXCAVATIONS

Any excavation of the subsoil, ancient or modern, is liable to promote crop-marks, regardless of its age. The grave-pit for a dead horse dug yesterday for convenience in the pasture where it fell will appear in terms of crop-marks, once the field is ploughed and sown, just as readily as a pit dug for the same purpose two thousand years ago. All that the interpreter can do is to note a positive crop-mark of a certain size and shape and to conclude that it is likely to represent a pit. The purpose and the age of the pit cannot be determined, though they may sometimes be surmised (not always correctly) from the context in which it occurs.

Some excavations nevertheless have such definite characteristics of shape or size or position that their function can be deduced with tolerable certainty.

Pipelines and sewer trenches

Trenches for pipelines and sewers are dug by machine and may extend for considerable distances across country. They run in straight lines from point to point, with abrupt changes of direction that are sometimes very marked, even right angles not being excluded. Such changes tend to be made close to, but not actually on, a field boundary, so as to give the trench-digging machine some room in which to operate. In rare instances where the pipeline is to cross some feature of acknowledged amenity value or historical importance a tunnel is dug to accommodate it, but in general its course is marked by demolished hedges and scarred earthworks. On some of the more important earthwork sites an attempt is made to restore the original form after the pipeline has been laid, but this is impossible on complex sites and is sometimes quaintly bungled when the wrong sections of bank are subsequently joined together (73)! It is clearly important in the interpretation of earthwork sites to be able to recognize the path of a pipeline across them, for although this may be difficult to trace after a few years have passed, it may have permanently altered the external appearance of the earthworks.

The course of a pipeline can be traced across fields in bare soil as a blurred mark caused by the presence of subsoil brought up into the filling of its excavated trench. The strength of this mark will depend on the brightness of the subsoil. In crops, there is a broad and well-defined band of disturbance which may appear as either a positive or a negative mark according to local circumstances (32). This band may be over 15m wide and at first blots out all archaeological features in its track. The disturbance is superficial, however, and archaeological marks can reappear after a year or two (114). The trench in which the pipe is actually laid is the only place where destruction of buried features takes place to any depth; and this has a width of 1–2m.

Crop-marks of pipelines may be confused with those of Roman or later roads or of linear earthworks with a broad single ditch. They are distinguished by their sharp changes of direction, by the damage to hedges through which they pass, and occasionally by association with a pumping station. On some pipelines there are reflective red markers at intervals, usually on field boundaries, which appear as bright spots of light tone on panchromatic photographs. A comparison between pipelines and anti-tank ditches has been made above (p 173). Underground aqueducts like that from the Elan Reservoirs to Birmingham are in many instances long-established features and differ from oil and gas pipelines in not being associated with visible damage to the environment. Their course is shown on the Ordnance Survey one-inch map, now obsolete, though not on the 1:50,000 map which replaces it.

a

b

114 *Crop-marks near Beeston, Nottinghamshire: (a) 30 June 1975, (b) 29 June 1976*
The photographs show where a pipeline has cut through an unsuspected Iron Age or Romano-British farmstead. Crop-marks reveal one round-house sited at the centre of a rectangular enclosure whose ditch appears to impinge upon another, while a second enclosure, earlier or later than the first, is joined to its northern side. The pipeline goes through one of the junctions between the two enclosures; in the earlier photograph it appears to have destroyed a strip about 16m broad. The later photograph shows that although there has been considerable damage, attested by narrowing of the marks of the prehistoric ditches, total destruction has been very limited. Even the bottoms of some of the medieval furrows seem to have survived.

Sewers are distinguished from other pipelines by their destination: when revealed by crop-marks they are already well on their way towards a sewage works.

Pits and quarries

Small pits and quarries in good agricultural land have always tended to be filled in promptly and reconditioned for continuing agricultural use. Their crop-marks are distinctive and often seen. The steep sides and deep filling of the pits cause strong positive crop-marks with notably sharp edges, often with an outline of reversed tone where the ploughsoil is shallow at the rim of the pit (104, 106). The well-defined edge is very characteristic and permits identification even when the interior of the pit makes a confused pattern because of variations in its filling. Access would normally have been from one side or one corner of the field, but sometimes a softer, more blurred margin to the crop-marks betrays the existence of a sloping ramp down to the floor of the pit.

The irregular outlines of most pits of this kind (51) bear witness to the small scale and unsystematic method of work typical of sand and gravel extraction until very recent times. Sometimes the area dug has evidently been constrained by property boundaries that no longer exist (92). This is particularly striking where the village fields have continued to be held in strips until a late date and the pits conform to these strips (Benson & Miles 1974, map 20). On some sites only a small area was kept open at any one time, successive portions

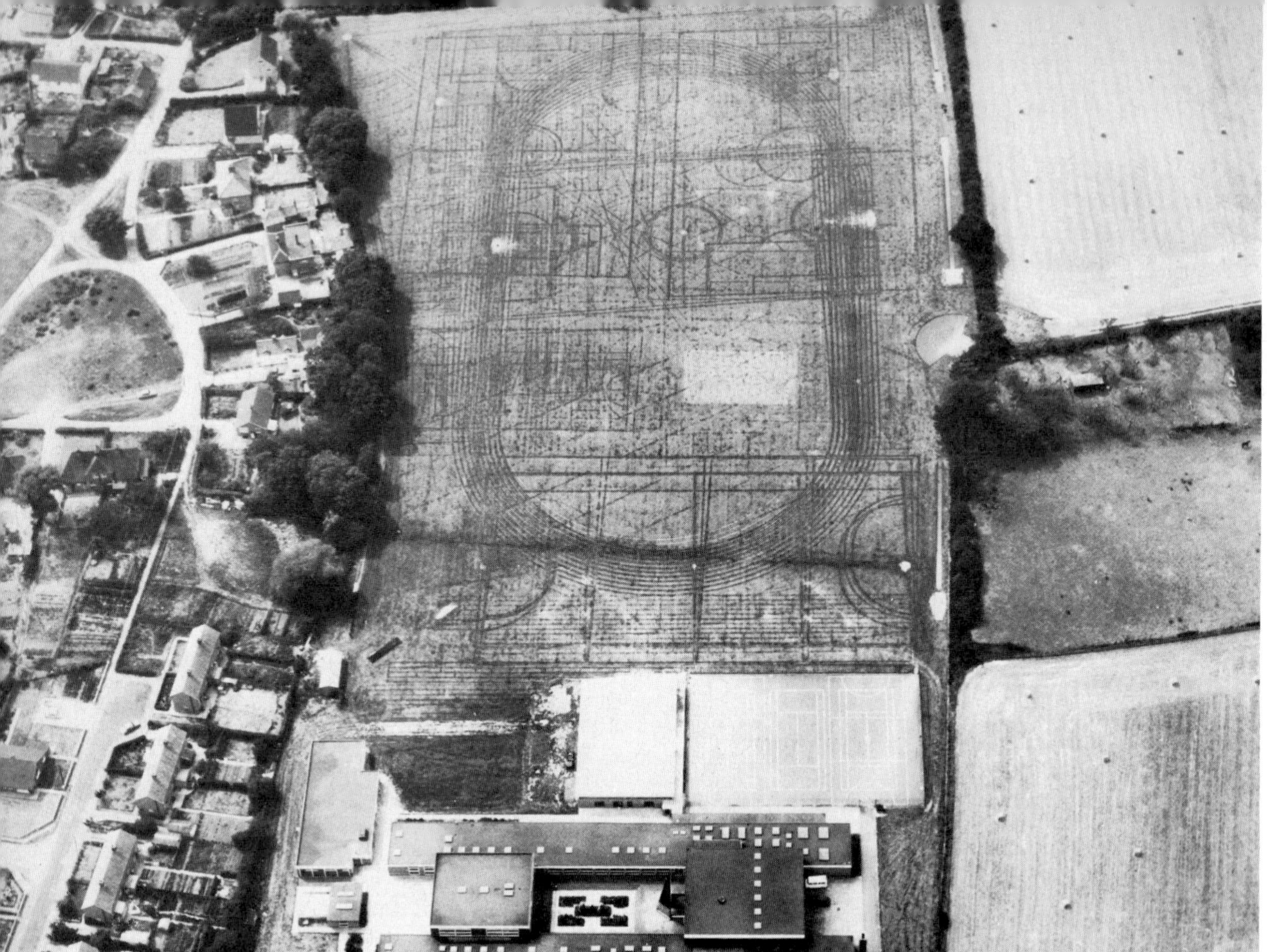

115 *Playing field, Harleston, Norfolk, 5 August 1976*
Severe drought has caused the turf of a school playing field to parch everywhere except over field-drains and along the formerly white lines marking out games pitches and athletics tracks. The layout of at least three successive seasons can be traced for football, hockey and netball as well as for track and field athletics. A pale rectangle near the centre marks the cricket square, and a pale circle near the top seems to be the well-mown green of a one-hole pitch-and-putt course for golf practice.

being dug and backfilled seasonally to maintain maximum agricultural production. To stabilize the ground and to define the limits of the work completed, baulks were left undug between the individual working areas, giving rise to a curious compartmented pattern in the crop-marks. Similar methods of work were used by nineteenth-century coprolite diggers near Cambridge, who opened a succession of parallel trenches, apparently leaving half of the ground undug (St Joseph 1974).

Archaeological excavations

Archaeological sites, once excavated, should be either conserved for permanent display or else reburied, and plans of the remains and of the position of trenches in the excavation should be published. Unfortunately, this does not always happen. When trenches are left open or spoil heaps unlevelled, the overgrown remnants may come to resemble an earthwork site of greater antiquity. There have also been cases where excavation was limited to simple wall-tracing and the unfilled trenches now furnish the only surviving record of the plan then unearthed (67a).

When an excavated site is reburied and restored to agricultural use, there is usually little alteration in the appearance of its crop-marks. Sections through roads or gravel banks, where solid material has been removed, show clearly enough, and when the bottoms of trenches have penetrated into the natural subsoil some marks of these may also be present. This may cause a mottled pattern to come into view on a site dug on the grid system; despite the regularity of the grid itself the effect is variegated by differences in the depth to which individual trenches have penetrated. Provided the excavation has been published, the explanation is easily deduced.

RECREATIONAL USE

Playing fields

Mention has already been made of the white lines used to mark out the field of play, court or track on which many sports take place. The lines are made by applying a solution of ground chalk to the mown grass and they are renewed at intervals during the playing season. The effect can often be to inhibit growth along these lines, but elsewhere it proves beneficial, leaving lines of darker grass after the surface chalk has washed away. If the field should be ploughed, there is a sufficient local concentration of calcium in the soil to reproduce the same pattern of lines both in bare soil, where a difference in water retention causes them to appear as darker damp-marks (information from R. Agache), and in growing crops, where they may form positive crop-marks (Agache 1964, fig 256). On a permanent playing field not subject to ploughing the effects produced by chalk lines survive in the soil for at least three years. Fig 115 shows a school playing field in which severe drought has brought back into view the layouts of three successive seasons.

The markings for each sport are standard, though not always correctly executed (7), and the interpreter should be able to recognize them even from isolated fragments. The most misleading, as well as one of the commonest, of such fragments is the circle at the centre of a football pitch. The regular shape catches the eye, but the eye should also note a straight line bisecting the circle, which proves on close inxpection to be the centre line of the pitch (115). Also deceptive is the penalty box in front of the goal (84). Pitches for rugby, hockey and other games are superficially similar but do not contain such easily misleading elements.

Cricket grounds and tennis courts are most likely to cause confusion if they are associated with a country house. When occasional cricket matches have been played on the lawns in front of some great mansion, traces of the creases combine with the rectangular shape of the closely mown central 'square' to form a pattern that seems to hint at the foundations of an earlier house lying underneath. Similarly, the faded lines of tennis courts, especially if laid out on a levelled terrace, may suggest the former existence of gardens or of buildings of much greater age.

It is rare for genuine buried archaeological features to be detected in playing fields and parks except in times of drought. When a drought does occur, therefore, it is particularly necessary to be on the look-out for marks of sporting origin.

Fêtes, shows and race meetings

Public assemblies in the open air leave their mark on the ground principally through the tramp of many feet. Distinctive patterns are created when crowds of people are attracted to some areas and excluded from others, the worn grass appearing light in tone and the unworn grass darker. This shows up the position not only of stalls and sideshows, but even of parked cars (117). Temporary wooden flooring protects the grass in the short term, but causes yellowing if left down for very long. Thus, a busy tent with no floor will show up as a pale rectangle, while one with a floor in use for only a few hours will be conspicuous for its lack of visible wear (116). The supports for temporary wooden stands, stalls and other buildings will usually leave behind clear lines in the grass defining the shape and type of structure. From a combination of such traces it is relatively simple to identify and distinguish fairs, fêtes, gymkhanas, agricultural shows and point-to-point meetings. Grass-track motor racing, although less familiar, has

116 *Site of a fête, Orsett Heath, Essex, 3 June 1971*
The light-toned marks at the centre of the picture are caused by trampled grass in what was evidently a successful fête on the playing field of the Technical College. The main concourse was surrounded by stalls and tents; an open-fronted marquee with a wooden floor was presumably the refreshment tent. In the middle were a number of stalls of the hoop-la type, in which a central stand is separated from the outer barrier by an open space in which the stall-holder circulates.

117 *Playing field north of Worcester, 12 July 1975*
The playing field furnishes evidence both for its past history and for its recent use. Darker lines in the parched grass trace the boundaries of the smaller fields out of which it has been created. Other lines crossing these obliquely possibly indicate an earlier field-system. At the top of the picture a triple-ditched four-sided enclosure is likely to have been a late-prehistoric farmstead. Further down, the very faint traces of three football pitches are overlain by the marks left by grass-track racing. The actual circuit is of much the same size and shape as an athletics track (cf fig 115), but shows considerable wear and no lane divisions. All round it have been lines of parked cars, their positions marked by rectangles of untrodden grass round which crowds of spectators have walked back and forth.

118 *Riding school, Wramplingham, Norfolk, 1 June 1977*
Late-evening sun picks out every variation of growth in a grass field, revealing the exercise tracks of a riding school as well as other tracks left by vehicles. The older tracks, where the grass has had some time to recover, are fainter than the recent ones; and there are overlaps. At the top of the photograph riders have made circles and figures-of-eight within a series of rectangular outlines, whose sharp corners have been imprinted on the turf by lengths of portable wooden fencing.

its own distinctive patterns (117). Individual features such as hoop-la stalls or racing circuits may appear to simulate archaeological sites, but if viewed in their full context, the correct interpretation should not remain in doubt.

Riding schools

Fields used for riding instruction are identifiable by the worn tracks left by pupil riders. These are usually simple ovals or circles, but more elaborate figures are used in advanced schooling and these may be guided by temporary movable rails (118). As long as the field continues in use, the fresh tracks provide an explanation for the older ones; but once riding ceases, there is a danger of seeming to see circular or oval archaeological enclosures. Sometimes the field also contains jumps, but usually the only clues are provided by the pattern of the tracks themselves and the variation in strength of the marks.

PHOTOGRAPHIC BLEMISHES

Air-photographs are intended to be a full and accurate record of the appearance of a particular piece of ground. Unfortunately, other marks can appear on the final print that have nothing to do with the subject matter of the photograph. The utmost care and cleanliness are required at all stages of the photographic process if such blemishes are to be avoided. The extraneous marks are misleading because of the enormous difference of scale between the photograph itself and the scene it represents. A speck of dust which appears tiny in relation to the size of the negative will seem to be a substantial feature if interpreted as part of the landscape being pictured.

Ideally, of course, such blemishes should not occur; but air-photographs are sometimes taken in hectic and difficult conditions, and they cannot be repeated at will if faults are later detected. When it is possible to take similar photographs on a subsequent occasion, they frequently fail to show significant detail which was present on the flawed original exposures. As to blemishes occurring in the darkroom, the reader should remember that the standard size of roll film for a survey camera is 241mm ($9\frac{1}{2}$in) wide and 76·2m (250ft) long and feel some sympathy for the difficulties of handling it. In practical terms, we must make use of the photographs we have, whatever their source and condition, and make the best of them we can.

The photo-interpreter must be on his guard against blemishes produced by a wide variety of causes.

a *Dust* on the lens will be so far out of focus as to be invisible; but when it occurs on the register glass, fitted in front of the film in some aerial cameras, the specks are reproduced full-size in the photographic image, blotting out the equivalent portion of the intended picture. Similarly, dust on the negative will appear in the corresponding print. In either case the intrusive specks may seem to be features of the actual landscape (cf 96).

b *Smears and fingerprints* on the negative are the result of inadequate wiping down and careless handling. They are reproduced on the print as marks overriding the original image, but when the background is even-toned they appear to be integrated with it, so perhaps creating bogus crop-marks. It is nevertheless essential that the film *is* wiped clean of water after the final wash, or else drying marks will result, individual drops of water leaving discoloured spots behind them on the surface as they dry. These too may assume the guise of crop-marks.

c *Physical damage* to the emulsion can occur in a variety of ways. The commonest is scratching, caused principally nowadays by plush lining the mouths of cassettes, but possible whenever the undeveloped film is wound on or off its spool. Scratches normally appear on the print as narrow dark lines parallel to the sides of the film (8, cf 46); whether they are vertical or horizontal depends on the design of the camera. Besides scratches and other forms of abrasion (34, 82), the emulsion is also damaged by excessive pressure. This can occur even

during routine processing. The end of the film is regularly attached to the spool by clamping it into a narrow slot in the spool's surface; on emerging from this slot the body of the film does not take up the curve of the spool instantly, causing slight but definite outward pressure in a bar across the format. This can be felt through several layers of film as it is wound back and forth and causes pressure marks across any exposed frames in this position. Damage also occurs if the film flexes and buckles during winding; this produces a crescent-like mark, appearing dark on the print.

d *Electrostatic charges* affecting the photo-

119 *Green Dikes under snow, north of Nafferton, Humberside, 1 January 1971*
Winter lighting and a thin mantle of snow combine to pick out the low mound of a prehistoric dyke crossing ploughed fields on the Yorkshire Wolds. A light-toned band running from top to bottom of the picture near its right edge is caused by a variation in sensitivity of the photographic emulsion. At the same time, however, irregular marks of slightly darkened tone seen in many of the fields in this landscape are not photographic blemishes, but are caused by variations in the scouring action of the wind on the snow-covered surface, some of which are due to gaps in windbreaks (p 36).

graphic image can build up during photography on either a very cold or a hot and humid day. This is most troublesome with cameras in which the film is transported by pinwheels engaging in the margins of the film. Irregular marks centred on the pinholes loop across the picture from either or both of the margins; their blurred edges and the combination of light and dark tone give them a spurious resemblance to soil-marks. Static marks may also occur during processing, if the film is not handled correctly.

e *Faults in manufacture* are not normally to be expected since production standards are very high. If certain rarely encountered blemishes are placed provisionally under this heading, this should not be construed as criticism of any individual manufacturer or of the industry as a whole. The first of these blemishes is an irregular, sometimes intricate, mark recurring like a blot at intervals through the film. The lateral position within the format is constant but the vertical position changes, since the spacing is usually out of phase with that of exposures on the film. Even if the shape of the blot is plausible and interesting, it is shown to be intrusive by its exact repetition on later photographs of different subjects. The second blemish is a variation of photographic sensitivity, causing a slightly wavy line of darker or lighter tone running more or less vertically at a variable distance from one edge of the film (52, 119). When seen against an appropriate background, this can be mistaken for an archaeological feature such as a linear earthwork or a Roman road.

This list is not exhaustive, but it is sufficient to indicate that the interpreter must stay alert for marks of purely photographic origin. They are most easily detected on the negative, where both physical damage and surface smears are readily seen by anyone looking for them, and any mark extending into the unexposed margins of the film must be a photographic blemish of some kind. When looking at prints, it is useful to see successive exposures, or at least several views of the same site taken on the same occasion. Marks reappearing on all the prints in the same position *in relation to the ground* are genuinely part of the landscape and may be considered for possible archaeological significance; but those reappearing in the same position *in relation to the frame of the photograph*, however convincing they may seem to be, must be judged as spurious. Similarly, a mark of distinct shape that recurs in identical form on different photographs, even though in varying positions, can only be a blemish of photographic origin. Photographic blemishes, being independent of the scene portrayed, run across details of every kind. What appears to be a linear crop-mark may be seen on close inspection to go over the top of a hedge or a house or even onto some portion of the aircraft if that is included in the picture.

5

Interpretation

Successful photo-interpretation is based on twin foundations: a good understanding of the *medium*—that is the mechanisms whereby archaeological sites are made visible on air-photographs—and a detailed familiarity with the *material*—that is with the appearance of both archaeological and other features on the photographs. These have been the subjects of preceding chapters. Proficiency is achieved by practice and experience; but, while there is no substitute for these, some guidance can usefully be given on suitable procedures to be followed and on valid principles of interpretation. In particular, attention must be drawn to the limitations of the evidence especially of crop-marks, which will often exclude what might at first sight seem to be attractive conclusions.

Aids to interpretation

Photo-interpretation requires few mechanical aids but there is almost no limit to the amount of background information that may prove to be of value.

The most important general aid is a magnifying glass. The serious interpreter can no more be separated from his magnifying glass than the excavator from his trowel. The diameter should be not less than 100mm (4in), to allow both eyes to focus on a sufficient area of the print at the same time. In use the glass should be held quite close to the face, for the same reason, and the print then brought up to the point where it is in focus. The correct positions are determined by experiment in relation to the individual eye. High magnification is not what is needed: × 2 is sufficient to reveal fine detail that might otherwise be missed with the naked eye. The object is to recognise significant pattern, not to study the individual elements (plants, clods or tussocks) of which it is composed, still less the photographic grain by which they are represented.

When the photographs include some in overlapping series, each overlapping pair should be viewed with a stereoscope so as to recapture the third dimension. This is of greatest use in studying earthworks but gives additional precision to the interpretation of all types of site. The two overlapping prints are laid out side by side so that their similar portions are placed next to one another (120). When examined through a stereoscope, part of the left-hand print is seen by the left eye and part of the right-hand print is seen by the right eye. If corresponding parts of the two prints are correctly related to each other and to the stereoscope, the two separate images are fused and a three-dimensional image then results. For this to turn out successfully, the size of the stereoscope should be appropriate to that of the prints. Thus, a pocket stereoscope, with fields of view separated by only 60–65mm ($2\frac{1}{2}$in), cannot be used properly with prints larger than 125mm (5in) wide. For vertical photographs in the standard format, 230mm (9in) square, a mirror stereoscope is needed. This type of instrument normally has a binocular attachment allowing small selected areas to be scrutinized at a magnification × 4; this is ideal for detailed study of low earthworks.

The most useful topographical map for purposes of photo-interpretation in Britain is the Ordnance Survey map at 1:25,000. This gives the subtlest rendering of contours, while including full details of field and property boundaries. The nearer the date of revision of the map sheet to the date of photography, the

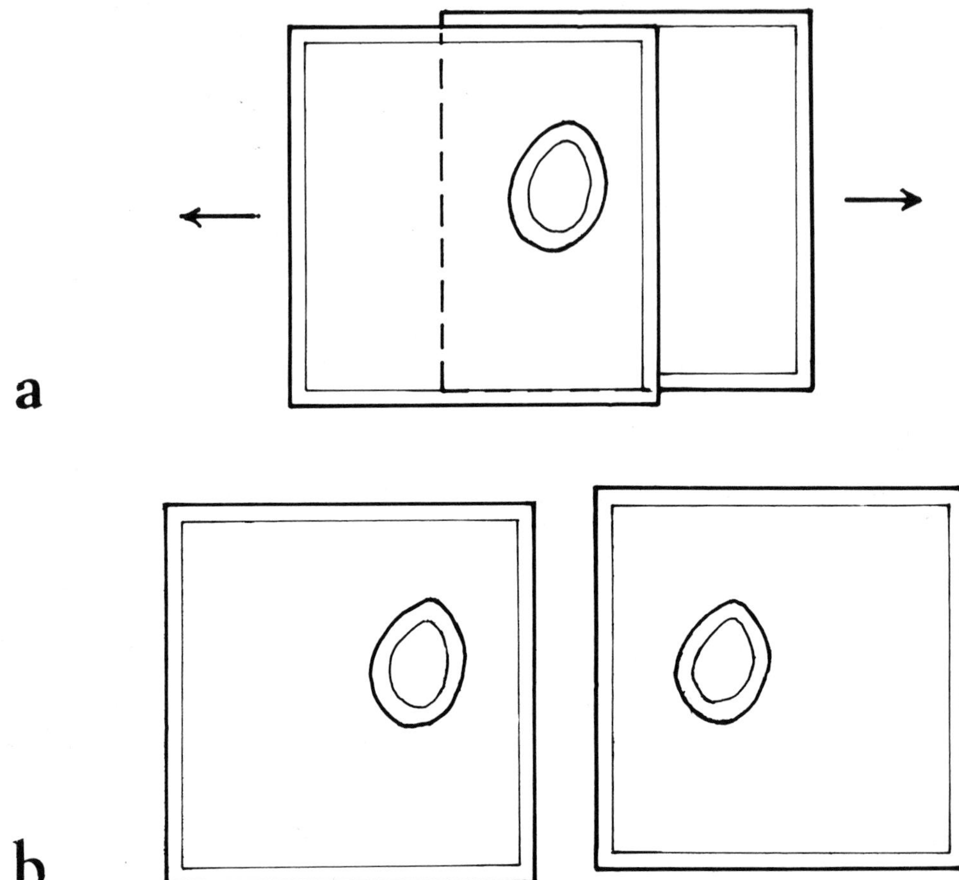

120 *How to position a stereo-pair correctly for viewing with the stereoscope*
(*a*) The two photographs with their corresponding portions overlapped: they should then be drawn apart in the direction of the arrows, as at (*b*).

closer the correspondence to be expected between details on the photograph and map. We should not, however, overlook the usefulness of older editions which, being outdated, show details of field boundaries, woods and buildings that have now gone but may have left traces still to be seen on the photograph.

Geological information is given on the maps of the Institute of Geological Sciences at 1:63,360 or 1:50,000. Solid and drift geology are sometimes represented together, sometimes printed on separate sheets. Reference should also be made to the maps of the Soil Surveys of England and Wales and of Scotland at 1:63,360 or 1:25,000, where these exist. For most archaeological purposes, however, and certainly for analysing the development of crop-marks, the classification of soils used on these maps is too fine; their data need to be understood in the framework of a broader classification like that of Avery (1973).

The archaeological information required for interpretation is both general and particular. In general, the interpreter should be familiar with the character, and especially the ground-plans, of the different types of archaeological sites so far known in Britain and the nearer parts of Europe. He should also have some knowledge of what kinds of site have turned up in the district with which he is concerned, forming what may be provisionally regarded as the local archaeological repertoire. More particularly, he needs details of all archaeological finds made on or near the spot being studied on the photographs. Such details should be available in the County Sites and Monuments Record or equivalent archive and may be supplemented by the results of fieldwalking newly undertaken for the purpose.

Looking at the photographs

It should not be necessary to repeat that all available air-photographs of a given site should be examined. This gives the best chance of benefitting from differences of viewpoint, of lighting, of cultivation and of plant growth, according to the time of day, the season and the year. Numerous examples have been given in earlier chapters of the additional information to be derived from photographs taken in different conditions (eg pp 29, 65, 68) or at intervals over a period of time (pp 68–9, 167). Where the site extends over several fields, it may take photography over many years to establish its complete plan. Moreover, when a site, large or small, has been photographed regularly over a long period, the photographs record its history during that time, including the results of progressive erosion or destruction, if this has been taking place. Earthworks may then be compared with successive soil-marks and crop-marks; or changing patterns of soil-marks may bear witness to continuing damage by the plough.

The careful archaeologist will always hesitate to interpret from a single photograph. Even if it is the best there is—and how can he say without seeing the others?—there are so many possibilities for misunderstanding and error in a single view that to rely on that alone must be counted a desperate expedient. If there are several photographs, taken on the same occasion but at least from different viewpoints, this is a little better, for he can then begin to see the site in the round, in a figurative as well as in a literal sense. But it will not be until he has seen the site on a number of different occasions that he will feel he is getting to know it at all well. What appears very striking one year may seem less important in another, or even spurious. Conversely, those features that reappear over several seasons, even if initially unconvincing, cannot be dismissed as mere agricultural accidents or photographic blemishes, but call for some deeper explanation.

Despite these comments, it will usually be convenient to select some of the best or most informative photographs to work with during the main phase of interpretation. This selection should naturally be made on the basis of a critical review of all the relevant photographic material. Furthermore, the rejected photographs should not then be simply forgotten. After study of the selected few, the interpreter should return to the remainder for a further scrutiny, in case there should be missed details, previously unintelligible or unobtrusive, whose meaning had now become plain.

Every photograph should be studied both with the magnifying glass and with the naked eye. This is not just a question of optics but also of mental receptivity. There is a danger of becoming so preoccupied with fine detail that large patterns become virtually invisible. A conscious effort does, in fact, have to be made to search for features at widely varying scales, and this requires considerable mental readjustments. It can be valuable to relax the attention slightly for a moment while scanning the print; recognition of a previously unseen feature will often follow. This is something which is liable to happen during conversation with a colleague, for instance.

It will be found that the naked eye and the magnifying glass do not always seem to tell the same story. When viewed through a magnifier, some suspected features become more definite, but others seem to disintegrate entirely. This vagueness in close-up must be taken into account, but it does not automatically disqualify the candidate. Both methods of inspection are equally valid, and each must be evaluated independently. If at the second and third look the feature still appears to have reality, it can be accepted, whatever its appearance beneath the magnifying glass. It is in fact possible sometimes to get too close to something to see it clearly.

When air-photographs are used as an aid to field survey, the best results are obtained if the photographs themselves are taken into the field for comparison with the ground. This is as true for archaeological fieldwork as it is for geology, ecology and environmental studies. In combination air-photographs and fieldwork make a whole that is greater than the sum of its component parts. Understanding of features on the ground is improved by reference to their appearance from the air, while understanding of the photograph is enhanced by the identification and examination of the features on the ground. Fieldwork also serves to re-establish a sense of human scale that is easily lost in the bird's-eye view. At a mundane and very practical level routine field checks can sometimes prevent or correct elementary errors of interpretation, like the circles seen by O G S Crawford on a photograph, which proved on local investigation to have been made by tethered goats (p 165).

Analysis

Analysis of an air-photograph should begin with appreciation of the topography, geology and modern land use. This comes to be done semi-automatically, and in familiar terrain it is hardly done consciously at all; yet for effective interpretation it remains essential to maintain a real awareness of the scene as a whole. An example may be taken from those areas where old irregular small fields have been amalgamated in recent times into much larger parcels. It usually happens that crop-marks of the vanished field-boundaries are the clearest crop-marks in the area. For anyone viewing the landscape as a whole identification of these former fields is obvious and immediate from the patterns that they make in relation to surviving boundaries, but if attention is concentrated exclusively on areas of crop-marks without reference to the modern world around them, the old hedge-lines may easily be misunderstood and misidentified.

Before seeking archaeological features on the photograph it is, in fact, useful to try to recognize (and thereby eliminate) any marks or structures of non-archaeological origin.

By far the commonest crop-marks are those produced by modern farming. These are bound to occur in all places where there is a crop capable of furnishing crop-marks at all. Numerous instances were cited in Chapter 4 of potentially misleading markings. Some of the warnings given there may be summarized in a single comprehensive rule: *be suspicious of all lines that run parallel to any of the modern field boundaries, or bisect the angles made by the corners of the fields, or happen to emerge from gateways.* They *may* represent archaeological features, but they are far more likely to be agricultural, and it is best not to accept any such mark as having archaeological significance without a really compelling reason. It does, nevertheless, need only a slightly divergent angle to distinguish a given line from the general cultivation pattern (cf 88); and while this does not guarantee its archaeological respectability, its credentials are undoubtedly enhanced. Might it then be a drain or a pipeline? If neither of them is plausible, it is probably time to consider an archaeological explanation.

Geological crop-marks are less widely seen, yet are always potentially present. They are distinguished from archaeological marks principally by their pattern, if not too fragmentary; yet it can be remarkably difficult to do this, especially where archaeological and geological patterns of similar scale overlap. When this happens, the archaeological marks can generally be recognised by their greater coherence and more precise outlines (85, 89, 95). Geological marks, by contrast, are often blurred, meandering or incomplete. This presupposes, of course, that the archaeological features are well preserved and the crop-marks tolerably clear. If the sides of a ditch have fallen in and part of its course has been lost through erosion, it will hardly be surprising if it begins to look rather more 'geological'.

Careful attention needs to be paid to the identification and understanding of repetitive patterns. It often happens that only one or two elements of such a pattern are clearly seen, either because of the growth of the crops or from the nature of the pattern itself. It is not unusual for clear crop-marks to be limited to certain parts of a field because of variations in the depth of soil. Although apparently unrewarding, it is then essential to scrutinize the remainder of the field in detail, for if a general pattern can be detected there, however dimly, it may transform the interpretation of the marks first noted. In this way a pair of parallel ditches may be seen to form part of a system of field-drains, or the ditches apparently defending a local summit may prove to be linked to the outcrop of certain geological strata.

A different effect is seen where marks of similar or identical shape are repeated across a field with gradually diminishing strength. This is not due to variations in the soil, but to the recent progress of some modern activity over a period of time. Examples are provided by controlled grazing of livestock (106), irrigation with movable sprinklers (102, 103), and the successive exercise-tracks of riding schools (118). If all the marks are faint, only the strongest will readily catch the eye and will tend to be interpreted in isolation. It follows that, whatever he may be looking at, the interpreter should remain alert for similar shapes nearby, however unobtrusive, faintly echoing those that he has already seen.

The extent of any pattern should be considered in relation to the modern fields and to archaeological sites already identified. If it is coextensive with a single modern field, there is a good chance that it results from the agricultural treatment of that field, even if the pattern itself is puzzling and the process responsible therefore obscure. Similarly, a pattern that is limited to the interior of some archaeological enclosure is likely to be directly related to it, like pits within a settlement. Such conclusions must, however, be based securely: are all the supposed pits contained within the perimeter ditch of the settlement, or is it just that the presence of the ditch makes those particular pits more conspicuous? If, on further inspection, they are found to continue across some of the rest of the field, it will no longer be safe to attach any archaeological significance to their presence within the enclosure. It is worth giving some thought to the siting of the settlement also. If this is closely controlled by the topography, perhaps occupying an island formerly surrounded by marsh, distribution alone can hardly serve as a basis for distinguishing between geological and archaeological marks, which can only be separated on their intrinsic appearance.

In seeking for significant pattern, whether in earthworks, soil- or crop-marks, the interpreter should recognise his own predisposition to see regular figures, especially continuous lines and circles. A critical inspection will often show that such figures have little basis in observable fact, being chance associations of a variety of agricultural, geological and indeed archaeological marks, unrelated to each other except in their accidental juxtaposition. The eye tends to leap on from one mark to another and the mind reads them as if they were really one. It would be unrealistic to expect every genuine archaeological feature to appear on the photograph complete, uninterrupted and unblemished; but it is vital to be clear how much of it is really visible and how much is legitimate conjecture or simple speculation.

It is in this context that putting down your interpretation on paper can provide a valuable discipline, since this entails definite decisions on what is sure enough to draw and what is safer left out. Such decisions are not easy and, although we must be careful not to fudge the evidence, they do not depend on the visible appearance alone. The level of confidence commanded by a particular series of marks is at least partly a function of our existing knowledge of the site. Thus, when identifying an archaeological site from crop-marks for the first time, we have to see them with a very fair degree of clarity in order to recognise the site at all; yet once it is known, its position can be detected from marks that previously would have been thought too faint or indistinct for interpretation, and some of these faint marks may even be accepted as adding new details to what is known. There is nothing unscholarly in making use of prior knowledge in this way, but it makes it all the more essential to be rigorous in noting explicitly what marks are really present and what are merely wishful thinking.

121 *Crop-marks near Barton-under-Needwood, Staffordshire, 30 June 1975*
A variety of archaeological marks are revealed by parching in grass: these include a double pit-alignment (bottom left), a ring ditch (centre) and an overall pattern of medieval furrows. A farm track crosses the ring ditch at two places, obliterating it on one side but not the other. The ring is surrounded by a wheel-like arrangement of smallish pits (p 76), of which less than half are actually visible on the present photograph.

Crop-marks may be incomplete or imperfect for a variety of reasons that have nothing to do with the underlying archaeological features. One of the commonest reasons is variation in the depth of soil. This may be caused by the filling up of natural hollows such as dry valleys, old river channels or kettle holes, by the accumulation of hillwash at the foot of slopes, or by rivers spreading alluvium over their flood-plains. Wherever the soil is deeper than normal there will be an overall positive crop-mark in which individual archaeological marks cannot be traced. This affects our knowledge of a number of Neolithic causewayed enclosures sited close to streams, for which crop-marks reveal perhaps three-quarters of an oval circuit but leave the side nearest to the stream largely undefined. Although there is ample room for the circuit to have been completed in each case, this cannot be verified by air-photography, as the depth of alluvium along that side precludes the appearance of any archaeological detail.

Agricultural patterns also interfere with the

visibility of crop-marks. The headlands along the ends of arable fields are particularly awkward areas: the confused patterns of over-lapping tracks make a difficult background on which to trace archaeological features, especially if they bear any resemblance to a tractor's turning circle. The same is true of the diagonal 'headlands' produced by cultivations on the square, which are associated with a peculiarly distracting fertilizer pattern made of triangles arranged like the teeth of a saw. By contrast, the smooth textures typical of cereal crops in other parts of the field generally give less trouble, but even there the cultivation pattern can cause narrow marks running across the 'grain' of the field to break up and lose continuity. Even field-drains have been observed picked out entirely in lines of dots. This re-emphasizes the value of seeing the appearance of all archaeological features, but especially crop-marks, in more than one season so that allowance can be made for freakish manifestations.

In grassland much of the visible pattern, in the absence of earthworks, is caused by surface texture. Rough long grass appears darker on the photograph than a mown sward because of the texture alone, and the carefully rolled surface of a golf green or cricket square stands out as an area of specially pale tone (115). For this reason tracks made by pedestrians or vehicles, even if not worn down to bare soil, show up as clear pale lines where the grass has been flattened. These patterns of modern use often override any archaeological marks that may be present and simply obliterate them. Thus a vehicle track crossing the dark line of an archaeological ditch can press down the grass into a smooth surface that is lighter in tone, thereby creating the impression that the ditch is interrupted by an entrance causeway (121). Similarly bogus entrances can also be caused by simple destruction of the archaeological remains, as when an unobtrusive pipeline slices through an earlier ditch; if the crop-marks of the ditch are much more obvious than those of the pipeline, the latter may escape notice altogether.

The advantages of a snow-covered landscape for the study of earthworks were described in Chapter 2. This does not alter the fact that such a landscape is unfamiliar and may contain paradoxical features. If the snowfall is not heavy, some sheltered spots may receive none at all and appear conspicuously dark-toned. This often produces a kind of 'snow-shadow' in the lee of hedges or behind trees and buildings, on their south or southwest side. When the sun comes out, it throws a conventional shadow on the north side of the same features, but this is less dark because it falls on unbroken snow. Thus the darker side of the hedge is in fact the sunny side, which is contrary to normal experience and easily leads to misunderstanding. Archaeological earthworks may then be inadvertently understood as if 'inside out', with banks appearing as hollows and vice versa. As the snow melts in the sun, it is the shadowed areas that remain white the longest, thereby continuing to produce an effect contrary to what is ordinarily expected.

Archaeological interpretation

There are two essentially different questions that the interpreter must ask himself:

1 What can I see on the photograph?

2 What do I think it means?

These represent successive stages in interpretation and are concerned with different data; their answers, although often closely linked, must always be treated as separate.

The first question is one of *recognition* of archaeological features; it is concerned with the photographic image and seeks to infer the physical remains portrayed. This involves interpretative judgments, but the answer is expressed in purely descriptive terms: '*a pear-shaped arrangement of pits at 2m intervals*'.

The second question is one of *archaeological interpretation*; it is concerned with the physical remains already identified and seeks to explain them in terms of current archaeological thinking. It is thus the second storey in a house of cards, equally vulnerable to the collapse of the lower storey and to its own instability. This should not be forgotten.

It is easiest to distinguish between archaeological interpretation in this sense and simple recognition when the interpretation is actually unknown. In the example already cited we can say virtually nothing about the archaeological character of the site; even to describe it as a fenced enclosure is tendentious and quite possibly mistaken. With more familiar types of site it is easy to fall into the way of treating the obvious archaeological interpretation as if it were a straightforward factual description: '*What is it?*' . . . '*It is a cursus*'. This does no harm provided that a more deliberate and cautious analysis is invoked in retrospect, by going on to ask, '*Yes, but is it really?*' This questioning of archaeological assumptions, however obvious they may seem to be, must be completely automatic. Indeed, no archaeological interpretation, however long established, should be free from occasional sceptical reappraisal. Examples of the latter will be given in the next section of this chapter.

In attempting to characterize a particular archaeological site we might hope to attain greater precision by referring to other indications than simply that of shape. These might include topographical situation, siting in relation to other archaeological features of known age or function, finds made in field-walking and, for earthworks, the degree of weathering. None of these is as conclusive as one might at first suppose.

The topographical situation is of some value in excluding certain interpretations; thus neither a windmill nor a watchtower is likely to have been placed in a deep hollow, nor would drains follow the contours across a slope. Many types of site do have preferred locations, but they are not unique to themselves, and not every example actually conforms to the general custom. In assessing a likely position for a Roman fort, for example, it is standard practice to check that there is a convenient water-supply; yet to bring water to the surviving Roman fort on Hod Hill (Dorset) involved an upward climb of over 100m in a length of 500m by the least arduous available route! The frequent occurrence of multi-period sites in all manner of topographical situations is in itself sufficient evidence that no situation is the preserve of one type of site only.

When we turn to siting in relation to other archaeological features, we have to remember that coincidence, chance association and accidental resemblance are the commonplaces of photointerpretation. Mere juxtaposition can mean nothing: it may look suggestive, but mental association is a far cry from archaeological association and neighbouring sites can be of totally different age, despite appearances (Wilson 1975b, fig 2 reversed). When one feature is seen inside another, this may be quite fortuitous. Narrow ring and penannular ditches have often been observed as crop-marks inside rectilinear or oval enclosures (54, 95, 114) and excavated examples have been found to belong to circular Iron Age houses; but this is no guarantee that any particular instance will prove to be a house or in genuine association with the surrounding enclosure. Similarly, military watchtowers surrounded by a bank and ditch are known to occur at intervals along strategic Roman roads in Scotland; yet circular banks or penannular ditches seen alongside such roads in suitable positions have, almost as often as not, proved to be the sites of prehistoric burials or circular houses. As to resemblances, we have already remarked on the difficulty of distinguishing the crop-marks of round barrows from those of round houses, but who would expect them to be mixed up together on the same site? This is what has been found in excavation, however (Parrington 1978), and similarly curious and confusing combinations must be expected from time to time in the study of crop-marks.

The finds made in field-walking are derived from layers disturbed by the plough. There should be a good correlation with soil-marks because these too are the product of plough-damage. Crop-marks, by contrast, represent layers that are still intact, and the contents of the plough-soil will relate to them only in some cases and not in others. When pits and ditches have been dug down from a layer that has now been disturbed by ploughing, contemporary artefacts may well appear among the material recovered from the surface. This will not happen, however, if that layer was in general archaeologically sterile (the only datable finds being within the pits and ditches themselves), nor again if the relevant layer still survives untouched below plough-level. The evidence of field-walking is of immense value both in its own right and as a guide to the interpretation of air-photographs, but in relation to crop-marks it must be used with a fair degree of circumspection.

To assess the age of earthworks from their appearance also requires circumspection, as well as much experience. Damage and erosion do not act consistently and even quite recent earthworks may appear considerably denuded. It is not therefore a matter of deducing how old an earthwork might be, but rather how young it is. To someone familiar with the appearance of Roman and prehistoric earthworks a particular enclosure will be too fresh-looking and too sharply defined to carry conviction as being older than medieval at the earliest. The precision is no greater than that, to say that something is more likely to be post-medieval than Roman; but even that can be information worth having.

It is fair to expect that many of the sites encountered will belong to types already familiar in the local archaeological repertoire, even though this is likely to be incompletely known. But there will also be others that are unique, or at least thus far unrepresented. The photo-interpreter must be equally alert to recognise the familiar and not to miss the unexpected.

Another thing with which archaeological interpretation is concerned is analysing the plan of groups of earthworks, soil-marks or crop-marks with a view to establishing a structural, and therefore chronological, sequence. Where earthworks survive in relief, it is sometimes possible to perceive that one bank definitely overrides part of another or is cut by a particular ditch. After ploughing, this evidence is either lost or else blurred into ambiguity. In a group of ploughed-down Celtic fields south of Wonston (Hampshire) a long barrow and a round barrow are sited at or near the corners of some of the fields (St Joseph & Wilson 1976), but it is no longer possible from mere inspection of the soil-marks to deduce if either or both of the barrows was in position before the fields were laid out. Soil-marks are mostly too imprecise in outline to leave much scope for this kind of inference, but crop-marks at their best are very clear and definite, at least in their rendering of pits and ditches. Associated mounds and banks usually leave no trace, but their former presence must be allowed for in any interpretation.

The clearest relationship is when two ditches meet in a T-junction. Unless they have been laid out as part of a single scheme, which is one possibility, the down-stroke of the T will be structurally later than the cross-bar. The time lapse may be quite minimal, but it will not be so great that the earlier ditch has ceased to be visible and probably also functional. A common instance of this relationship is where one enclosure is attached to another (30, 40): the former is possibly secondary, but certainly came into use during the lifetime of the latter.

If two ditches cross, their relationship is much more problematical and usually cannot be directly determined. Which was the earlier, or whether both were actually contemporary, can only be shown (if at all) by study of their positions in relation to less ambiguous portions of the plan. Occasionally, however, the filling of the two ditches is so different that they cause marks that are visibly different in appearance; one ditch can then be seen to have cut through the other. A considerable time interval must have elapsed to allow sufficient consolidation of the filling of the earlier ditch. In fig 58 the overlapping archaeological ditches cannot be distinguished in this way, but the ditch of the central enclosure can be traced across some of the fossil ice-wedges.

Care must be taken in interpreting the relationship between ditches of parallel or concentric course. If the two ditches follow a closely similar line, it is evident that they must have coexisted during part of their lifetime, but it is far from certain that they were constructed at the same time or were even in contemporary use for any significant period. It was argued in Chapter 3 that truly concentric compass-drawn ring ditches were likely to be of identical age because of the difficulty of placing additional circles accurately; but these constitute a special case. It is certainly true that in a number of double-ditched enclosures known from crop-marks excavation has shown that the outer ditch replaced the inner one as soon as it had been added. The same may be true of Neolithic causewayed enclosures known from crop-marks, whose main circuit is usually composed of two or three broken lines of ditch. In an earlier study (Wilson 1975c) it was assumed that these formed an obstacle in depth, but it now seems more probable that the ditches were successive. Such an interpretation fits better with the location of a palisade *between* the inner and outer ditches at Freston (43), and it agrees well with the new evidence from excavations that the filling-in of such ditches had some ritual importance.

It is all too easy to assume that because certain crop-marks look as though they belong together they really do so. Sometimes they do and sometimes they do not. This is what is meant when the crop-mark record is described as a *palimpsest*, that is to say, a piece of parchment that has been used more than once and carries more than one text. Such superimposed texts interfere with each other and are difficult to read.Another comparison is with an excavation plan that omits all stratigraphical relationships and has no convention for distinguishing different phases. Furthermore, it would appear that the excavator responsible has failed to recognise some of the archaeological features despite including on his plan various geological and other features of doubtful archaeological relevance. Each feature must therefore be read initially in isolation and only joined with others when there is real justification for doing so.

Reinterpretation

Archaeological interpretations inevitably reflect the state of knowledge current at the time, so it is scarcely surprising if some call for revision as archaeological knowledge grows. It would be useful if all relevant air photographs could be critically re-examined every ten years, but the effort required would be prodigious, and the reward probably no more than one photograph in a thousand yielding new information. As things are, there must be a substantial number of photographs buried in the major collections holding secrets that have yet to be revealed. We may take fig 63 as an example. This photograph was taken in June 1962 and crop-marks of timber buildings noted, but the significance of their distinctive plan was not at that time generally appreciated. The site was effectively rediscovered fifteen years later, when someone looking through a box of photographs to find a Saxon settlement in the Thames valley that had been photographed on the same flight found himself looking (quite by chance) at a Saxon settlement in Cambridgeshire. Knowledge of Saxon settlement and building types had advanced so far in the intervening period that there was no longer any doubt about the character of the site. Such 'rediscoveries' provide striking evidence of the progress of archaeological photo-interpretation—though it may yet prove that to identify a Saxon settlement from the presence of a single type of building is a crude over-simplification.

Revised interpretations come about in various ways. New photographs may show the site with greater clarity or reveal new features that significantly alter its apparent character. If the site is excavated, or reliably identified in documentary sources, this may well show the original interpretation to have been mistaken. A better understanding may also be derived from the photography or excavation of similar sites elsewhere.

A few examples may be given of each of these processes.

In Chapter 3 we saw how two lines of pits near the Thornborough South Circle, when seen in apparent isolation, had been originally supposed to indicate an aisled hall of four bays. It was only when drought conditions revealed the presence of lines of smaller pits on the same alignments that the marks first encountered were seen to form one part of a long 'avenue' (46). Similarly, at East Tilbury (Essex) a penannular ditch was found in the drought of 1976 to contain a hitherto unsuspected central cross, showing it to be the site of a vanished medieval windmill. Elsewhere, the appearance of clearer crop-marks was sufficient to cause several rectangular enclosures, once thought to be Roman fortlets, to be reclassified as native homesteads; such sites include that at Fairholm (Dumfriesshire), which was deleted from the fourth edition of the Ordnance Survey *Map of Roman Britain* (1978), and probably that at Carkin Moor (N Yorkshire), which was not so deleted, but well might have been.

The ultimate test for any interpretation is that of excavation. When circular enclosures at Thwing (Humberside) and Mucking (Essex) were first photographed, the closest parallels that could be adduced for them were henges (St Joseph 1964a, 1968b). At Thwing the crop-marks were not very clear in detail, but at Mucking they showed two concentric circles with one or possibly two entrances each and an overall diameter of over 70m (54). The proportions were virtually the same as those of the Big Rings at Dorchester (Oxfordshire), though the size was smaller (Crawford 1927, pl 1). Nevertheless, excavation at both sites discovered apparently domestic occupation of the Later Bronze Age (Manby 1979, Jones & Bond 1980). At three hillforts in southern Britain the Iron-Age ramparts were seen to surround a much slighter and obviously earlier defensive circuit (Curwen 1930). After excavation at the Trundle (W. Sussex) had shown the inner defences to be of Neolithic date it was natural to assume that the same was true of Scratchbury and Yarnbury (Wiltshire); but excavations there showed that both were actually of Iron-Age date. This is a salutary reminder that, however illuminating the exploration of a superficially similar site may be, its actual history may prove to have been entirely different.

Documentary evidence bearing on the interpretation of crop-marks is not always of great age or difficult to find. Even quite recent maps are sufficient to show that certain ring ditches mark the sites of circular parkland groves rather than round barrows or prehistoric settlements (Wilson 1975b, fig 5) or that other marks are those of former field boundaries rather than cursuses or Roman camps. Thus, the supposed Roman camp on Walwick Fell (Northumberland) turned out to be the site of a former plantation. So indeed it did, but is that the end of the matter? We may still enquire why the plantation had its distinctive and unusual playing-card shape. It would not be unparalleled for an existing earthwork to be planted with trees; so there is still the possibility that excavation could restore the original interpretation by finding evidence of military use.

The most obvious examples of excavation and new photography leading to a better understanding of whole classes of sites seem to relate to Roman military works, and it is possible that some early interpretations betrayed too much eagerness to recognise signs of the former presence of the Roman army. Confusion between Roman fortlets and native farmsteads has already been mentioned. Correction of the original interpretation does not necessarily depend on obtaining better photographs, but may be achieved through a more refined appreciation of what has already been seen. Thus, the photograph that was originally used to infer the existence of a small Roman fort near Hadleigh (Essex) (St Joseph 1953, pl 16) will now serve to refute the same interpretation. Despite the regularity of the outer ditch with its sweeping curves on the four corners, the inner ditch makes a less regular figure, the inner and outer ditches are not parallel, and the entrances through the two ditches do not correspond. This site now looks like a native settlement—though, to be fair, the same could be said of the excavated Roman fort at Bawtry (Nottinghamshire). Similarly, the photograph that was once claimed to identify a Roman signal-station (ie watchtower) at Thornhill (Dumfriesshire) has been selected in this book to illustrate what is now a well-known type of Iron-Age circular house (45a). It is always dangerous to argue from the non-appearance of crop-marks, but at Thornhill it is not unreasonable to conclude that if the narrow circular foundation-slot for a house or palisade is visible, we could hardly fail to see the four great post-pits for a watch-tower, if they were really there. These, however, are conspicuous by their absence and there remain no grounds for claiming a Roman military function for the site.

Not all examples of misinterpretation feature prehistoric or Romano-British sites masquerading as Roman military posts; sometimes the process works the other way. At Huntingtower (Perthshire) a double line of irregular pits was observed in proximity to a henge, another circular (perhaps ceremonial) site and a possible cursus. Some kind of avenue seemed to be indicated, though the pits were surprisingly irregular even for holding unshaped boulders. Observation of the crop-marks of quarry-pits alongside the Roman road from Ardoch to Strageath eventually furnished the clue that led to the Huntingtower pits being reinterpreted as quarry-pits for the same Roman road as it continued on its way to Bertha (St Joseph 1977, pl 13). In the meantime excavation had shown the 'cursus' to be formed of two medieval ditches, though the two circular monuments still appear to be genuine enough.

It should be appreciated that now, just as much as before, the choices available are sometimes not sufficiently well established to allow a securely based interpretation. The supposed Roman signal-station on Stoke Hill, north of Exeter (Devon) (St Joseph 1955, pl 21) bears some resemblance to the first-century Roman fortlets on the north Devon coast at Countisbury and Martinhoe Beacon, and also to a settlement of prehistoric type known from crop-marks beside the river Torridge east of Merton (Devon). Neither resemblance is close enough to guarantee genuine equivalence, however. The site at Stoke Hill has a plan that is more regular than that of the settlement near Merton, yet of different proportions from the fortlets at Martinhoe and Countisbury. Even excavation has failed to find clear evidence in favour of either domestic or military occupation; so until we have more comparative material to work on, the question remains open.

The examples of reinterpretation, past and present, given above have been presented to illustrate the processes involved; but what is more important is to provide for reinterpretation in the future. It should be the concern of the custodian of any collection of air-photographs to ensure that this is possible, by affording opportunities and encouragement for their re-examination. Equally, anybody working with air-photographs or with data derived from air-photographs should be ready to challenge accepted interpretations.

In conclusion, it should be remembered that two alternative interpretations are not necessarily mutually exclusive. Sites of one kind do get adapted to new purposes in a way that transforms them into sites of another kind entirely. The henge at Maumbury Rings (Dorset) was converted to an amphitheatre for the Roman town of *Durnovaria*. A smaller henge at Llandegai (Gwynedd) was turned into an Iron-Age farmstead. Some Irish cashels were re-used to house early Celtic monasteries. Many Roman forts and prehistoric hillforts were adapted to form the outer defences of Norman and later castles. Medieval windmills were placed, where possible, on existing mounds including round barrows. Much of this is incapable of being deduced from air-photographs, but sites with complicated histories certainly occur on air-photographs and give us yet another warning, if that were needed, not to be too rigid in our attitude to interpretation.

6

Transcription and Data Retrieval

An interpretation, once made, is of little lasting value unless it is also recorded; and even that record is of limited use unless it can be found when wanted. That, in a nutshell, is the reason for including here a discussion of transcription and data retrieval. The only adequate way to record what you think you can see on an air-photograph is to draw it out on paper. The archaeological interpretation can be noted in words. However these records are stored, there has to be some kind of index if the information contained is to be readily accessible. It is outside our scope to provide a manual of photogrammetric survey or data handling, but we should certainly review possible strategies, with the needs of interpretation in mind.

TRANSCRIPTION

The need for accuracy

It is essential for serious archaeological study that any transcription of data from air-photographs should not only be meticulous in its rendering of detail but should be metrically accurate. This affects both the representation of individual features and their location in relation to each other. The size and shape of an archaeological feature are key elements in its interpretation, so any distortion would be likely to result in misinterpretation. It is also important that the various parts of a site are recorded in their correct spatial relationships. This can often be done only by plotting them all with reference to nearby modern features, a procedure that is inescapable if some of the archaeological data appear on different photographs from others.

Transcription is the only way in which information from a number of photographs can be combined in a form capable of being read as a single whole. A simple instance would be that of a small enclosure being divided between two modern fields; although seldom visible at the same time on the ground, the two halves could be simply reassembled on paper. With a large site many modern fields may have to be studied and the crop-marks painstakingly plotted to build up a composite picture. When there is much complicated detail seen intermittently over many years, as for the Roman town at Wroxeter (Shropshire), it will be necessary to extract information from several hundred photographs. It is obvious that in such an exercise every detail must be drawn in with all possible accuracy, otherwise the pieces of the plan will not be put together correctly.

The survey problem

If we ignore purely photographic factors such as lens design, film flatness and paper stretch (summarized in Peak 1979, fig 16), there are two reasons why patterns seen on the ground do not ordinarily appear on air-photographs with the accuracy of a surveyed plan. Distortions are introduced into the image by the effects of camera tilt and of varying ground height (summarized in Peak 1979, fig 14).

The effect of tilting the camera so that the optical axis is no longer truly vertical is familiar enough. In oblique photographs of the kind mainly used to illustrate this book we can clearly see how shapes are distorted in accordance with the laws of perspective. Parallel lines receding into the distance appear to converge (5, 23); circles appear as ellipses and rectangles as trapeziums (48, 84). Features nearer to the camera (in the foreground of the picture) are represented at a larger scale than those that are further away. The more oblique the photograph is, the more rapid is the change of scale from foreground to background and the greater the degree of foreshortening. In near-vertical photographs the distortion is less evident, but it is still there.

The means of correcting tilt-distortion is simple in principle: the photograph is printed on a tilted baseboard carefully adjusted to the compensatory angle. This will usually be determined by registering the photographic image with the corresponding portion of a suitable map. Such rectified prints are regularly used in the production of photographic mosaics. That is not the end of the matter, however, since distortion is also caused by sloping or uneven ground. In a vertical photograph the higher ground, being nearer to the camera, appears at a larger scale than that which is lower down. The distortions associated with perspective are thus in a manner of speaking reintroduced into certain parts of the picture, but only in a variable and discontinuous way. The effect does not operate uniformly from one part to another, nor is it felt over the whole format, so that there can be no way of eliminating the distortion by applying a general correction to the photograph as a whole.

If we examine what happens to individual points within the photograph, we find that increasing ground height causes each of them to be systematically displaced in relation to its correct plan position. The point on the ground directly beneath the camera is called the *nadir point*; if the photograph is a true vertical, this will coincide with the centre (or *principal point*) of the photograph. This is the only point on the photograph at which ground height makes no difference to the apparent position. Everywhere else a variation in height brings a greater or less displacement along a line radiating from the nadir point.

This is most easily understood if we consider the photographic image of a flagpole. At the centre of a vertical photograph we are looking straight down on it and can see nothing but a single dot at the exact position which the flagpole occupies. If the pole appears in any other part of the photograph, we shall see it partly from the side. It will then seem to be leaning outwards, and its image will consist of a line running from tip to base. If the ground is level, the base will be represented in its correct plan position, but the tip of the flagpole will be displaced from that point radially outwards. The amount of this displacement (or *parallax*), ie the length of the visible line, is proportional to both the height of the pole and the scale of the photograph; the parallax can be measured in such a way as to allow the height of the pole to be calculated. Now, suppose the flagpole to be buried in a large mound of earth so that only the button at the top is visible at ground level. Its position is unaltered, but the base is now hidden; the height of the pole cannot be determined and its very existence is probably unsuspected; and if the earth mound is well spread and only gently sloping, the presence of the mound may not be noticed either. The top of the flagpole is still displaced on the photograph from its correct plan position, but this is no longer apparent from mere inspection. Other points on high ground are affected in the same way, and there is no way of correcting this displacement using only a single photograph.

With an overlapping pair of photographs the situation is quite different. Parallax can be exploited to yield a three-dimentional image in a stereoscope or to build a 'model' in a stereoplotter from which accurate measurements can be taken both in plan and in altitude. Looking at a single vertical photograph is like looking at the world through one eye: shapes become ambiguous and distances uncertain, unless already familiar. Nevertheless we often have to use single photographs. Most photographs taken for archaeological purposes are in any case oblique, and it is often the oblique photographs of a site that are the most informative. Even oblique photographs can yield accurate transcriptions, however, if they are handled correctly, though the more of them there are, the better the chance is of successful completion.

Two simple universal rules

Fortunately there are some characteristics of air-photographs that are constant, regardless of tilt and height distortions.

1 *On an oblique photograph, three or more points lying on the same direct line of sight from the camera are also all in line on the map.*

In normal photography, with the camera held upright, lines of sight in this sense run straight up and down the print. Such a line may appear on the photograph in the form of a field boundary or of a linear crop-mark, or it may be entirely notional. Provided it runs through two known points, represented on an existing map or fixed by local survey, this identifies an alignment on which the other point or points must lie. In this way it is possible to relate chosen points within an archaeological site to detail on the map. Such alignments are independent of ground height because the displacements caused by differences of height are made radially from the nadir point, which in this instance means up-and-down the picture along the line of sight.

2 *On an oblique photograph, lines that are horizontal on the print (and are also horizontal on the ground) are lines of constant scale.*

This is because they lie at an equal distance from the camera throughout their length. They may be lines that are already visible on the photograph like field boundaries, or they may be completely notional; the essential feature is that they should pass through two known points identifiable directly or indirectly on the map. Since the scale does not vary from one part to another, it is permissible to make proportional measurements, defining a given point as being, let us say, one half, or three fifths, or 17/32, of the way from one known point to the other. This proportion holds good for the map as well as the photograph, and so the position can be transferred from one to the other. The conversion of photo-scale to map-scale can be done mechanically with a pair of proportional dividers or mathematically with a calculator.

Note should be taken that not every horizontal line on an oblique photograph is genuinely square to the camera. It is possible for a field-boundary running diagonally away from the camera, for example, to appear as a horizontal line if the ground over which it runs is falling away. Its true course is easily established from a large-scale plan, however, while the lie of the land can be checked from other photographs or contoured maps or by personal ground inspection.

These two rules have been presented in a simplified form that holds good for most ordinary oblique views. For vertical and near-vertical photographs they require stricter definition. True alignments (Rule 1) radiate from the nadir point. On a vertical photograph this will lie at or very close to the principal point, but on a near-vertical steep oblique its position will have to be found by geometrical construction (Hampton 1979). Lines of constant scale (Rule 2) are concentric with the nadir point. On vertical and near-vertical photographs reliable measurements have therefore to be taken along an arc, which is inconvenient. On ordinary oblique photographs the curvature can be ignored, and lines of constant scale can be identified at right angles to the line of sight either geometrically (Palmer 1976b) or by computation (Hogg 1980, 233).

These rules can be applied successfully and with great accuracy to the plotting of photographic detail, and it is some comfort that it is the most oblique views, which in other respects are the least tractable, to which they can be most simply and accurately applied. Their effective use is nevertheless dependent on two conditions. There need to be plenty of photographs taken from different angles and there must also be enough known points to generate useable alignments and lines of constant scale in adequate quantity. When these conditions cannot be met, resort has to be made to other methods.

Methods for use on even ground

If the ground is even, ie a plane surface though not necessarily horizontal, then a variety of methods can be employed, as all straight lines traceable on the photograph will correspond to straight lines on the map and can be transferred, regardless of orientation. Whichever method or methods are selected, four or more identifiable points will be required to fix locations accurately. Ideally these should be so placed that a series of straight lines linking them into a polygon would enclose all the detail to be transcribed. The further outside such a polygon any of the details lies, the less accurately it can be plotted.

Several of the methods considered involve drawing lines onto the photograph as well as the map, but it is of utmost importance that the print being used for interpretation is not marked in any way, otherwise the evidence for the interpretation is actually obscured. If possible, a duplicate print should be obtained for annotation. Alternatively, but less satisfactorily, lines can be drawn on a sheet of clear acetate film laid over the photograph and fixed firmly in relation to it. It should be possible to lift the film as desired in order to verify the underlying photographic detail.

a *Möbius network* (Scollar 1975; Hogg 1980, 226). The aim here is to construct a network of lines, both on the photograph and on the map, which will serve as a guide to the interpreter in making a controlled sketch of the archaeological features. Lines are drawn between pairs of known points on the photograph and between the corresponding points on the map; the resulting intersections are then used to give new points for drawing in further lines until the weblike pattern reaches its optimum level of elaboration. If the network is sufficiently complex and appropriately positioned, the sketch can achieve a fair degree of accuracy. For this to be possible, the starting points must be well spaced and numerous; five is the minimum number and the more there are, the better.

b *Palmer's network* (Palmer 1976b; Hogg 1980, 228) is tied into a line of constant scale, as previously defined. Once such a line has been found or constructed on the photograph, it can be arbitrarily divided to give additional points in the places *where they are needed.* Thus, instead of the positions of lines being determined accidentally by that of points already known, they can now be drawn purposefully through chosen archaeological detail and produced to cut the line of constant scale at points that can be fixed by proportional measurement. If rays can be drawn in this way through the same detail from two known points, its position is thereby accurately fixed. This is a more efficient way of constructing a network for transcription, though it may require some intricate computation to transfer the line of constant scale correctly to the map.

c *Hogg's network* (Hogg 1980, 233) adds a second line of constant scale parallel to the first, positioned so that one lies each side of the features to be plotted. Once the first line has been correctly drawn, the second may be constructed parallel to it through any convenient known point, without further computation. Lines may now be drawn from one line of constant scale to the other in any direction that seems advantageous, both ends being now fixed by proportional measurement. This makes it possible either to build up a grid of evenly spaced lines across the area of interest, or more usefully to place lines in whatever positions and at whatever angles will give most assistance in producing an accurate plan.

d *The paper-strip method* (Scollar 1975; Hogg 1980, 228) uses intersecting rays to fix selected points on the archaeological features. The method of defining the rays on the photograph and transferring them to the map is simple, accurate and laborious; it is therefore an ideal method for computerization.

e *Computer transformation* (Palmer 1977, 1979) achieves the same result as the paper-strip method by computation instead of geometrical construction. It is necessary to have access to a computer with a digitizing table and a graphics plotter. The computer has two advantages over the other methods described above. The first is speed. Once the program has been adapted to the hardware available and run successfully, archaeological sites can be plotted in far greater numbers than could otherwise be contemplated. This makes it possible to undertake programmes of research requiring the transcription of hundreds of sites, eg for detailed morphological study. The other advantage is that the co-ordinates of the transformed image are computed virtually continuously, so that the line drawn by the computer has been checked throughout its length instead of being merely sketched in relation to a few measured reference points. The computer method is no more accurate in its basic survey than any other of the methods listed here, but it is more consistent in making use of the survey to achieve a satisfactory result.

f *Optical transformation.* Most optical devices to assist sketching from single air-photographs have the same effect as rectifying the print, ie they correct for perspective but not for parallax. An exception is the OMI Stereofacet Plotter, which by an ingenious optical mechanism is able to eliminate both distortions, provided the correct procedures are followed. This equipment is designed for vertical photographs with very modest tilts but can certainly be used on steep obliques. Although less expensive than the computer hardware used in method (*e*), such plotters are also less likely to be available except in a specialist cartographic or photo-interpretation laboratory.

In all the methods described at least four known points must be visible on the photograph to provide ground control for the survey. Many photographs of archaeological sites, admirable in other respects, fail to satisfy this condition, while those that do so may be only mediocre in their rendering of archaeological detail. The transcription may have to proceed in several stages, a general view being used to fix four or more points in or near the site which can then be used as the reference points in transcribing from more detailed photographs. These new points may be modern features such as bushes or fence posts, capable of being located equally by ground survey, or they may form part of the archaeological detail to be plotted, such as ditch intersections or the corners of enclosures. They should lie near the edge of the area of interest and a minimum of four must be visible in each photograph used.

In some large modern fields it is virtually impossible to take a satisfactory air-photograph of an archaeological site that also includes as many as four control points. Accurate transcription is then impossible except with the air of a geophysical survey or exploratory excavation.

Another problem is encountered when the ground surface does not in fact conform to a single plane. In theory it is possible to analyse the surface into a series of facets, each approximating to a plane, but in practice this is seldom possible because there are not enough control points. Each facet must be defined by at least four known points, thereby compounding an existing difficulty, that of providing adequate ground control. Typical examples of this problem in an archaeological context are furnished by defended settlements sited on a ridge (55), on the end of a spur, or on an isolated hillock, within a large field whose boundaries are sometimes hundreds of metres distant. The discrepancies between the plane defined by the control points and that passing through the archaeological features can result in distortions of size, shape and position. These distortions should be recognised, acknowledged, evaluated, and perhaps accepted. They are no greater than those present in any ground survey in which measurements are taken along the surface of the ground instead of on a true horizontal level.

Draughtsmanship

In four of the six methods presented in the previous section the interpretation is committed to paper in the form of a sketch. The accuracy of this sketch is controlled by a variety of measurements and guidelines, but its quality depends on possession of a good eye and a sensitive appreciation of possibly significant form. The same attributes are needed no less in tracing from the photograph or in following the outlines of archaeological features with the cursor of a digitizer. There are subtleties of form which can be captured or destroyed by deviations of no more than a line's width. In this respect transcription from air-photographs is not unlike drawing the profile of a pot: the outline may be perfectly measured at a number of points and yet fail to represent the shape which the experienced eye can see. For this reason it is important that every sketch, tracing or computer output should be compared directly with the photograph from which it is derived to check the rendering of the nuances. A plot that is entirely adequate to record the position and general character of an archaeological site may be quite misleading for detailed morphological analysis, unless this is done (cf Hogg 1980, fig 21.8).

Once it has been done, reference should be made to the other photographs on which the interpretation was originally based. New details may need to be added, either by eye or with the aid of one of the methods already mentioned, and some existing detail may need to be redrawn after considering photographs taken on another occasion and in different conditions.

Sometimes there is a conflict of evidence which cannot be resolved by simple scrutiny of the prints. If one picture of crop-marks shows an entrance into an enclosure at a certain place where another shows a continuous ditch, which one is more likely to be right? If the two photographs have been taken in different seasons, or are separated by an interval of weeks or days in the same season, the discrepancy may be explained by differences in the depth reached by roots of the growing crops (p 68). But if, as sometimes happens, the photographs are consecutive exposures made on the same occasion and the only detectable difference between them is of 20° in the angle of view, which picture is to be believed? There is no answer to this question, except by ground investigation (probing, geophysical survey, or excavation) or by obtaining subsequent photography of convincingly superior quality.

This is but one instance of the need to annotate transcriptions if they are to be adequate records of interpretation. Whatever threshold of significance is adopted, there will always be some marks whose value is less than certain but which it would be perverse to ignore completely. If they are drawn in without comment, it implies a spurious degree of confidence, but if they are omitted, we may well fail to take the chance to verify their character in future work. Nor is it satisfactory just to use the convention of a broken or dotted line, since this could be understood as representing a pit-alignment. Once a note is added to explain the convention used, the problem disappears and the crop-marks in question may be represented in any way that proves convenient.

Notes of a more general kind should also be provided, to allow assessment of the reliability of the interpretation and transcription (Hampton & Palmer 1978). What photographs have been examined?—which formed the basis of the interpretation, and which were used in the transcription? What was the quality of the earthworks/soil-marks/crop-marks? What survey method was used, and was it wholly successful? These details should all be recorded as a matter of routine in any programme of photo-interpretation.

In an archive such as a county Sites and Monuments Record transcriptions are most usefully presented on transparent overlays allowing the archaeological detail to be related to topographical and other information on maps of appropriate scale. The original transcription, if done by hand, is likely to have been based on the Ordnance Survey large-scale plan at 1:2,500: for only the simplest sites can be successfully plotted at 1:10,560, while the new map at 1:10,000 is unfortunately too generalized in its representation of detail to be of much value for purposes of survey. The overlay will usually, however, be at a scale of 1:10,560 or 1:10,000 so as to allow individual sites to be studied in a broader context and linked together into the historical landscape. Computer transcriptions have an advantage in that the program permits the output to be drawn at a variety of specified scales, to suit different subsequent uses.

If the same material is being prepared for publication, it is important to include enough of the background detail to put the archaeological features in their context and to explain variations in the extent of our knowledge of them (Hampton & Palmer 1978). Modern field boundaries should be shown, for example, since they mark the major divisions of agricultural use, between favourable and unfavourable crops or between ploughed and unploughed land. The presence of a hedge or fence between two arable fields, each with a headland alongside, could account for a sizable break in the otherwise continuous line of a crop-mark. If the hedge is not represented on the plan, there will appear to be an entrance causeway; but it would be wrong to draw the crop-mark as a continuous line since such an entrance may indeed exist. To include the hedgeline gives an appropriate degree of guidance in interpreting the plan.

Care should be taken to indicate areas on the plan where the absence of known archaeological features is unsurprising, being the result of non-archaeological causes. There are four of these, as follows.

a *Destruction*, eg by building foundations, landscaping, pits and quarries. Prehistoric settlement is attested in the Thames valley by abundant crop-marks from Cirencester to Reading, but few crop-marks are known below the immediate environs of Reading. While this is partly caused by the difficulty of approaching Heathrow for archaeological air-reconnaissance, the main reason is that so much of the river gravel has been either built over or removed in gravel-workings. Crop-marks cannot be expected, and no inference about prehistoric settlement can therefore be drawn from their absence on our maps.

b *Concealment*, eg by woodland, temporary housing or standing water, which may in time be removed to re-expose the archaeological features. The west end of the cursus discovered from the air at Springfield (Essex) in 1975 was revealed by parching of grass on the site of a recently dismantled housing estate, presumably composed of 'prefabs' (Hedges 1980, pl 1). Similarly, felled woodland is often found to contain surviving earthworks and, if subsequently ploughed, may also furnish crop-marks (107).

c *Unfavourable soil*, eg on clay or peat. Any map or plan showing crop-marks should also include the limit of soils favourable to their appearance (Taylor 1975a, figs 1–2; Wilson 1980). This is not to say that crop-marks will never appear on the unfavourable soils, either in exceptional conditions or on patches of better-drained soil too limited in extent to have been recognized during soil-mapping; but their appearance is not to be expected and their absence is therefore not archaeologically significant.

d *Unfavourable crop*, such as raspberries, potatoes, tulips or permanent grass. Fields subject to a normal crop rotation including cereals, sugar beet or green fodder crops are excluded from this category, since crop-marks may be expected to appear there in the end, if there are features to produce them. Grass is by far the commonest 'crop' to be grown without change over long periods. In normal conditions it is unrewarding for air-reconnaissance, but in times of drought grassland can yield very detailed crop-marks. In this context we must think not only of permanent pasture, but also of lawns, playing fields and parks. Even built-up areas may then yield archaeological information, as when the north side of the Roman fort at Ixworth (Suffolk) was traced across the back gardens of houses in the village because their lawns remained green over the Roman ditches.

Some care must thus be taken in delimiting the areas ascribed to each category. Although towns and villages are usually unproductive of crop-marks, this is not because archaeological features are everywhere destroyed or deeply buried; quite large areas may still fall in category (*d*).

Suitable conventions for representing these areas on maps and plans may be based on those suggested by Hampton and Palmer (1978):

a diagonal hatching
b medium stipple
c a bold dashed line
d fine stipple.

At the beginning of this chapter it was stated that transcription provided the only means of recording, and sometimes also of compiling, an interpretation of air-photographs. This is true, but it should not be supposed that even the most accurate and sensitive transcription can actually replace the photographs on which it is based. Just as pottery drawings provide a simple and efficient means of comparing the forms of pots which may be fragmentary or separated from each other by an inconvenient distance, but do not remove the need sometimes to look at actual potsherds, so too transcriptions of air-photographs provide a convenient means of record and comparison but do not remove the need sometimes to consult the original photographs, to resolve doubts or to allow reinterpretation.

DATA RETRIEVAL

The value of any index depends very largely on the foresight of the compiler in recognizing its possible future uses and on his skill in providing for them. We have to ask ourselves: is the aim to identify planning constraints affecting certain parcels of land?—to facilitate mapping of selected areas?—to document the use of the land at various periods of the past?—to undertake detailed morphological analysis of archaeological sites? To achieve these different aims will require the use of different systems of classification, of varying degrees of complexity.

A simple topographic system

The simplest way to organize a collection of air-photographs is to file them in topographical divisions. This is obviously appropriate when such a collection constitutes merely one section of a large archive like a county Sites and Monuments Record which is itself organized on a topographical basis. The same topographical divisions will be used throughout, and if these follow the lines of the National Grid, there is automatic correlation with Ordnance Survey map sheets on which sites of all kinds may be noted or transcribed.

This system works well in relation to enquiries that are themselves topographically based—in respect of planning applications, for example, or with a view to study of landscape history. It can do little to assist those whose queries relate to a particular type of site or to a given chronological period, unless it is supported by some kind of a subject index. When the area of study is small and the number of photographs not too great, this does not matter too much. Much can be done from memory or with lists of selected data or by systematic search of maps or overlays. But for a large collection a subject index is essential if interpretations, once made, are to serve any useful purpose. Provision of such an index is a normal function of a county Sites and Monuments Record (Benson 1973, 1975); it is one of the principal disadvantages of the English National Monuments Record that it affords no comparable facility.

Indexing by shape and by interpretation

Designing a subject index requires that a fundamental question be answered at the outset. Should the categories used be purely descriptive, based on morphology and association, or should they (where possible) be interpretative, allowing recognition of sites with a definite cultural and historical context? The advantage of a purely descriptive classification is that it can, in principle, be applied to all photographs with an archaeological content; furthermore there is less likelihood of error. The fact that it is also more objective need not be unduly emphasized: the search for total objectivity is as sterile in photo-interpretation as in excavation or indeed in most scientific research. It would certainly be perverse to ignore reliable identifications of Roman forts or deserted medieval villages simply on the grounds that these categories demand interpretative assumptions, or that some past identifications have proved to be incorrect. Interpretation undoubtedly has a place in any subject index of archaeological air-photographs, and it is to be hoped that with increasing knowledge that place will become larger and more secure. Interpretations must nevertheless be understood to be provisional and should perhaps always be supplementary to a basic morphological classification. Punched-card systems and computerized indexes will, of course, permit the same data to be sorted in terms of location, morphology, association and interpretation, singly or in combination, at will.

The next question concerns the degree of detail to be put into the index. It is all too easy to get carried away in devising a classification. Although general categories can answer few questions directly, the more intricate the classification becomes, the more work is involved in entering the data. However narrowly defined the individual categories may be, there will always be a proportion of sites that refuse to fit and demand difficult decisions, and it is no solution to continue to subdivide until every possibility is catered for. There are two extremes to be avoided, both equally unhelpful to the user. The first is to limit categories to over-generalized designations such as 'crop-marks' or 'earthworks', which by implication acknowledge some archaeological content but are not prepared to go any further. The other is to elaborate an over-detailed scheme in which every enclosure is the unique example of its size and shape. Somewhere between these extremes a middle course must be found, appropriate to the expected functions of the index. An index designed as a research tool to assist morphological analysis will clearly need to be more detailed than one serving merely to find photographs for a variety of purposes, but even so there will be a point beyond which benefits are only to be achieved in accordance with a law of diminishing returns.

Whatever the intended function, it will be more useful to have the whole photographic archive entered even in a rather general way than to have indexed one-tenth of the photographs in meticulous detail while leaving the remainder to be completed at some indefinite time in a possibly distant future. For this reason it will be prudent not to let the initial classification become too detailed, though room should be left for later development as required. The results of detailed study can then be incorporated as they become available without disrupting the whole framework. In a computerized index this can be done very readily; the full classification is programmed from the start, but it can be activated at whatever level or combination of levels is found to be most rewarding from time to time. This will be most effective if the classificatory scheme is organized on strictly hierarchical principles.

It is convenient to refer to the subject of each entry in the index as a 'site'. To do so does not imply that the compiler or the users of the index are wedded to 'site archaeology' (in which each site is studied in virtual isolation from its surroundings) which air-photography has done so much to make an outmoded concept. It does nevertheless acknowledge that recognizable foci of past settlement do exist and that even within the framework of landscape archaeology they require careful detailed examination. A general overview of past landscapes can be obtained from maps and overlays; correlation of the individual elements with the photographic evidence and with current interpretations is achieved by means of the index.

There are practical problems in defining a 'site' for the index. A solitary enclosure presents no difficulty, but what about an assumed prehistoric settlement composed of twenty such enclosures, some overlapping, as well as other crop-marks? Can we justify the labour of indexing each of those twenty enclosures individually, when they are bound to appear on much the same groups of photographs? Yet if we do not do so, there will be no means of tracing every example of that sort of enclosure. A possible strategy would be to adopt a two-stage indexing process, with enclosures entered as a group to begin with and treated individually later on. This would call for some interim arrangements: adequate cross referencing to allow the enclosures still to be found even if not yet indexed individually, and explicit notes of where there is still work to be completed.

The first of the two stages in such a process, being more concerned with economy of effort than with the niceties of archaeological classification, would call for a pragmatic approach. A well-defined group of crop-marks, for example, will tend to be photographed together on the same occasions and is therefore conveniently indexed together as a single site. Unfortunately, however, groups of crop-marks are often not well defined, and the impression they give of themselves on different occasions can be surprisingly varied. There are places where crop-marks of one kind or another extend more or less continuously over several kilometres. If that means that they are to be regarded as forming a single site, this must still be broken down for indexing purposes into convenient lots. Sometimes there will be apparent foci where the marks are more densely concentrated, which it seems reasonable to make the nucleus of 'sites' for indexing; but in another year, with different fields showing archaeological features, the obvious foci seem to be at other positions. In practical terms it is usually more satisfactory to make arbitrary divisions along modern lanes and field boundaries. Such divisions will have no archaeological meaning whatever, but since the appearance of crop-marks is controlled by modern agricultural use of the land, they have the advantage of corresponding closely to the groupings actually seen on the photographs. More archaeologically sensitive analysis would then be reserved to the second stage.

A final paradox concerns the indexing of photographs in terms of their archaeological interpretation. Elsewhere in this book the interpreter has been encouraged to maintain an attitude of vigilant scepticism, but for the purposes of indexing it pays not to be too rigorous. This is not a question of lowering critical standards but simply one of practical utility. According to most definitions of a cursus the parallel ditches at North Stoke (51) do not qualify for that description. Yet excavation appears to have shown their Neolithic date, and anyone studying cursuses would need to consider their relationship to cursuses in their normal form. Academic integrity can be maintained by adding one or two question-marks to the description; but until some better interpretation is forthcoming, is it more useful to index the North Stoke ditches as a '*cursus?*' than to relegate them to some indeterminate miscellaneous category. Similarly with the multitude of crop-mark enclosures that may or may not represent long barrows or long mortuary enclosures: to describe them as '*long barrows?*' is to place them beside genuine examples and to pose the question whether they are in fact equivalent. It is a question that needs to be asked, and asking it is not to prejudge the answer, which will eventually come from systematic study of the photographs coupled with selective excavation.

Glossary

of archaeological and other terms not defined in the text

AMPHITHEATRE a Roman place of entertainment like a bullring, with an elliptical arena surrounded by tiers of seats resting either on an earthen bank or on a masonry structure; also used by Roman soldiers for arms training.

BARROW a mound of earth covering a burial; normally classified by shape as 'long', 'round' or 'square'; ranging in date from Neolithic to Saxon.

BASILICA the official public hall of a Roman town, used as a place of assembly and law court, usually occupying one side of the forum.

BELL BARROW a round barrow whose surrounding ditch is separated from the mound by a level space (or berm); usually Early Bronze Age.

BOWL BARROW the commonest type of round barrow, in which the surrounding ditch (if present) lies immediately outside the mound; cf bell barrow, disc barrow.

BROCH defended homestead of circular plan with chambers constructed in its 5m thick drystone wall; found principally in northern Scotland in the later Iron Age; the more impressive examples were built up as towers.

CAUSEWAYED ENCLOSURE a name used especially for Early and Middle Neolithic roughly oval enclosures bounded by discontinuous lengths of bank and ditch; finds from the ditches suggest a ritual function.

CELTIC FIELDS small rectangular fields (0·1 to 0·6ha) of Bronze Age to Roman date; the name 'Celtic' has become traditional, but is no longer intended to be understood literally.

clavicula a defensive work screening the entrance into a Roman camp, shaped like a quarter circle (fig 56).

CROSSTREES intersecting horizontal beams supporting the central post of a post-mill; medieval examples were held firm by being imbedded in an artificial mound, later ones by being fixed in brick or masonry piers.

CURSUS an elongated and more or less rectangular enclosure of unknown (but presumably ceremonial) purpose and later Neolithic date.

DISC BARROW round barrow of small size with outlying ditch enclosing a broad berm; Early Bronze Age.

ENCLOSURE a piece of ground surrounded by a boundary such as a wall or bank and ditch; there is usually at least one entrance.

FORUM the courtyard or marketplace at the centre of a Roman town, surrounded by porticoes, shops and offices; the basilica usually occupied one side, and sometimes there were also public temples.

GEOPHYSICAL SURVEY non-destructive methods of exploring below the surface of the ground by measuring the soil's magnetic susceptibility, electrical resistivity and other properties.

HEADLAND strip left unploughed at each end of a field for the plough to turn on.

HENGE more or less circular enclosure, normally with the bank outside the main ditch and often enclosing a stone circle; probably a place of ceremony; Late Neolithic and Bronze Age.

HYPOCAUST heating system used in Roman buildings by which hot air was circulated beneath a concrete floor.

KETTLE HOLE a hollow produced by melting of a block of ice left behind imbedded in end moraine by a retreating ice-sheet.

LEGIONARY FORTRESS the permanent quarters of a Roman legion of about 5000 men.

LYNCHET artificial scarp, especially when produced in the cultivation of sloping ground.

MILEFORTLET one of a line of Roman fortlets spaced at one-mile intervals along the Cumbrian coast as part of Hadrian's frontier in Britain.

MORTUARY ENCLOSURE an enclosure believed to have been used for exposing the dead before eventual interment.

MOTTE conical earth mound supporting a timber or masonry castle.

OPPIDUM the Latin word for a town; in a prehistoric context this is used to describe a major settlement of the late Iron Age, often on level ground defended by dykes, especially when the site of a tribal mint.

PERIGLACIAL ZONE zone of severe cold (with a range between $-12°$ and $+2°C$) surrounding an ice-sheet; geological features typical of this environment are also termed 'periglacial'.

PILLOW MOUND a low mound, normally shaped like a long pillow or bolster and most often found in groups on moorland.

PIT ALIGNMENT land division composed of a line of circular or rectangular pits, presumably once accompanied by a bank; the pits are believed not to have ever held posts.

POST-MILL a windmill carried on a central post on which the main structure revolves; as opposed to a tower-mill, in which only the cap of the mill turns.

POSTGLACIAL belonging to the phase immediately following a glaciation.

RING DITCH a ditch enclosing a circular space.

SALTERN a place for making salt by boiling or evaporation.

SOLIFLUXION down-slope movement of water-saturated soil.

STEREOSCOPE optical device to allow two photographs to be viewed simultaneously, each by one eye only; when the two photographs are of the same subject seen from different positions, the images combine to form a three-dimensional picture.

TILLERING putting out lateral shoots from the base of the stem.

titulum a defensive work screening the entrance into a Roman camp, comprising a short length of rampart and ditch set forward from the main line (fig 56); called in English a 'traverse'.

VEXILLATION FORTRESS the permanent quarters of a composite garrison of Roman troops, comprising a detachment ('vexillation') of one or more cohorts from a legion with a body of auxiliaries.

VILLA the buildings of a Roman farm, especially when built in distinctively Roman fashion with stone foundations, and often with heated baths, concrete floors, etc.

Bibliography

ADAMS, R E W 1980 'Swamps, canals, and the locations of ancient Maya cities', *Antiquity* 54, 206-14

AGACHE, R 1964 *Archéologie aérienne de la Somme*, Société de Préhistoire du Nord, Amiens

— 1978 *La Somme pré-romaine et romaine,* Amiens

— 1979 'Nouveaux apports des prospections aériennes en archéologie pré-romaine et romaine de la Picardie', *Cahiers archéologiques de Picardie* 6, 33-90

ASHBEE, P 1960 *The Bronze Age Round Barrow in Britain*, London

AVERY, B W 1973 'Soil classification in the Soil Survey of England and Wales', *Journal of Soil Science* 24, 324-38

BAKER, W A 1975 'Infra-red techniques', in D R Wilson (ed), *Aerial Reconnaissance for Archaeology*, 46-51, Council for British Archaeology, London

BENSON, D 1973 'A Sites and Monuments Record for the Oxford region', *Oxoniensia* 37 (1972), 226-37

— 1975 'The application of aerial photography in the Oxford region', in D R Wilson (ed), *Aerial Reconnaissance for Archaeology*, 132-6, Council for British Archaeology, London

BERESFORD, M & HURST, J G 1971 *Deserted Medieval Villages*, London

BERESFORD, M W & ST JOSEPH, J K S 1979 *Medieval England: an aerial* survey (2nd ed), Cambridge

BINNEY, M & HILLS, A 1979 *Elysian Gardens*, London

BOWEN, H C 1961 *Ancient Fields*, British Association for the Advancement of Science, London

— 1972 'Air photography: some implications in the South of England', in E Fowler (ed.), *Field Survey in British Archaeology*, 38-49, Council for British Archaeology, London

BRADFORD, J 1957 *Ancient Landscapes: studies in field archaeology*, London

BROMWICH, J 1970 'Freshwater flooding along the Fen margins south of the Isle of Ely during the Roman period', in C W Phillips (ed), *The Fenland in Roman Times* (= Royal Geographical Society *Research Series*, 5), 114-26, London

BURGESS, C 1976 'Meldon Bridge: a neolithic defended promontory complex near Peebles', in C Burgess & R Miket (eds), *Settlement and Ecology in the Third and Second Millennia BC* (= *British Archaeological Reports* 33), 151-79, Oxford

CAPPER, J C 1907 'Photographs of Stonehenge as seen from a war balloon', *Archaeologia* 60, 571

CHOUQUER, G 1977 'Mottes féodales du Jura et de la Bresse décelées par les inondations de l'automne 1976', *Dossiers de l'archéologie* no 22, 44-7

COLWELL, R N 1960 (ed) *Manual of Photographic Interpretation.* American Society of Photogrammetry, Washington

CORBISHLEY, M J 1979 'A crop mark at Ramsey, Essex', *Aerial Archaeology* 2 (1978), 70-1

COUNCIL FOR BRITISH ARCHAEOLOGY, 1981 *Archaeology in Britain 1980*, London

CRAWFORD, O G S 1923 'Air survey and archaeology', *Geographical Journal*, May 1923, 324-66

— 1924 'The Stonehenge Avenue', *Antiquaries Journal* 4, 57-9

— 1925 'Air-photograph of Gainstrop, Lincs., *Antiquaries Journal* 5, 432-3

— 1927 'Air photographs near Dorchester, Oxon', *Antiquity* 1, 469-74

— 1928a 'History and bibliography of archaeology from the air', in O G S Crawford & A Keiller, *Wessex from the Air*, 3-7

— 1928b *Air Survey and Archaeology* (= Ordnance Survey *Professional Papers*, new series, 7), 2nd edition, London

— 1929 *Air Photography for Archaeologists* (= Ordnance Survey *Professional Papers*, new series, 12), London

— 1935a 'Rectangular enclosures: a note on Mr Leeds' paper', *Antiquaries Journal* 15, 77-8

— 1935b 'New air-photographs', *Antiquity* 9, 478-9

— 1938 'Luftbildaufnahmen von archäologischen Bodendenkmälern in England', *Luftbild und Vorgeschichte* (= *Luftbild und Luftbildmessung* 16), 9-18, 27-63

— 1954 'A century of air-photography', *Antiquity* 28, 206-10

CRAWFORD, O G S & KEILLER, A 1928 *Wessex from the Air*, Oxford

CRUMMY, P 1980 'Crop marks at Gosbecks, Colchester', *Aerial Archaeology* 4 (1979), 77-82

CULPIN, C 1981 Farm Machinery (10th ed). London.

CURWEN, E C 1930 'Neolithic camps', *Antiquity* 4, 22-54

DANIEL, G 1975 *A Hundred and Fifty Years of Archaeology*, London

DASSIÉ, J 1978 *Manuel de l'archéologie aérienne*, Paris

DEUEL, L 1971 *Flights into Yesterday: the story of aerial archaeology*, London

DOWNEY, R R 1980 *A History of Archaeological Air Photography in Great Britain* (= *Orbit* 1), London

DYMOND, D P 1966 'Ritual monuments at Rudston, E Yorkshire, England', *Proceedings of the Prehistoric Society* 32, 86-95

EBERT, J I & LYONS, T R 1980 *Remote Sensing in Archaeology, Cultural Resources Treatment and Anthropology: the United States of America in 1979* (= *Aerial Archaeology* 5), London

EDDOWES, M 1976 *Crop Production in Europe*, London

EDWARDS, D 1978a 'A soil mark at Roydon, Norfolk', *Aerial Archaeology* 1, 22-3

— 1978b 'Air photography and early fields in Norfolk', in H C Bowen & P J Fowler (eds.), *Early Land Allotment in the British Isles* (= *British Archaeological Reports* 48), 99-102, Oxford

ERITH, F H 1971 'The levelled long barrows', *Colchester Archaeological Group Bulletin* 14, 35-6

EVANS, J G 1972 'Ice-wedge casts at Broome Heath, Norfolk', *Proceedings of the Prehistoric Society* 38, 77-86

EVANS, R 1972 'Air photographs for soil survey in lowland England: soil patterns', *Photogrammetric Record* 7, 302-22

EVANS, R & JONES, R J A 1977 'Crop marks and soils at two archaeological sites in Britain', *Journal of Archaeological Science* 4, 63-76

FRENCH, H M 1976 *The Periglacial Environment*, London & New York

GRINSELL, L V 1953 *The Ancient Burial Mounds of England* (2nd edition), London.

HAMPTON, J N 1974 'An experiment in multi-spectral air photography for archaeological research', *Photogrammetric Record* 8, 37-64

— 1979 'The mapping and analysis of archaeological evidence provided by air photographs', *Aerial Archaeology* 2 (1978), 18-24

— forthcoming 'Some aspects of interpretation and mapping of archaeological evidence from air photography', in G S Maxwell (ed), *The Impact of Aerial Reconnaissance on Archaeology*, Council for British Archaeology, London

HAMPTON, J N & PALMER, R 1978 'Implications of aerial photography for archaeology', *Archaeological Journal* 134 (1977), 157-93

HAWKES, C F C 1948 'Britons, Romans and Saxons round Salisbury and in Cranborne Chase', *Archaeological Journal* 104 (1947), 27-81

HEDGES, J D 1980 'The Neolithic in Essex', in D G Buckley (ed), *Archaeology in Essex to AD 1500*, 26-39, Council for British Archaeology, London

HOGG, A H A 1980 *Surveying for Archaeologists and other Fieldworkers*, London

JOHNSON, N D forthcoming 'The results of air and ground survey on Bodmin Moor, Cornwall', in G S Maxwell (ed), *The Impact of Aerial Reconnaissance on Archaeology*, Council for British Archaeology, London

JONES, G D B 1976 'The western extension of Hadrian's Wall: Bowness to Cardurnock', *Britannia* 7, 236-43

JONES, M U 1980 'Mucking, Essex: the reality beneath the crop marks', *Aerial Archaeology* 4 (1979), 65-76

JONES, M U & BOND, D 1980 'Later Bronze Age settlement at Mucking, Essex', in J Barrett & R Bradley (eds), *Settlement and Society in the British Later Bronze Age* (= *British Archaeological Reports*, British Series, 83), 471-82, Oxford

JONES, R J A & EVANS, R 1975 'Soil and crop marks in the recognition of archaeological sites by air photography', in D R Wilson (ed), *Aerial Reconnaissance for Archaeology*, 1-11, Council for British Archaeology, London

KILFORD, W K 1979 *Elementary Air Survey* (4th ed), London

KNOWLES, D & ST JOSEPH, J K S 1952 *Monastic Sites from the Air*, Cambridge

LAMBRICK, G 1977 *Archaeology and Agriculture*, Council for British Archaeology and Oxfordshire Archaeological Unit

LEEDS, E T 1934 'Rectangular enclosures of the Bronze Age in the Upper Thames Valley', *Antiquaries Journal* 14, 414-6

LÉVA, C & HUS, J J 1975 'Recent archaeological discoveries in Belgium by low-level aerial photography and geophysical survey', in D R Wilson (ed), *Aerial Reconnaissance for Archaeology*, 81-102, Council for British Archaeology, London

LUEDER, D R 1959 *Aerial Photographic Interpretation*, New York

MACKRETH, D 1979 'Durobrivae', *Durobrivae* 7, 19-21

MANBY, T 1979 'Thwing', *Current Archaeology* 67, 240-1

MAXWELL, G 1979 'Air photography and the work of the Royal Commission on the Ancient and Historical Monuments of Scotland', *Aerial Archaeology* 2 (1978), 37-44

— (forthcoming) (ed) *The Impact of Aerial Reconnaissance on Archaeology*, Council for British Archaeology, London

MAY, J 1972 'An Iron Age square enclosure at Aston upon Trent, Derbyshire', *Derbyshire Archaeological Journal* 90 (1970), 10-21

MAY, L H & MILTHORPE, F L 1962 'Drought resistance of crop plants', *Field Crop Abstracts* 15, 171-9

MILES, D, (forthcoming) 'An integrated approach to the study of ancient landscapes: the Claydon Pike project', in G Maxwell (ed), *The Impact of Aerial Reconnaissance on Archaeology*

MONGUILAN, L 1977 'Particularités de la Provence qui influent sur les phénomènes révelateurs en archéologie aérienne', *Dossiers de l'archéologie* no 22, 112-5

NORMAN, E R & ST JOSEPH, J K S 1969 *The Early Development of Irish Society*, Cambridge

ORDNANCE SURVEY, 1973 *Field Archaeology in Great Britain* (5th ed), Southampton

PALMER, R, 1976a 'Interrupted ditch enclosures in Britain: the use of aerial photography for comparative studies', *Proceedings of the Prehistoric Society* 42, 161-86

— 1976b 'A method of transcribing archaeological sites from oblique aerial photographs', *Journal of Archaeological Science* 3, 391-4

— 1977 'A computer method for transcribing information graphically from oblique aerial photographs', *Journal of Archaeological Science*, 4, 283-90

— 1978 'Aerial archaeology and sampling', in J F Cherry, C Gamble and S Shennan (eds), *Sampling in Contemporary British Archaeology* (= *British Archaeological Reports* 50), 129-48

— 1979 'Computer transcription from air photographs: an explanation', *Aerial Archaeology* 2 (1978), 5-8

— *forthcoming* 'Analysis of settlement features in the landscape of prehistoric Wessex', in G Maxwell (ed), *The Impact of Aerial Reconnaissance on Archaeology*

PARRINGTON, M 1978 *The Excavation of an Iron Age Settlement, Bronze Age Ring Ditches and Roman Features at Ashville Trading Estate, Abingdon (Oxfordshire) 1974-76*, Oxfordshire Archaeological Unit & Council for British Archaeology, London

PARSONS, R 1980 'Aerial photography in archaeology: some practical points', *Aerial Archaeology* 4 (1979), 16-17

PEAK, K D 1979 'In perspective: a photogrammetrist's view of the use of oblique photography', *Aerial Archaeology* 2 (1978), 24-7

PENMAN, H L 1948 'Natural evaporation from open water, bare soil and grass', *Proceedings of the Royal Society*, Series A, 193, 120-45

PERRY, B T 1970 'Iron Age enclosures and settlements on the Hampshire chalklands', *Archaeological Journal* 126 (1969), 29-43

PIGGOTT, S 1931 'Ladle Hill—an unfinished hillfort', *Antiquity* 5, 474-85

RACKHAM, O 1972 'Responses of the barley crop to soil water stress', in A R Rees *et al* (eds), *Crop Processes in Controlled Environments*, 127-38, London

— 1976 *Trees and Woodland in the British Landscape*, London

RICHMOND, I A 1943 'Recent discoveries in Roman Britain from the air and in the field', *Journal of Roman Studies* 33, 45-54

RILEY, D N 1944 'The technique of air-archaeology', *Archaeological Journal* 101, 1-16

— 1946 'Groups of circles in the Silt Fens', *Antiquity* 20, 150-3

— 1980a 'Factors in the development of crop marks', *Aerial Archaeology* 4 (1979), 28-32

— 1980b *Early Landscape from the Air: studies of crop marks in South Yorkshire and north Nottinghamshire*, Sheffield

ROYAL COMMISSION ON HISTORICAL MONUMENTS (ENGLAND), 1960 *A Matter of Time: an archaeological survey*, London

— 1969 *Peterborough New Town*, London

— 1972 *North-East Cambridgeshire* (= *An Inventory of Historical Monuments in the County of Cambridge* 2), London

— 1976 *Iron Age and Romano-British Monuments in the Gloucestershire Cotswolds* (*An Inventory of Ancient and Historical Monuments in the County of Gloucester* 1), London

— 1979 *Long Barrows in Hampshire and the Isle of Wight*, London

— 1981 *Archaeological Sites in North-West Northamptonshire* (= *An Inventory of the Historical Monuments in the County of Northampton* 3), London

RUSSELL, E W 1961 *Soil Conditions and Plant Growth*, London

ST JOSEPH, J K S 1951a 'A survey of pioneering in air photography', in W F Grimes (ed), *Aspects of Archaeology*, 303-15, London

— 1951b 'Air reconnaissance of North Britain', *Journal of Roman Studies* 41, 52-65

— 1953 'Air reconnaissance of South Britain', *Journal of Roman Studies* 43, 81-97

— 1955 'Air reconnaissance of Britain, 1951-5', *Journal of Roman Studies* 45, 82-91

— 1958 'Air reconnaissance in Britain, 1955-7', *Journal of Roman Studies* 48, 86-101

— 1961 'Air reconnaissance in Britain, 1958-1960', *Journal of Roman Studies* 51, 119-35

— 1964a 'Air reconnaissance: recent results', *Antiquity* 38, 217-8

— 1964b 'Air reconnaissance: recent results, 2', *Antiquity* 38, 290-2

— 1965a 'Air reconnaissance: recent results, 3', *Antiquity* 39, 60-3

— 1965b 'Air reconnaissance: recent results, 5', *Antiquity* 39, 223-5

— 1965c 'Air reconnaissance in Britain, 1961-64', *Journal of Roman Studies* 55, 74-89

— 1966a 'Air reconnaissance: recent results, 6', *Antiquity* 40, 58-9

— 1966b 'Air reconnaissance: recent results, 7', *Antiquity* 40, 142-4

— 1966c 'The towns of Roman Britain: the contribution of aerial reconnaissance', in J S Wacher (ed), *The Civitas Capitals of Roman Britain*, 21-30, Leicester

— 1967a 'Air reconnaissance: recent results, 10', *Antiquity* 41, 148-9

— 1967b 'Air reconnaissance: recent results, 12', *Antiquity* 41, 312-3

— 1968a 'Air reconnaissance: recent results, 13', *Antiquity* 42, 46-7

— 1968b 'Air reconnaissance: recent results, 14', *Antiquity* 42, 130-1

— 1968c 'Air reconnaissance: recent results, 15', *Antiquity* 42, 311-4

— 1969a 'Air reconnaissance: recent results, 18', *Antiquity* 43, 314-5

— 1969b 'Air reconnaissance in Britain, 1965-68', *Journal of Roman Studies* 59, 104-28

— 1970a 'Air reconnaissance: recent results, 22', *Antiquity* 44, 308-10

— 1970b 'The camps at Ardoch, Stracathro and Ythan Wells: recent excavations', *Britannia* 1, 163-78

— 1971 'Air reconnaissance: recent results, 26', *Antiquity* 45, 298-9

— 1972a 'Air reconnaissance: recent results, 28', *Antiquity* 46, 224-6

— 1972b 'Air reconnaissance: recent results, 29', *Antiquity* 46, 313-4

— 1973a 'Air reconnaissance: recent results, 30', *Antiquity* 47, 144-7

— 1973b 'Air reconnaissance: recent results, 31', *Antiquity* 47, 236-8

— 1973c 'Air reconnaissance in Britain, 1969-72', *Journal of Roman Studies* 63, 214-46

— 1974 'Air reconnaissance: recent results, 35', *Antiquity* 48, 213-5

— 1975 'Air reconnaissance: recent results, 38', *Antiquity* 49, 207-11

— 1976a 'Air reconnaissance: recent results, 40', *Antiquity* 50, 55-7

— 1976b 'Air reconnaissance of Roman Scotland, 1939-75', *Glasgow Archaeological Journal* 4, 1-28

— 1977a 'Air reconnaissance: recent results, 43', *Antiquity* 51, 143-5

— 1977b 'Air reconnaissance in Roman Britain, 1973-76', *Journal of Roman Studies* 67, 125-61

— 1978a 'Air reconnaissance: recent results, 44', *Antiquity* 52, 47-50

— 1978b 'Air reconnaissance: recent results, 45', *Antiquity* 52, 137-40

— 1980 'Air reconnaissance: recent results, 49', *Antiquity* 54, 47-51

ST JOSEPH, J K & WILSON, D R 1976 'Air reconnaissance: recent results, 41', *Antiquity* 50, 237-9

SCOLLAR, I 1964 'Physical conditions tending to produce crop sites in the Rhineland', in R Chevallier (ed), *Colloque international d'archéologie aérienne 31 août-3 Septembre 1963*, 39-47, Paris

— 1975 'Transformation of extreme oblique aerial photographs to maps or plans by conventional means or by computer', in D R Wilson (ed), *Aerial Reconnaissance in Archaeology*, 52-9, Council for British Archaeology, London

— 1979 'Progress in aerial photography in Germany and computer methods', *Aerial Archaeology* 2 (1978), 8-18

SIMPSON, W G 966 'Romano-British settlement on the Welland gravels', in C. Thomas (ed.), *Rural Settlement in Roman Britain*, 15-25, Council for British Archaeology, London

SMITH, L P 1967 *Potential Transpiration*. Ministry of Agriculture, Fisheries and Food, London

STURDY, D 1973 'The Temple of Diana and the Devil's Quoits', in D E Strong (ed), *Archaeological Theory and Practice*, 27-43, London & New York

TAYLOR, C C 1975a 'Aerial photography and the field archaeologist', in D R Wilson (ed), *Aerial Reconnaissance in Archaeology*, 136-41. Council for British Archaeology, London

— 1975b *Fields in the English Landscape*, London

TRAFFORD, B D 1970 'The farmer's guide to agricultural research 1970: field drainage', *Journal of the Royal Agricultural Society* 131, 129-52

WEBSTER, G & HOBLEY, B 1965 'Aerial reconnaissance over the Warwickshire Avon', *Archaeological Journal* 121 (1964), 1-22

WEST, R G 1977 *Pleostocene Geology and Biology* (2nd ed), London

WHIMSTER, R 1981 *Burial Practice in Iron Age Britain* (= *British Archaeological Reports*, British Series, 90), Oxford

— forthcoming 'Aerial reconnaissance from Cambridge: a retrospective view 1945-80', in G S Maxwell (ed), *The Impact of Aerial Reconnaissance on Archaeology*, Council for British Archaeology, London

WILLIAMS, R B G 1973 'Frost and the works of man', *Antiquity* 47, 19-31

WILSON, D R 1974a 'Roman camps in Britain', *Actes du Congrès International d'Études sur les Frontières Romaines*, 341-50, Bucuresti & Wien

— 1974b 'Romano-British villas from the air', *Britannia* 5, 251-61

— 1975a 'Photographic techniques in the air', in D R Wilson (ed), *Aerial Reconnaissance for Archaeology*, 12-31, Council for British Archaeology, London

— 1975b 'Some pitfalls in the interpretation of air photographs', in D R Wilson (ed), *Aerial Reconnaissance in Archaeology*, 59-69, Council for British Archaeology, London

— 1975c '"Causewayed camps" and "interrupted ditch-systems"', *Antiquity* 49, 178-86

— 1975d 'The "small towns" of Roman Britain from the air', in W Rodwell & T Rowley (eds), *The 'Small Towns' of Roman Britain* (= *British Archaeological Reports* 15), 9-49, Oxford

— 1975e 'The evidence of air-photographs', in J G Evans, S Limbrey, & H Cleere (eds), *The Effect of Man on the Landscape: the Highland Zone*, 108-11, Council for British Archaeology, London

— 1977 'A first-century fort near Gosbecks, Essex', *Britannia* 8, 185-7

— 1978 'Pit alignments: distribution and function', in H C Bowen & P J Fowler, (eds), *Early Land Allotment in the British Isles* (= *British Archaeological Reports* 48), 3-5, Oxford

— 1979a 'Groups of circles in the silt fens', *Proceedings of the Cambridge Antiquarian Society* 68, 42-6

— 1979b 'Light soils and heavy soils: a question of priorities', *Aerial Archaeology* 2 (1978), 46-9

— 1980 'Factors affecting the distribution of crop marks in the Anglian Region', *Aerial Archaeology* 4 (1979), 32-6

— 1982 'Deployment of Roman troops as revealed by air-photographs', in C Léva, J J Hus & G Heldenbergh (eds), *Photographie aérienne et prospection géophysique en archéologie*, Bruxelles

WILSON, J & WILSON, D R 1982 'The site of the Elvetham entertainment', *Antiquity* 56, 46-7

WOOD, E S 1979 *Collins Field Guide to Archaeology in Britain* (5th ed), London

Index